# C'mon City!

*for Bart*

# C'mon City!

## A Hundred Years of the Bluebirds

## Grahame Lloyd

seren

seren is the book imprint of
Poetry Wales Press Ltd
Wyndham Street, Bridgend, CF31 1EF, Wales

ISBN 1-85411-271-6

A CIP record for this title is available from
the British Library

*The publisher works with the financial assistance of the
Arts Council of Wales*

Main cover photograph: Huw Evans

Printed in Plantin by CPD Wales, Ebbw Vale

# Contents

7   Acknowledgements

9   Foreword

11   Prologue: Dream On

14   Down by the Riverside (It's Not Just Cricket)

29   What a Load of Rubbish!

55   The Bluebirds Take Flight

70   Always the Bridesmaids

90   Third Time Lucky

104   Happy Days Are Here Again?

132   The Yo-yo Years

159   Flying the Welsh Flag

185   A Man for Thirteen Seasons

212   A Woman's Place

230   Pleasure before Business

255   Never Go Back?

277   Epilogue: Last Thoughts on Bart Wilson

283   Select Bibliography

# Acknowledgements

As befits a book about a football club, the writing of this centenary celebration has been a real team effort. I would like to thank everyone involved at Cardiff City for their co-operation and all the people who have kindly agreed to be interviewed, especially Dannie Abse, Peter Corrigan, Brian Clark, Phil Dwyer, Sue Goodfriend, Tony Clemo and Frank Burrows.

I am especially grateful to Bart Wilson's grandchildren, John Head and Alma Vosper, for showing such patience and understanding as the incredible story of the club's founder gradually unfolded. My thanks must also go to Pat Connies-Laing and Gwyneth Lewis, the granddaughters of Walter Parker, Cardiff City's chairman when the club won the F.A. Cup in 1927. Their memorabilia, including priceless early programmes, enabled me to piece together the club's history, especially the pre-Football League days. Alan Jenkins and Derrick Jenkins provided important information about the Riverside years and Graham Keenor's recollections of his father Fred were most welcome. Thanks too must go to Terry Phillips of the *South Wales Echo* for his help in tracing the origins of the club's nickname and to Steve Groves who solved the mystery surrounding the pseudonmyn of one of his predecessors as match programme editor.

I am indebted to my consultant Richard Shepherd and my next-door neighbour Peter Walker for their meticulous reading of the manuscript and to Frank Keating for a crucial editorial suggestion. My appreciation is particularly due to Seren's managing editor, Mick Felton, whose commitment and advice have been invaluable. The creativity of Simon Hicks at Seren is also much appreciated. I would also like to thank Phil Jardine, one of the new directors on the Cardiff City board, for his support and enthusiasm as the book developed.

A final word of thanks to my backroom team – my wife

Nicola and children Tom, Becca and Alys as well as a couple of friends – one old, the others new. The inspirational music of Bob Dylan and Catatonia kept me going through many a long night. Catatonia were magnificent in the mud at Margam in May, performing songs from their new album, *Equally Cursed and Blessed*, which, I suppose, rather neatly sums up Cardiff City during their first hundred years. C'mon You Bluebirds!

*G.L. Cardiff, July 1999*

# Foreword

Trevor Ford was the big name at Ninian Park when I began watching Cardiff City. He scored in the first game I saw – a 3-2 home defeat by Portsmouth in the old Division One on April 2nd 1956. Little did I realise that while the fiery Welsh international centre-forward was the idol of the fans, the outspoken Ford was not the most popular person with his directors and manager because he never considered himself subservient to them.

But over the past forty-three years of watching the Bluebirds – as spectator, radio broadcaster and programme editor – my insight into the club, their players and staff over that period has grown. Results, goalscroers and attendances are interesting up to a point, but I was particularly fascinated in the stories behind the scenes.

When Grahame Lloyd, a sports broadcasting colleague for many years, came up with the concept of writing Cardiff City's official centenary celebration via the people involved from the start, I was enthusiastic about an idea which gave the story a different slant. John Crooks' excellent 1992 *Official History*, togther with my detailed records on Cardiff City, formed a solid starting point for Grahame's project. A dusty search together through an old and disused store cupboard at Ninian Park produced a number of heavry, leather-bound ledgers which contained the minutes of board meetings held between 1915 and 1972. They made remarkable reading, solved a number of 'mysteries' and revealed the thoughts and actions of directors and managers.

If it's a record of matches, players and goals you're looking for I'm afraid you won't find them in this book. But if you want to know about the battle that Bartley Wilson fought to change the name of the club from Riverside to Cardiff City in the early 1900s, the feelings of Brian Clark on the night he scored the memorable winner against Real Madrid in 1971 or why John Toshack did not return from Liverpool to Ninian Park in 1978, then all is revealed in *C'mon City!* The book tells the story of a club that made history by winning the F.A.Cup just four months after their legendary skipper Fred Keenor decided that he wanted to leave because he couldn't get back into the first team after recovering from injury.

*C'mon City!* contains many stories which have never reached the ears of the press but which were waiting to be discovered. Grahame Lloyd's detective work would do credit to City's record appearance holder Phil 'Joe' Dwyer, now a CID officer in the South Wales Police. Why the nickname? Phil explains its origins in a book that will tell you everything you ever wanted to know about the Bluebirds but were afraid to ask.

*Richard Shepherd*
*Football commentator and archivist*
*Cardiff City programme editor*

# Prologue: Dream On

There's only one Cardiff City! When the team won promotion to the Second Division on Saturday May 1st 1999, that particular chant rang around Ninian Park as nearly 13,000 fans celebrated the club's success. A scoreless draw with Scunthorpe United had secured the necessary point. The champagne flowed as the players and manager Frank Burrows acknowledged the crowd's acclaim and the directors allowed themselves more than the occasional smile of satisfaction.

It had been a long, hard and, towards the end, nerve-racking season but Cardiff City had made it back to the Second Division. Nothing unusual about that – the club had already won promotion eight times since joining the Football League in 1920. But there's still only one Cardiff City.

All football supporters believe that their favourite team is unique but Cardiff City really are a one-off. And unless Welsh football undergoes a remarkable transformation, it seems likely that they will remain so.

No other team has ever taken the F.A.Cup out of England. Cardiff City did it by beating Arsenal 1-0 at Wembley in 1927. Over the years, that fact has become the club's main claim to fame and a standard football quiz question. The game was memorable not only for the result. Community singing made its pre-final debut and, for the very first time, British football fans were able to follow the action of an F.A.Cup Final via the B.B.C. and a page of the *Radio Times* on which the pitch was divided into a grid.

Three years earlier, Cardiff City had come within 0.024 of a goal of winning the First Division after a missed penalty in their last game cost them the title. No team has come closer to lifting football's major championship. The club also staged the first closed-circuit television transmission of a league match when they lost 2-1 to Jimmy Hill's Coventry City in October 1965 –

two more reasons why there's only one Cardiff City.

Some cynics have unkindly suggested that, after helping to make history, it was all downhill after that 1927 win. Certainly it rounded off a glorious period in the Twenties during which they reached two F.A.Cup Finals, and it's true that in the intervening seventy-two years, Cardiff City have had to make do with occasional promotions, exciting cup runs and a few unforgettable nights in Europe.

But, as with any football club, the roll of honour tells only a fraction of the story. For managers and players, the game is all about winning: fair enough, it's their profession and, as the late Billy Bremner once said, "you get nowt for coming second". It's different for fans. They obviously want their team to be successful but in the main they continue to support them – whatever the results. From the moment they attend their first match, many are hooked for life. Each generation hails heroes and vilifies villains as Saturday afternoon becomes one of the most important parts of their week. Loyalty can sometimes be stretched to breaking point but usually remains intact.

The absence of another major trophy since 1927 is more than a little misleading because it masks the contribution made by the football club to both Cardiff and South Wales, before and after that historic Wembley victory. The exploits of Cardiff City have enriched the lives of thousands of people, giving some a focal point and providing all with a rich store of stories and souvenirs – some tragic, some comic, but all of them precious.

Not everyone who has pulled on the blue shirt is featured wihtin these pages but I hope all the key players have been included. Precise details of goalscorers, appearances and attendances can be found elsewhere in other publications. *C'mon City!* is about memories rather than matches. It tells the story of Cardiff City's first hundred years through the eyes of some of the club's most loyal supporters – managers, players, chairmen, writers and fans, starting with the remarkable disabled man who founded Riverside A.F.C. in the summer of 1899.

Bart Wilson was a lithographic artist who never lost sight of the big picture. He loved to paint because he loved create, to use his imagination. But Bart was no idle daydreamer. He had the foresight to see that the biggest town in Wales could support a football team and his dream culminated in the creation of a successful Cardiff City. Without his single-minded devotion, the Bluebirds would never have become airborne, let alone take flight. Bart was 'Mr Cardiff City' and this book is a celebration of his vision, the club's centenary and their 1999 promotion to the Second Division.

There's only one Cardiff City – and don't let anyone tell you otherwise.

# Down by the Riverside
## (It's Not Just Cricket)

Plot 246, Section I, Western Cemetery, Ely, on the outskirts of Cardiff. That's where you'll find him.

Go in through the Cowbridge Road entrance, walk right down the middle of the cemetery for about a quarter of a mile and there, tucked away on the left, you'll come across Bart Wilson's grave.

For nearly forty-five years, he rested in peace because very few people knew he was buried there. Bart Wilson lay in an unmarked grave – no headstone, no flowers, no memorial at all to the disabled lithographic artist who created the blueprint for the Welsh capital's football team. A fluffy club mascot, a blue-bird, but not a tombstone, bore his name.

But in June 1999, a century after almost single-handedly founding what became a unique football club, the contribution of the 'Grand Old Man' of Cardiff City was officially recognized.

When Walter Bartley Wilson died on November 19th 1954, everything was in place. His wife, Sarah Ellen, mother of John Bartley, Alma May and Donald Bartley – also known as Jim – had passed away in August 1951 and Bart bought plot 246 from Cardiff City Council for £2.10s. In December 1952, he arranged for a local monumental mason to provide and inscribe a headstone for their grave.

Nearly two years later, after a short illness, Bart died, aged eighty-four. After his funeral at a packed St. John's Church in Canton – attended by many of the Cardiff City players – the burial was due to take place at midday at Western Cemetery, gentlemen only, as was the custom. But it rained so much on Tuesday November 23rd 1954 that when the mourners arrived at plot 246, they found the grave flooded and the burial had to

14

be postponed. The headstone was put aside under a nearby tree, and when Bart was laid to rest the next day it wasn't returned to the local monumental mason for inscription.

After the discovery of his unmarked grave in December 1998, a new memorial to Bart Wilson was commissioned by Cardiff City to commemorate his pivotal role in the club's formation. Work on the replacement headstone was about to begin when the original was discovered by chance just yards from his final resting place. For nearly half a century, it had lain in a line of trees bordering Section I – face down, unnoticed and therefore undisturbed. In May 1999, Cardiff City won promotion for the ninth time in their history. A month later, close family and club representatives attended the rededication of the updated headstone in Western Cemetery as part of the centenary celebrations of the club to which Bart Wilson devoted his life.

From the day he resolved to set up a football section of Riverside Cricket Club, Bart laboured tirelessly for the good of Cardiff City as inspirational founder, enthusiastic first secretary and even, for a disastrous six months in the Thirties, as manager. Indeed, when he died at his home in Llanfair Road, Canton, he had only recently retired as assistant secretary at Ninian Park, the club's home since 1910.

As the last year of the nineteenth century, 1899 was always going to be pretty momentous. Huge changes were taking place in what had become Bart's adopted home since he had arrived from Bristol to work in the burgeoning former market town two years earlier. Coal, 'Black Gold' from the Valleys, had firmly established Cardiff as the jewel in the Welsh crown. Despite the growing competition from the new Barry Docks, it had developed into the biggest coal-exporting port in the world with a population of nearly 160,000 – an increase of more than 120,000 in just thirty years.

King Coal had enabled Cardiff to become, in 1885, the first borough in Wales to provide a public electricity supply, councillors were considering introducing trams into the town and, having just bought Cathays Park, they were about to design and build Britain's first planned civic centre. They were also looking to extend the borough boundaries by swallowing up

Llandaff and Llanishen and were eyeing up Penarth, Cogan, Llandough and Whitchurch.

The exact date of the formation of Riverside A.F.C. is not known but, over the years, the story has been handed down – folklore-like from generation to generation – that Bart Wilson set the ball rolling sometime during the late summer of 1899. In the absence of conclusive documentary evidence, let us suppose that it began something like this...

It was growing dark as Bart stepped onto Canton Bridge to cross Westbourne Crescent – the last part of Cowbridge Road as it was later to become – which overlooked the River Taff, opposite Cardiff Castle. He was returning home to 1 Coldstream Terrace, after watching members of Riverside Cricket Club play in nearby Sophia Gardens, the first of an eventual 2,000 acres of parks and recreation grounds to which the people of Cardiff were given free access by the Bute family.

Nearly a decade later when they helped create Ninian Park, Bart was to have good reason to thank the borough councillors for their generosity. That night, as he prepared to cross the road, he was pleased to have heard that, at last, the corporation were going to illuminate Canton Bridge – possibly before the end of that year. It would make his journey home easier because, as Cardiff's population grew, Westbourne Crescent was becoming busier all the time. In the last five years, the number of grand late-Victorian houses in nearby Cathedral Road had risen from sixteen to over two hundred as the green fields of Canton started to disappear under bricks-and-mortar. You had to have your wits about you in late nineteenth-century Cardiff. Those horse-cabs, trams and buses could be pretty dangerous as they clattered across Canton Bridge – especially if, like Bart, you were on crutches.

As he made his way towards his end-of-terrace house about a hundred yards from the bridge, the solution to the problem which had been preoccupying him all summer suddenly became clear. Not quite as dramatic as the incident on the road to Damascus but life-changing in its own way for both Bart and professional football in Cardiff. Riverside's officials, worried that their cricket team might disband once the season ended, had been wondering how to keep the players together during the winter.

Bart thought he had the answer: why not start a Riverside football team? Association football was still rugby's poor relation but it was gaining in popularity all the time. Bart had witnessed at first-hand the growth of the round-ball game in his native Bristol where City and Rovers had both become professional clubs in 1897.

The next day, Bart put up a poster in the Riverside pavilion to let everyone know about his idea. Two meetings were held in the front room of 1 Coldstream Terrace during that time of year when the cricket and football seasons overlap. The first was so badly attended – only five members turned up – that Bart nearly gave up there and then. If nobody else could bother, then why should he?

Shortly afterwards, he tried again. This time, he received a much better response – about a dozen members attended – and Riverside A.F.C. was formed. Precisely when this historic meeting took place isn't clear. What is known is that Bart Wilson was elected as secretary and the committee was made up of A.J. Stone, George Pearce, Jimmy Redfern, Stanley Barrett, Andrew Sheen, E.W. Holder, Billy Canter and Frank Burfitt – some of whom were to feature in early team line-ups. After agreeing to levy an annual membership fee of half a crown – 2s 6d – and selecting a strip of chocolate and amber quartered shirts, all they needed now were some opponents and somewhere to play.

The delay in setting up the club had cost Riverside a place in the recently-formed Cardiff and District League for the 1899-1900 season. But, almost immediately, Bart arranged for them to play the first of a series of friendlies against Barry West End. The match took place on Saturday October 7th at Sophia Gardens, and in the previous day's *South Wales Echo* the team was listed as:

Goal – G.A. Sheen. Backs – H.G. Pearce and P. Whitcombe. Half-backs – F. Drake (captain), B. Stone, T. Mann. Forwards - J. Holder, S. Barrett, W. Jenkins, J.F. Pearce and W. Hill.

It was not the most auspicious of debuts – Barry fell a goal short of double figures and Riverside were lucky to get one – but at least it was a start and something on which Bart Wilson was determined to build. During his life, he would often reminisce about those early days:

> We wanted to keep the boys together in the winter. We decided to be different and go for soccer and we've been different ever since!
> Although we lost 9-1 to Barry West End, the funny thing was that, after the game, most of the Barry fellows wanted to play for us. Several eventually did, including their captain, George Travis.

For the moment though, Riverside had to rely on their own members as they played occasional games against the likes of Barry District Juniors, Llanbradach and Penarth Parish Church. In fact, there was so much interest that the club almost immediately started fielding two sides nearly every Saturday. As secretary, it was Bart's job to make sure that details of Riverside's teams were supplied to the *South Wales Echo*. He didn't always manage it. On Friday November 10th, he received a mild rebuke when, under the headline 'Notice to Secretaries', the paper issued the following warning:

> We have to inform certain club secretaries, who have expressed surprise at the omission of their players from our weekly list of teams, that the fault is their own. Teams not arriving by 9.30 on Friday morning cannot be inserted. A most frequent cause of non-insertion is that secretaries do not state the full name of their club and that of their opponents and where the match is to be played.

The paper then announced that the line-ups of Canton Villa v Riverside Reserves, among other sides, had accordingly been omitted.

A fortnight later, knuckles gently rapped, Bart had sorted himself out. The *South Wales Echo* revealed that on Saturday November 25th, Riverside were playing Cadoxton United at Sophia Gardens while the reserves travelled north to meet Llandaff City Boys Brigade.

The third week of December 1899 proved a turning point in the history of the embryonic football club. Encouraged by results after the Barry West End thrashing, Bart decided that Riverside could spread their wings. It was the first of many tests for his fledgling footballers. At this stage, they played for just one of hundreds of local amateur parks teams in South Wales. In Cardiff alone, you could find clubs such as Clare Stars, Roath Road Wesleyans, St Catherine's Athletic and Cardiff Corinthians with which Jack Sandiford, one of the pioneers of football in South Wales, was involved. In 1890, Sandiford had helped form and finance a Cardiff A.F.C. which lasted only a couple of years.

Ten years later, the game was much better established in the town and, although Riverside may have been nothing out of the ordinary, Bart was very ambitious. As part of his vision for the future of football in Cardiff, he believed passionately in Riverside's potential and during that December week, he took the first steps towards helping them to realise it. The secretary had a lot on his plate during December. Apart from work, his wife Sarah had just given birth to their second child, Alma May, but after choosing the teams for their matches against Penarth Parish Church and Barry Boys Brigade, Bart found time to put pen to paper.

As 1899 drew to a close, Charles Axtell, the honorary secretary and treasurer of the South Wales and Monmouthshire Football Association, was feeling pretty satisfied with life. Since August, there had been the usual irregular flow of annual subscriptions and affiliation and entry fees for the Senior, Junior and Junior Medal Cup competitions run by the Association, the game's governing body in South Wales. Football was on the up and so were the Association's finances. In September, Axtell had submitted the annual accounts to the AGM and was able to report, for the first time in its history, a credit balance of £30.11s.1d. Two Senior Cup semi-final teams had drawn three games and given the association an unexpected windfall of £17.

On Saturday December 16th, Charles Axtell opened his post at his home in Caerleon in Monmouthshire to find a payment from a team he had never heard of before. W.B. Wilson, of 1 Coldstream Terrace in Cardiff, had sent him 2s 6d to enable Riverside Reserves to take part in the Junior Medal Cup. This entry fee – more than a little late – meant that Charles Axtell had to begin a new receipt book and, as befitted a meticulous secretary, he duly entered Bart's contribution into the S.W.&

M.F.A's records – appropriately for Riverside's first competitive fixture, receipt number 1. The club's history had officially begun.

Bart Wilson's was a name with which the football authorities in South Wales were to become infuriatingly familiar over the next decade as Riverside's honorary secretary doggedly pursued his dream of forming a professional team in Cardiff. His logic was simple: if it could happen in Bristol, then why not on this side of the Severn? When he arrived in Cardiff from Bristol to work as a lithographic artist, Bart saw the opportunity to emulate the success of football in his home town.

For most of his twenty-nine years, Bart Wilson had been a fighter. Struggling to overcome major misfortune had become a deeply-ingrained habit. Born in Bristol, with a clubfoot, on January 3rd 1870, Bart was the son of a publican-turned-brush-maker and a teacher. He was orphaned as a boy and brought up with his cousin Arthur Spurll by their grandmother Jane Hathaway. Arthur, twelve years his junior, came to live with Bart and Jane in Barossa Place, Bristol, after losing both his parents, and later become editor of the *Bristol Evening Post*.

Bart married Sarah two days after Christmas in 1894 and by the time their son John was born in the following October, the couple had moved to 6 Green Street in Riverside. And by entering the S.W.&M.F.A.'s Junior Medal Cup, Riverside were on their way. Over the next ten years, he was to prove the proverbial thorn in the Association's side but, without him as midwife, Riverside A.F.C. might well have been stillborn and Cardiff City would not now be celebrating their centenary.

A hundred years ago, football's growing popularity was proving a double-edged sword for the S.W.&M.F.A. More clubs meant more money but also more problems for the administrators whose relations with the Football Association of Wales, the game's parent organisation, were often rather tense as a result of a North v South power struggle. During the 1899-1900 season, they had to deal with a variety of disciplinary matters including stone-throwing at Barry, an alleged professional playing for Llandrindod Wells and a Builth goalkeeper who refused to leave the field after being sent off for using foul language to the referee. There were also regular protests about results – including the one involving Riverside Reserves in their first match in the Association's Junior Medal Cup.

The result of the round one tie against Roath Road Wesleyans on February 24th 1900 isn't known but it can be assumed that Riverside lost and were unhappy about it. A fortnight later, at an association committee meeting at the Alexandra Hotel in Queen Street in Cardiff, the result was discussed and members resolved "that Riverside be requested to provide definite statements as to their objections and that players objected to attend the next meeting if required."

It seems that Bart had complained about the eligibility of certain opposition players, but the protest came to nothing. Roath Road Wesleyans were awarded their semi-final tie when Mardy failed to turn up and then went on to beat Trelewis 4-3 to win the cup. Bart's fingers had been burnt by Riverside's baptism of fire. It was to be another three years before he re-entered the club in any competition run by the S.W.&M.F.A. although links with the governing body were maintained from a distance through annual subscriptions and affiliation fees.

Then as now, money was beginning to play a much bigger role in the running of football at all levels. Jack Sandiford, the S.W.&M.F.A.'s first chairman when it was formed in 1890 and still a leading member of the governing body, informed his colleagues that "professionalism is not only rife in South Wales but rampant!". Meanwhile, Bart and the Riverside committee members were trudging around the touchline at Sophia Gardens with small collecting boxes. Any donation was gratefully accepted and anything between 15s and £1 on a Saturday afternoon was considered a bonus. Normally, they were lucky to raise 10s (50p in modern-day money).

The stooped but unbowed figure of the mustachioed secretary, with a crutch under each arm, became a permanent fixture at Riverside's home games. There were other calls on their spectators' generosity: the S.W.&M.F.A. had invited all clubs to make collections for the relatives of the "Soldiers and Sailors of the Principality engaged in the Boer War in South Africa".

Bart was indefatigable. He was so committed to Riverside's survival and subsequent success that, when not working for a local printing firm, he would help run the club's headquarters, a disused stable in the back garden of 23 Mark Street in

Riverside. Access was gained via a lane off Green Street, just fifty yards from Bart's new home in Coldstream Terrace. When Cardiff City celebrated their first half-century, the editor of the club handbook recalled how the stable had been converted into Riverside's HQ:

> The old stalwarts tell of how the boys set to work fitting the place for a clubroom by pulling down the mangers, erecting partitions, the expenditure of much whitewash and the installation of water, gas and a full-sized billiards table – the latter on the monthly payment system – and not one single month did the committee default in their payments to the makers.

In 1910, when Cardiff City became a professional club, all twenty-six members of Riverside A.F.C. were made life members and given four half-sovereign shares each. One of them, Herbert Frew Jones, later recalled the early days of the amateur club:

> In the old clubhouse, we had a billiard table and played cards, the boys buying 12 chips for a penny to play games like solo. Bart Wilson used to run a little shop so we could buy sweets. I well remember how the lane behind Green Street became very notorious but our headquarters were all right. I must say at once that it was always Bart who was the prime mover. Cardiff City would never have been Cardiff City if it had not been for Bart. He was a tremendous worker.

As well as running his shop, Bart also used to charge club members 2d a game to use the billiards table – the proceeds going towards buying equipment and kit for the team. The players only had to provide their boots. Like the club, 23 Mark Street, one of a row of terraced houses, is about to enter its second century. Not so the clubroom. It survived the German bombs, but was demolished after the Second World War when owners Les and Daisy Aplin decided that the derelict building was too dangerous for their children to play in.

After their first season of friendlies, Riverside entered the Cardiff and District League in 1900 as, after their Junior Medal Cup experience, Bart seemed to have opted for a period of consolidation. In typical footballing fashion, the club concentrated on the league but did not sever their connections with the S.W.&M.F.A. According to Charles Axtell's records, a spate of letter-writing in the autumn of 1900 saw Bart first pay a 5s annual subscription on behalf of the Cardiff and District Junior League with which he was now involved. Three days later on October 20th, he applied for the league to be affiliated to the S.W.&M.F.A. and a month later, he was asked to submit a copy of the League's rules. When Bart eventually complied with the request, the Association confirmed the Riverside affiliation in late December.

The following season, Bart paid the C.D.J.L.'s annual subscriptions in September 1901. Then in December 1902, for the first time, he sent Riverside's annual subscriptions to Charles Axtell but still declined to enter any more competitions. At the end of the year, Riverside was one of a number of affiliated clubs in Cardiff – its registered address being recorded as 23 Mark Street.

After two seasons of Cardiff and District League football, Bart was getting restless. It was time to move onwards and hopefully upwards with the next rung on the ladder being the South Wales Amateur League – created in 1894 and containing sides such as Merthyr, Aberdare, Ton Pentre and Treharris. As part of their plan to improve the standard of their teams, Riverside amalgamated with their close rivals, Riverside Albions in 1902. They continued playing in the Cardiff and District League before, in season 1903-04, Bart decided it was time to dip their toes into the choppy waters of knockout football again. In September 1903, he sent 10s to the S.W.&M.F.A to cover both Riverside's annual subscriptions and the entry fee for the Junior Cup.

The game turned out to be another hiccup on Riverside's controversial journey towards professionalism. They drew 0-0 with Roath but then lost what appears to have been a bad-tempered replay 5-1. At their January meeting, the Association decided to suspend one player from each side "for conduct as reported by the referee."

In the next round, Roath were drawn against Bargoed Albions and the Association was so concerned about the possibility of bad behaviour that it resolved "that Roath be cautioned as to any recurrence of their conduct in their last match. The team must not leave the field without permission of the referee."

Later that season, Riverside were hit by another occupational hazard – the unfulfilled fixture. When Llanbradach let them down, Bart complained and the S.W.&M.F.A. decided "that the explanation by Llanbradach be accepted as satisfactory, as Llanbradach gives the assurance that they will, if possible, offer Riverside a date this season upon the same terms, and, failing that, will do so early next season".

Riverside had a miserable Junior Cup experience during the next season when, after a bye in the first round, they crashed out 6-1 to Cwmaman in the second. But trouble on the field was now being replaced by problems off it. A week before Christmas 1904, Bart, now living in nearby De Burgh Street, received a reprimand over the Riverside balance sheet from the S.W.&M.F.A. The finance committee had resolved "that the Honorary Secretary write to Mr Bartley Wilson and inform him that his letter does not meet with the approval of this committee".

Whatever the reason for his reprimand, Bart was out of the bad books by the following October because Riverside were not included on a list of fourteen clubs threatened with suspension for failing to produce satisfactory balance sheets. By that time, Riverside's first trophy had found its way into the club cabinet. In 1905, they won the Bevan Shield, a local competition sanctioned by the S.W.&M.F.A.

This was the breakthrough Bart had been waiting for. After five years of league football, Riverside had proved they could be successful – albeit in a minor cup competition – and he felt it was time for the club to move forward again. On October 28th 1905, as a result of its phenomenal growth and increasing importance to Wales, Cardiff was officially made a city. A week later, Bart made his way to a meeting of the S.W.&M.F.A at the Alexandra Hotel with Charles Kyd, a local stock-keeper. They wanted to change the name of the club to Cardiff City. The city needed a capital football team in keeping with its new-found status and they believed Riverside was that team. As the two men entered the hotel, Bart was optimistic that their request would be granted. Not for the first time, they were to be disappointed. The Association had heard rumours that Riverside were already calling themselves Cardiff City.

At an emergency committee meeting of the Association, it was resolved:

(i) that the explanation of assumption of title be accepted and the club's officials exonerated
(ii) that this Association withhold all sanction to this title for the present season
(iii) Riverside's application shall again be considered at the end of the season in view of there being no other application.

As is often the case, minutes of meetings seldom tell the whole story. The real reason for the refusal was that Riverside were not playing in a good enough grade of football. They would have to join the South Wales League if they wanted to become Cardiff City. Bart was only too keen to accept the challenge and Riverside successfully applied for election and began competing in the South Wales League in the autumn of 1906.

In the meantime, their miserable record in the Junior Cup continued as they drew 2-2 and were then beaten 2-1 in a replay by Penarth Parish Church in the first round. Two days before Christmas 1905, Riverside found themselves embroiled in another dispute – this time involving the non-payment of travelling expenses for their players by Pontlottyn in the Llanbradach Charity Cup. Like the Bevan Shield, the L.C.C. was sanctioned by the S.W.&M.F.A. to whom Riverside appealed for help.

The row rumbled on through most of 1905 as the Association tried in vain to persuade the tournament's organisers to explain what had happened to the gate receipts from the game. At a meeting on July 26th, the general committee had both good and bad news for Riverside. They warned the honorary secretary of the Llanbradach Charity Cup that further delay in supplying the Association with information would affect next season's competition and then decided that the club's proposed change of name to Cardiff City should again not be sanctioned.

Both items were on the agenda at a meeting held on September 15th. Again, the news was mixed. A sub-committee consisting of Bart, his opposite number at Pontlottyn and four Association members would examine the whole gate receipts issue. Then, after Bart and Charles Kyd had made another appeal for Riverside to become Cardiff City, the Association decided to lay down the law. It was resolved:

(i) that the application be not granted
(ii) that the Association is now fully convinced that the officials of Riverside A.F.C. have adopted the name of Cardiff City A.F.C. in direct opposition to the ruling of this Association. In the event of any repetition of this offence, the club will render itself liable to suspension.

Both Riverside and the Football Association of Wales were notified of the resolution but Bart had little time to either worry or sulk – he was also involved in the Pontlottyn inquiry. Four days later, the six wise men delivered their verdict. Riverside had to settle for a not very honourable draw as the sub-committee only hinted at dark deeds and skulduggery. It unanimously decided:

that while there was some laxity on the gate arrangements by both sides, there is no unfair handling of the monies. It is a matter of regret that the gate did not allow of payment of fares of visiting players – but that is one of the risks of a cup-tie.

Pontlottyn were fined 2s.6d. for ignoring an order to submit details of the incident, the rules of the competition were amended and the Association decided that all minute books and records should be kept. The following resolution provided cold comfort for the Riverside committee: "This Association regrets that the ex-secretary of the Llanbradach Charity Cup Competition has destroyed the documents which this Association ordered to be produced and the non-production of such documents caused great delay in the settlement of this case."

Riverside's first season in the South Wales League from the autumn of 1906 was a real struggle. They lost most of their matches with Newport, Cwmparc-and-Treorchy and Treharris all putting six past them. During a 4-1 defeat by Barry District, they fell foul of the referee who sent off a Riverside player for remarking "Well, I'm blowed, you take the cake!" in response to one of his generally contentious decisions.

There was little improvement in the next few seasons as Riverside continued to lose far more games than they won.

Aberdare, Treharris and Ebbw Vale scored seven against them, while Ton Pentre inflicted an 8-2 drubbing. As well as competing in the South Wales League, Riverside were now taking part in the S.W.&M.F.A's Senior Cup. A change of competition failed to produce a change of fortune – they were knocked out in successive years in first round matches by Barry Dock Albions and Ebbw Vale.

Relations between Riverside and the S.W.&M.F.A. remained strained when a request for financial help was turned down in August 1907. The Association resolved "that no further applications for grants can be entertained." But just over a year later, Riverside were to land the most coveted prize of all.

Thursday, September 5th 1908 will always be celebrated as one of the most important milestones in the history of Cardiff City A.F.C. Once again, the Alexandra Hotel in Queen Street was the venue and once again an application by Cardiff Riverside – as they were now being called – to change their name to Cardiff City was on the agenda. Bart and his committee were taking nothing for granted. They just hoped that this time the S.W.&M.F.A. would acknowledge and then accommodate Riverside's ambition. The resolution was short – but oh so sweet:

> that permission be given on the condition that if a professional team should be started in Cardiff in the near future, they would relinquish the name.

Nobody knows how Bart Wilson reacted to the news for which he had worked so diligently for more than eight years. It would be natural to suppose though that he could hardly contain his delight. Recognition at last! It must have been a wonderful feeling – and well worth all the effort. Already Bart must have been looking forward to the next exciting chapter in Riverside's history.

As their members celebrated back in the clubhouse that evening, Bart, his crutches propped up against the wall, might well have been found in a quiet corner, studying the precise wording of the Association's decision. Relinquish the name!? After struggling so hard to acquire it? What were the S.W.&

M.F.A. thinking? The only professional team that would be started in Cardiff in the near future would be started by *him*. Let nobody be in any doubt about that. The Southern League beckoned – as did, in the distance, the Football League. With a new name came a new resolve – who or what could stop Cardiff City now?

# What a Load of Rubbish!

Bart was in something of a dilemma. Winning the right to call the club Cardiff City was a remarkable achievement for the honorary secretary and his loyal band of Riverside enthusiasts. Almost nine years after starting life as a local parks side, they had gone some way towards fulfilling his dream of establishing a professional team in the city. Riverside may not have been the best side in South Wales – or even in Cardiff – but they had taken the crucial first step of being recognized as the organisation most likely to represent the fastest-growing area of the Principality on the football field. In fact, they were in danger of becoming victims of their own success. Other clubs in the city had now been alerted to the potential of transforming association football from a pastime into a profession.

What to do next? Bart needed to act quickly to head off any rivals but Riverside also had to make sure they could walk before they started to run. It would make no sense to set up camp in the traditional rugby stronghold of Cardiff and then be forced out of town through lack of support. Teams such as Aberdare, Merthyr and Treharris had not regretted taking the plunge by joining the Second Division of the Southern League and regularly attracted home crowds of up to 12,000; Cardiff's General Railway Station was bursting with supporters on alternate Saturdays as they made their way to Ashton Gate to watch Bristol City in Division One of the Football League. Sandwiched between these two hotbeds of the game, Cardiff seemed ripe for conversion but although soccer was starting to become the main sport in schools in the city, Bart was still wary. Timing was everything – and the time wasn't right.

Neither were the facilities. The secretary of the Southern League, Harry Bradshaw, approached Cardiff City about joining but, without an enclosed ground, they had to decline his offer. So the newly-named club continued to play in the South

Wales League as Bart and the committee weighed up their options. By treading water, they were wisely treading carefully. Top-class soccer was their ultimate aim but the groundwork for the arrival of the professional game in Cardiff had to be first-class too. Anything less and it wouldn't take root.

When results started to improve – Cardiff City won or drew half of their South Wales League matches in 1908-09 – the committee decided it was time for action. They could wait no longer – they had to test the water. Would the public support professional football in Cardiff? There was only one way to find out.

The first of three friendlies played during the 1909-10 season was staged on October 5th at Cardiff Arms Park, the national home of Welsh rugby, alongside the cricket ground where Glamorgan had played their games for the last twenty years. Crystal Palace from the Southern League were the opposition and Cardiff emerged with a creditable 3-3 draw and gate receipts of £33.

The financial success of this inaugural exhibition game proved a great incentive to the committee. Six weeks later on November 17th, Bristol City were in action against another Cardiff City XI made up of promising local amateurs rather than the club's normal South Wales League side. In front of 2,000 spectators, Cardiff came horribly unstuck. Despite the presence of the local left winger, Ted Vizard, who went on to win 22 Welsh caps while playing for Bolton Wanderers, Bristol easily brushed them aside.

According to a report in that day's *South Wales Echo*, "The game commenced at a furious pace, and was fought with keenness by both sides. The visitors, as expected, exerted most pressure, but it was far from being a one-sided game."

With the First Division side 3-0 ahead at half-time, the reporter had to change tack. "When the second half opened, it was soon apparent that Bristol had settled down to their game. Simmonds, the Cardiff goalkeeper, had to save twice within a few minutes of the re-start from warm shots, one of which he dealt with by falling full length."

It was to get even hotter for the Cardiff side as Bristol City eventually ran out 7-1 winners. To add insult to injury, the gate receipts of £50 immediately disappeared as part of Bristol City's match guarantee.

Despite "putting in some fast work on the left wing", Ted Vizard learned that it was a long way from Cogan Old Boys in the Cardiff and District League to the English First Division. It was a gulf he was soon to bridge as he helped Bolton gain promotion to the top flight in his first season the following year.

Cardiff City may have lost money and the game but their confidence was sky high. In fact, the public's response to the two matches convinced Bart Wilson that a first-class association football side could now be set up in the city. Any doubts he might have harboured immediately disappeared and, in the aftermath of the Bristol result, Bart focused all his attention on overcoming the final hurdle – finding a new home for the new club.

The public pitches, which had served both Riverside and Cardiff City so well since 1899, had now been outgrown. Although Cardiff Arms Park had been ideal for the exhibition games, Bart knew there was no permanent future for a football team at a rugby ground. He had shown missionary zeal – some might say cheek – in taking the game into the heart of enemy territory, but he had pulled it off.

If soccer were to succeed, the dribbling game had to be independent of the running game of rugby. It could not rely on the goodwill of a group of people who viewed this new-fangled form of football as a threat to their own great passion which then was justifiably considered as the national sport of Wales.

As the twentieth century moved into its second decade, Bart Wilson moved up a gear. He knew he had to act quickly so the search for a ground began. After scouring the city for a suitable site, Bart opened negotiations with the Bute Estate to buy a plot in the Leckwith Common area to the west of the city. When he met a leading city councillor, John Mander, in Cathays Park, he took pains to outline his plan. But Councillor Mander immediately suggested an alternative: would Bart be interested in some waste land owned by Cardiff Corporation on Sloper Road on the edge of the common? If the club moved there, then he promised the Corporation would do all it could to help.

Bart went to inspect the Sloper Road site with a keen Cardiff

City player and local printer, Ivor Parker. At the age of twenty-three, Ivor was to become the youngest member of the original board of directors when the club turned professional in April 1910. In an interview in the *South Wales Echo* nearly fifty years later, Ivor recalled Bart Wilson's crucial contribution to the choice of the club's new home. The pair had examined some ground near a junction in Sloper Road which seemed to fit the bill but Bart wasn't convinced:

> I can see Bart now, leaning on his crutches. He said "let's go further down the road. If we go there, there will be no room for expansion." How right he turned out to be.
> His foresight was remarkable. We decided that this bigger plot of land could hold at least 10,000 – we never realised that one day it would hold 60,000!

But the sweet smell of success was unlikely to be found at Cardiff City's new home – the Corporation's former rubbish tip between Sloper Road and the Taff Vale Railway Embankment. As he made his way back to De Burgh Street, Bart wondered if Councillor Mander would be able to keep his promise. He felt a letter – or two – might be in order.

On January 17th 1910, Bart wrote to the Parks, Open Spaces and Burial Board Committee asking if Cardiff City could rent the Sloper Road land. The five acres had to be in "a compact form suitable for the purposes of a football ground, on a seven year lease, with the optimum of renewal for fourteen or twenty-one years."

He offered £60 rent for the first year, with an annual increase of £10 rising up to £100. The club would be prepared to lease the land from April 1st, pay half a year's rent in advance and provide satisfactory sureties. Five days later, Bart wrote to the Committee again. On second thoughts, his football club were now willing to offer fresh terms for fourteen rather than twenty-one years when the initial seven-year lease ended.

Two days after Bart's second letter, the Parks Committee resolved to ask the Property and Markets Committee to instruct the city engineer to "report forthwith." Before the end of the month, councillors on the Electrical Lighting and Tramways sub-committee had also lent their support. Following the lead taken by some English cities, Cardiff had developed a tram road system and members liked the idea of running a special service to Cardiff City's new home. It was resolved that:

> in the opinion of this committee, the establishment of a football ground would be advantageous in as much as a large percentage of persons proceeding and returning from the matches would be conveyed by means of tram cars.

The sub-committee urged the Parks Committee to take their observations on board and on February 17th – a month to the day that Bart had written his first letter – his offer was accepted. From April 1st, the club would be the proud lessees – in effect owners – of a former rubbish tip. Where there's muck, there's brass – Bart passionately hoped that the proverb would prove true.

The deal was done if not quite dusted. The club had to provide two or more guarantors and when one of the original backers withdrew his support, the whole project was temporarily in doubt. At another meeting of the Parks, Open Spaces and Burial Board Committee on March 30th, a letter from Norman Robertson, the club's acting solicitor, was read to members including the Lord Mayor John Chappell.

Mr Roberston explained that because of the unsettled state of the coal industry, "there had been great difficulties in obtaining promises of support" but now five men had provisionally agreed to become guarantors. They were given as D.A. Thomas (Lord Rhondda), J. Bell Harrison, Councillors H.C. Vivian and Charles Wall and most crucially Lord Ninian Crichton-Stuart. The latter, second son of the third Marquess of Bute – and future MP for Cardiff Boroughs – had stepped into the breach and in recognition of his help, the new ground was named after him.

After councillors were told that another twenty-four men were willing to become sureties if their liability was limited to £5, two members made significant contributions to the debate. True to his word, Councillor Mander said that in the interests of Cardiff generally, as well as of football, the committee should do all they could to reach an agreement with the club.

Then Councillor Wall, soon to become a Cardiff City director, suggested that the enclosed ground could be used in the summer for baseball. He said it was a very popular game which would become even more so on a properly protected pitch. The Lord Mayor and his colleagues were sympathetic and, after visiting Sloper Road, they agreed that the Corporation should give Cardiff City the chance to develop the site.

On the very same day, final confirmation of Bart's intuitive feeling that professional football's time in Cardiff had arrived was being provided. Less than a mile away from City Hall, the club's third exhibition match took place at the former Harlequins Rugby Ground near the tram terminus on Newport Road. After Crystal Palace and Bristol City, it was Middlesbrough's turn to take on a Cardiff City XI.

Middlesbrough were another First Division team who boasted two of England's finest goalscorers in Alf Common and Steve Bloomer. Common had become British football's first four-figure transfer player when he moved from Sunderland to Middlesbrough for £1,000 in 1905 while Bloomer had scored five goals in England's 9-1 annihilation of Wales at Cardiff Arms Park in 1896. Quite what this distinguished pair of internationals made of having to change in the Royal Oak pub, on the corner of Beresford Road and Broadway, was not recorded for posterity. The result was: City beat Middlesbrough 2-1.

The home side was again made up of the best local talent – a mixture of players from City, Cardiff Camerons, Cardiff Corinthians and the Post Office. The local newspaper headlines accurately summed up the match:

MIDDLESBROUGH TAKEN OFF THEIR GUARD.
CARDIFF SNATCH VICTORY IN FINAL STAGES.
LEAGUE CRACKS BEATEN.

There was no score at half-time but Middlesbrough took the lead on the hour when Bloomer

the famous shooter, gave Pritchard no chance with a stinger from the left.

For the next quarter of an hour, the Northerners, who all along had played pretty football, slackened down a bit, and then, following a strong attack on Williamson, Evans sent in a nice dropping centre from the left wing, which was only partially cleared by McLeod. The ball came to Boswell, who sent in a high shot, which Williamson caught and threw away. The ball, however, had entered the net, and the large crowd cheered with delight as the referee pointed to the centre.

A few minutes later, another attack on the visitors' goal forced Williamson to concede a corner, and from the resultant kick, Wilson headed through out of Williamson's reach.

Another Wilson, Bart (no relation), was the toast of Cardiff City on March 30th 1910. As well as winning over the Parks, Open Spaces and Burial Board Committee, Bart's boys had beaten one of the best teams in English football – albeit in an exhibition match – and the public had voted with their feet. Eight thousand had turned up to show their support for the third friendly match to be held on a weekday. And to cap it all, the club had made a profit of £39.

Bart knew there was no going back. The future was bright. The future would be blue – the colour of the club's new strip, replacing the Battenburg look of chocolate and amber quarters. Cardiff City now had a potential team, a ground and a following – what they needed next was a professional organisation to pull everything together and an experienced man to run the side. This letter to the *Western Mail* in early April reflected the growing enthusiasm for football in the city:

> Sir. Cardiff being somewhat late in starting a first-class Association club, it is absolutely essential that a manager of experience, with sound judgement, carrying weight and respect in the administration of the laws of the game, should be secured, if possible. A good start means success in the end. As regards the financial support being forthcoming, I do not doubt this for one moment in a fair-minded, sport-loving city like Cardiff. My final words are: Hurry up!

Bart took the hint. Within three weeks of receiving the Corporation's approval, the first professional football club in Cardiff was up and running. Bart had never worked so hard in his life. Having sorted out the guarantors, he and Norman Robertson spent hours drawing up the legal documents and the first prospectus was filed with the Registrar of Joint Stock Companies. Cardiff City Association Football Club Ltd was officially incorporated on April 21st 1910 with its registered office at 9 Park Place – from where Robertson practiced as a solicitor. Lloyds were appointed the club's bankers, Bart Wilson was confirmed as secretary and the directors were named as Frank Burfitt, a dairyman, clerk Percy Hansford, Charlie Kyd the stock-keeper, Job McGill, an electrical engineer who lived down the road from Bart in De Burgh Street, Lew Nash, a builder, Ivor Parker the printer and John Taylor, a clerk.

As a limited liability company, Cardiff City A.F.C. had £3,000 in capital, divided up into 6,000 shares worth 10s each. The seven directors all bought twenty shares each and Lord Rhondda became the first non-board shareholder. To help him become involved, Ivor Parker had to borrow £5 from his father Walter, a rugby fan and the owner of the Imperial Printing Company. In 1915, Walter Parker followed Ivor onto the board after his son had emigrated to Australia a few years earlier, and was chairman when they won the F.A.Cup in 1927. In the *South Wales Echo* article of 1959, Ivor recalled his father's conversion to football:

> Dad was not very keen to lend me the money. He was a most staunch rugby man and did not like the idea of men playing for money. Anyway, he gave the £5 as my contribution towards drawing up the articles of association under the Companies (Consolidation) Act 1908.
>
> Dad first came to see the City while Cardiff rugby were away and he liked the fewer stoppages there were in the game. The turning point came one day when he decided to go to Newport to watch a soccer match while Cardiff rugby were playing at home to Newport.
>
> On the way he told me what really attracted him to soccer. "It's a business and no business can stand still. It must go ahead and build"'

The club had ostensibly been set up to promote first-class football in the Cardiff area but that was not the only reason for their formation – as the original Memorandum of Association shows:

> The objects for which the company is established are:
>
> To carry on, and manage, the affairs, or business, of a club for fostering, practising and generally promoting, or stimulating proficiency, in the game, or sport, of football, or any other lawful old English or other games, sports or pastimes, including cricket, golf, lacrosse, hockey, polo, running, jumping, cycling, motoring, tennis, bowls, quoits, and the like; and generally to encourage all such athletics, exercises, practices, and proceedings as are deemed conducive to the efficient training and development of the human frame, with full

authority to the company to own, lease, or hire, level, drain, play, lay
out, adapt, prepare and maintain any grounds for the purposes of the
company as may from time to time be deemed expedient.

No mention there of Councillor Wall's baseball, or indeed
boxing which would feature in Ninian Park's future, but it is
interesting to note that Cardiff City hadn't forgotten their crick-
eting roots. In fact, virtually any sport would be catered for at
the new ground. There were more surprises to come because,
after explaining how Cardiff City would operate as "social club
proprietors and refreshment contractors", the list of objectives
continued:

To lend money to such persons and on such terms as may seem expedient and, in particular, to customers of, and any persons having
dealings with, the company and to give any guarantee or indemnity as
may seem expedient.

As well as making sure that the supporters and directors were
supplied with their half-time cup of tea or tot of whisky, Cardiff
City were to become moneylenders. And the club's activities
were not only confined to Cardiff, so wide-ranging was the brief
of the new organisation:

To do all, or any, of the above things in any part of the world, and
either as principals, agents, contractors, trustees, or otherwise, and by,
or through, trustees, agents or otherwise and either alone or in
conjunction with others.

Not too many of the club's supporters would have been
worried by the small print – even if they had found the time to
read it. The only thing that mattered was that Cardiff City was
in business. Now came the job of selling the shares, and a fortnight later, Bart arranged a public meeting at the Grand Hotel.
A newspaper report the following day revealed that five of the
company's directors and its secretary attended the meeting.
Financial details of the launch were revealed and potential
shareholders were told that the subscription would close in just
over a week's time. The paper revealed that Cardiff City had
been invited to join the Second Division of the Southern League
as well as the Western League.

Despite the reference to moneylending in the Memorandum of Association, the newspaper report showed that club officials were keen to play down the financial importance of the new organisation:

> Mr Norman Robertson said the company was not being promoted merely to make money but primarily to foster the Association game. Soccer had made rapid strides in the Valleys during the last few years and it was played by 80 per cent of the schoolboys of Cardiff. Their ambition was to get into the Second Division of the English League and to do that it would be necessary to engage the services of first-class players.

Just over a fortnight later towards the end of May, Cardiff City launched another offensive. This time, the venue was the Oddfellows Hall in Charles Street for what one newspaper called "a largely-attended meeting". Again, Norman Robertson and Bart attended – along with a representative of the Great Western Railway Company. Details of the corporation lease and the new company were explained before the club's solicitor put forward the main reason for the meeting:

> Mr Robertson said he wished to correct the impression in some quarters that the movement was primarily a money-making concern. Its primary object was the promotion of the Soccer code in the district but, of course, dividends would be declared according to the success of the undertaking. The directors would, however, receive no promotion or other fees.
>
> Shareholders would get a reduction of 25 per cent on their season tickets, so that, even if no dividends were declared, they would have their money back within a few seasons.

Norman Robertson then revealed that the new ground would be levelled and enclosed very soon. The site was "ideal in every respect. It was even drier than the St. Helen's ground, Swansea. There was plenty of scope in Cardiff with its teeming population inside and in the immediate neighbourhood, for first-class clubs of both codes to be run side-by-side amicably."

Enough shares had been taken up to justify the directors going to allotment, when the shares would be divided up. The board would be filled with directors at the first statutory meeting at which "the shareholders would have perfect freedom to propose any gentlemen they chose for vacancies".

The newspaper reported that the gentleman from GWR had confirmed the claim that association football in South Wales was becoming more popular all the time. "Even on the day of the Scotland v Wales rugby match at Cardiff," he told the meeting, "an important soccer match was being played at Bristol, and four trains were run from South Wales conveying 1,700 people. When Ton Pentre played a match at Bristol, 936 passengers travelled up from the Rhondda and 800 made the journey from Aberystwyth."

It was Bart's job to bring everyone up to date with the players and the man who would run the team. The newspaper reported:

> The secretary stated that a good manager would be appointed and he was receiving 20 or 30 letters a week from players offering their services. Practically every player in the Rhondda district had applied for a position and he had also received applications from players in the First and Second Divisions and the Southern League. He thought they would be able to fix up an exceptionally good team and one that should next season be a credit to Cardiff.

Bart had now achieved his first aim: a professional football team for Cardiff. It marked the end of a long struggle for the enthusiastic group of cricketers who had gathered at the secretary's home more than ten years before to form Riverside A.F.C. They had travelled a long way in a very short space of time but Bart knew that their journey was not yet over. Eventually, Cardiff City had to become a successful side in the English Football League. In the short term, the more pressing problems of building a football ground, appointing a manager and recruiting some quality players had to be tackled. There was still much to do.

In early June, the Cardiff City board was re-vamped. The former Wales and Cardiff rugby union forward Sid Nicholls became chairman, Charles Kyd was elected vice-chairman and the original seven directors were supplemented by Joseph Brain, the former Glamorgan cricket captain and a member of the brewing family, John Pritchard, Councillor Charlie Wall and Walter Riden.

The recruitment of Sid Nicholls to the board was crucial to the club's early survival. The brother of Gwyn – the more famous of the two rugby-playing brothers – gave Cardiff City a certain credibility which negated much of the anti-soccer bias engendered by some members of the Arms Park club.

In the short-term absence of a manager, Bart assumed responsibility for running the team and his first professional signing turned out to be one of the best in Cardiff City's history. Jack 'Bala' Evans had come to South Wales to look for work as a printer after badly injuring his shoulder while playing for Wrexham. He later recalled how he came to play for Cardiff: "The doctor told me that was only one cure and that I would have to have a complete rest but I was not all that well-off and couldn't afford to. I did a light job and my shoulder became strong again and the old urge to play forced itself on me and I signed for Cwmparc-and-Treorchy."

Jack was spotted playing against Cardiff City in the South Wales League and the new club snapped him up. "Jack's signing bonus was 6s," Bart later recalled with a chuckle. "It was all we had and it included his train fare from Treorchy!"

By the time Jack Evans had put pen to paper, work on transforming the former rubbish tip into a football ground had just begun. The club and their supporters were faced with an enormous task. The five acres had to be levelled and then enclosed – all within three months because the club's application to join the Second Division of the Southern League had been accepted. Bart was keen to enlist the help of any volunteer labourers so when one anonymous supporter approached the secretary about lending a hand, Bart asked him and some friends to report back to the site one evening in early June. Years later, that supporter explained how Ninian Park was created:

> It had been decided that the area which sloped away from the railway should be built up to form an embankment along the length of the playing pitch, the site of which had been staked out and ran parallel to Sloper Road.
>
> We proceeded to dig and level the site of the pitch, wheeling the spoil in barrows to the far side where it was tipped to form the bank. The contractors arranged with the Corporation for refuse to be tipped onto the bank, while the local factories and the gasworks on Penarth

Road sent along ashes and clinker from their furnaces, until enough material had been tipped to form quite a substantial bank.

The spectators who later came to stand on this bank suffered whenever there was a stiff wind, since the dust and ashes flew up causing them to resemble coal-miners who had worked a hard day at the pit. To complete the embankment, large wooden hoardings were built along the top to prevent free viewing and access to the railway.

Eventually, low ash banks were raised on all four sides of the pitch which was enclosed by a white picket fence. A small wooden grandstand – with a canvas roof and room for about 200 spectators – was built and turnstiles were installed at the Grangetown and Canton Ends. Dressing rooms and offices were provided in a wooden building in the corner of the field at the Canton End. The pitch, having been laid out on an old rubbish dump, was rough and needed a lot of rolling. On match-days, players and spectators would have to remove pieces of coke and glass which had worked their way to the surface. Jack Evans later recalled how the players were able to earn an unexpected bonus:

When our first-ever professional team reported for training, we were told we would be paid 6d an hour for picking up glass from the playing pitch.

Everybody jumped at the offer, and indeed it was a strange sight to see all the players walking up and down the pitch, mornings and afternoons, doing this job – we certainly did not look like footballers! Unfortunately, even I missed one piece of glass but found it during a match when I fell. My knee was permanently scarred.

The facilities may have been spartan – they were certainly not fit for a king – but Lord Ninian Crichton-Stuart seemed happy enough with them when he officially opened the ground on September 1st 1910.

The former rubbish tip wasn't the only part of Cardiff City's operation to be transformed. Once Bart had appointed Davy McDougall as player-manager and captain, their squad of players became unrecognisable from the collection of local amateurs. McDougall was signed from Glasgow Rangers and he began recruiting players mainly from the North of England and Scotland. An exception was goalkeeper Ted Husbands who joined from Wrexham after a season with Liverpool Reserves.

Cardiff City's playing staff for the 1910-11 season also included James McKenzie (Middlesbrough), Jock Duffy (Dundee Harps), Bob Lawrie (Third Lanark), Jack Ramsey (Dundee), James McDonald (Aberdeen), Jimmy Malloch (Dundee) and Billy Watts (Glossop). Apart from Jack Evans, South Wales was represented by Tom Abley (Treharris) and Bob Peake (Cwmparc-and-Treorchy). With a squad of fourteen full-time professionals, the rest of the club's players were local amateurs who made up the numbers when City had to put our more than one team.

There really was no alternative to importing players with proven track records. Although he may have regretted the absence of former local heroes, Bart knew a solid, confidence-building start was essential if the club were to survive. In preparation for the big day, a couple of trial matches pitching professionals against amateurs were held at Ninian Park, the second attracting a gate of more than 2,000.

On Thursday September 1st – five months to the day since being granted the lease to the ground – Cardiff City made their debut as a professional club against the First Division champions Aston Villa in front of 7,000 spectators. The match was kicked off at five o'clock by Lord Ninian Crichton-Stuart and ended in a narrow 2-1 defeat for the new boys. Villa, with half a dozen first-team regulars, were 2-0 up at half-time and the honour of scoring the first Cardiff goal at Ninian Park appropriately fell to the club's first professional, Jack Evans. The following day's *Western Mail* was fulsome in its praise:

> The Cardiff City Association Football Club has every reason to congratulate itself on the success of the inaugural match with Aston Villa yesterday. Not only did the players give an excellent account of themselves, but they managed to raise the enthusiasm of some 7,000 spectators. Besides Lord Ninian Stuart and Mr. D.A. Thomas, MP, there were many prominent people among the spectators, as well as a number of Welsh Rugby players, who evinced much interest in the game.

After the Villa defeat, Cardiff City hit a Bristol League XI for six before opening their Glamorgan League campaign by beating Ton Pentre 3-2 in front of nearly 5,000 spectators.

Professional soccer had well and truly arrived in South Wales, it was here to stay and, according to Harry Bradshaw, there was no limit to what could be achieved. On a flying visit to inspect Ninian Park in the middle of September, the Southern League's secretary voiced his amazement at the progress made at the new ground:

> I am simply astounded with what has been accomplished. You have done wonders and I would not have believed you could have done so much. It is already a very fine ground and it is nothing to what you can make of it.
>
> I can see endless possibilities in this – there is the making of the finest football ground in the country, because there is nothing to undo, and you can go straight ahead with your improvements.

With that unequivocal endorsement ringing in their ears, Cardiff City took Ton Pentre to the cleaners in their very first Southern League game. In front of 8,000 at Ninian Park, they beat their South Wales rivals 4-1 – a shattering blow to Ton who were also making their Southern League debut. The headlines said it all:

A 'FIGHT' FOR POINTS
CARDIFF CITY'S ROUGH PASSAGE
CLEAN FOOTBALL TRIUMPHS

'Citizen' of the *Western Mail* wrote of a game "marred by several unfortunate incidents, due mainly to the over-excitement of the visiting team, which culminated when one of the Ton Pentre players was sent off the field for a deliberate and very bad foul."

He praised Cardiff for not losing their heads and for sticking to clean football but lambasted the referee – "an old Rugby official in charge of his first Association match of importance"– for losing his grip on the game. In his report, 'Citizen' also fired the first warning shots across the bows of the rugby community who were rightly starting to view football as a threat:

> The game had all the intensity of a cup-tie, being fast and furious – sometimes literally furious – from beginning to end, and as an example of the concentrated excitement that can be conveyed by Association football, must have gone far to complete the conversion of the many one-time Rugby enthusiasts who witnessed the sport.

A week later, this time in front of a record crowd at Ninian Park, Cardiff were knocked out of the F.A.Cup when they lost 1-0 to Merthyr in the third preliminary round. A regular rugby writer on the *Western Mail* sporting the nom-de-plume of 'Forward' could contain himself no longer. 'Soccer's Menace to the Rugby Game' screamed the headline as 'Forward' came out fighting:

> Eight thousand strong was the army that marched down to see Ton Pentre at Ninian Park just over a week ago, and everybody wondered. Last Saturday, a still greater army of over twelve thousand invaded a district which had been unexplored till the advent of the City club.... To argue any longer that Soccer is not a serious menace to Rugger in the Welsh metropolis is tantamount to betraying an ignorance of existing facts and a narrow, prejudiced outlook of possible future developments. It was only a qualifying round between two second-rate teams in the English Cup competition and yet the match magnetised an assemblage of nearly thirteen thousand souls.

'Forward' then proceeded to bemoan the decline of rugby in Merthyr and Aberdare before predicting its imminent demise in the Rhondda. The Welsh Rugby Union was berated for showing, "with characteristic apathy, a masterly inactivity which makes one despair". The WRU seemed content to "follow a policy of drift" as Cardiff Rugby Club suffered successive defeats by Pontypool and Bristol which had led to many supporters making "open declarations of intentions to transfer allegiance to the Cardiff City Club".

'Forward' then described soccer as "a very real and a very serious menace to the existence of Rugby in some localities" before taking the gloves off altogether:

> That menace will be all the greater should it ever to come to pass that Cardiff gain promotion from the Southern League into the First Division of the English League. Stranger things have happened, and for practical illustration, one need not go beyond the rapid rise, within the past few years only, of such clubs as Bradford, Oldham Athletic and Leeds.

Just over a decade later, a strange thing had happened. Cardiff City were in Division One of the Football League – and rugby was still alive and kicking in South Wales. One can only imagine Bart Wilson's reaction to such hysterical hyperbole generated by the club's first season as a professional team. His faith had been justified, the football bandwagon was rolling and, although it had not been his intention, the running game seemed to be on the run.

In the event, the club's first experience of competitive football proved something of an anti-climax. Having been among the promotion contenders for most of the season, they finished a very creditable fourth after losing at Ninian Park on successive days over Easter to Reading and Stoke – both of whom went up.

The following season they went one better after a complete overhaul of the team by the experienced Fred Stewart who had been managing Stockport County for eighteen years. Cardiff City had decided a full time secretary-manager was needed if they were to make progress in football's pyramid so they advertised the position in the *Athletic News*, a magazine read by the football community throughout Britain.

Stewart proved an inspired choice, becoming Cardiff's most successful manager. After signing a three-year agreement at £4 a week – the players' maximum wage at the time – plus bonuses, he set about the task of rebuilding the team. Not for the first time in his twenty-two years at Ninian Park, Stewart used his vast knowledge of League football to improve Cardiff City. Out went all but four of the players he had inherited from Davy McDougall – Husbands, Bob Lawrie, Tom Abley and Jack Evans. Like McDougall, Stewart used Scotland and the North of England as recruiting grounds.

The former player-manager saw the writing on the wall when left-half Billy Hardy joined Cardiff from Heart of Midlothian, having worked with Stewart at Stockport County. The new man in charge was so keen to sign the nineteen-year-old North Easterner that he paid the £25 transfer fee himself and was later reimbursed by the club. Other new signings included Arthur Waters (Stockport County), Bob Leah (Colne), Harry Featherstone (St. Mirren), Harry Tracey (Colne) and Eddie Thompson and Jack Burton who both joined from Nelson in Lancashire.

Ninian Park was changing too. A wooden grandstand had

been started in October 1910, built by some supporters and players – including Jack Evans. "I got 35s a week as wages," recalled Cardiff's first professional player, "and I was promised a job as soon as possible. I had a job all right – I helped to build the first grandstand at Ninian Park!" By August 1911, gas and water had been connected to the manager's office and the dressing rooms.

In front of enthusiastic and ever-increasing crowds, Cardiff City had looked well set for promotion until mid-February when they lost consecutive matches to Portsmouth and Merthyr – again, the two clubs which were eventually promoted. Merthyr finished top and were recognised as the best team in South Wales.

But the 1911-12 season was not without its rewards. History was made when Cardiff City beat Pontypridd 3-0 to win the Welsh Cup for the first time. A South Wales team had never lifted the trophy before and the victory was marked by a wonderful gesture of sportsmanship by Cardiff's player-coach, the Newtown-born Welsh international George Latham who had joined City from Stoke eighteen months earlier.

After drawing 0-0 with Pontypridd at Ninian Park, Cardiff lost half-back Bob Lawrie through injury for the replay. He was replaced by Latham, now only an occasional player, but the coach's personal pride in helping City lift the Welsh Cup didn't prevent him from giving his winner's medal to the unfortunate Lawrie.

It was a case of third time lucky for City in the 1912-13 season. After finishing fourth and then third, they were promoted to the First Division of the Southern League by winning the championship. With a new goalkeeper, Jack Kneeshaw from Colne, and a stronger defence thanks to the signings of Tommy Doncaster (Barnsley), Henry 'Kidder' Harvey (Wallsend) and Pat Cassidy (Bradford City), the club lost only one of their 24 league matches. Extra money provided by the board for team strengthening had been spent wisely by Fred Stewart.

From the opening 1-1 draw with debutants Swansea at the Vetch Field to the 3-2 defeat of Aberdare Athletic in April, Cardiff dominated the division. The highlight was their 3-0 win over Luton Town in front of a record 20,000 at Ninian Park while the club's defence of the Welsh Cup was abruptly ended by Swansea – 4-2 winners at the new ground in front of a 12,000 crowd.

Fred Stewart's mid-summer shopping spree saw more fresh faces arriving at Ninian Park in time for the new season – most of them from the North East. Jim Henderson was signed from Scotswood, George West and Tom Witts from Wallsend, Joe Clarke from Hebburn Argyle and Billy Davidson came from Wallsend Shipway.

The 1913-14 season also saw the introduction of a modern-style match day programme – courtesy of the Imperial Printing Company. The programme provides a fascinating insight into Cardiff – the club and the city – just before the First World War. The first issue was produced for a match against Newport on September 3rd in the Southern Alliance, a midweek competition for First and Second Division clubs in the Southern League. The programme's authors were obviously proud of their creation:

> In introducing the first number of an Official Programme and Journal dealing with the doings of Cardiff's Premier Soccer Club and the only team in the Metropolis of Wales who has ever attained the honour of admission to a First Division League, we avail ourselves of the opportunity of stating some of our plans for the future.

These included a results service on a score board, "one of the finest in the country" which could be seen from any part of the field and exclusive news of the players. Photographs and pen portraits of Sid Nicholls, Fred Stewart and Bart Wilson were included in the first issue. Bart, the supporters were informed, would be in charge of the reserves who "this season will be a very formidable lot, a hard nut to crack. Mr Wilson has been overheard chuckling to himself very much recently."

The programme notes reminded the supporters that they would be expected to buy the publication for 1d from sellers – "all of whom will wear a distinguishing coat, supplied to our order by the Civic Clothiers, St. John's Square, Cardiff." Apart from the club's official tailors, a variety of businesses advertised in the programme – florists, sports shops, cab companies providing "high-class motor char-a-bancs for football and cricket teams and picnic parties" and a number of hotels, including one with a certain S.H. Nicholls as proprietor. Readers were encouraged to enter a football joke competition and win a 2s 6d prize and the programme was peppered with one-liners like "Generally speaking, women are – generally speaking" to less sexist contributions such as this word of advice to disheartened supporters. "If you get 'down in the mouth' don't worry. Jonah was further down than you will ever be – and he got out all right!"

Much of the humour was provided by an anonymous columnist who went by the mysterious name of 'Fels Naptha'. It could well have been Walter Parker whose company printed the programme. Fels Naptha is a heavy duty laundry soap which, like Cardiff City, celebrated its centenary in 1999, and which, according to its publicity, is "ideal for pre-wash spotting!" Shakespeare, Sterne and Dickens were frequently quoted in the 'Fels Naptha' notes and his wide-ranging brief meant that no subject was out of bounds.

Not surprisingly, he was usually supportive of the club and its directors. One week, the board members would be praised for their attendance at matches, the next disgruntled fans found themselves being reprimanded. Secretary-manager Fred Stewart was complimented for his transactions in the transfer market:

> It is a comparatively easy task to sign on a team of "stars" if you can pay out cheques of three and four figures ad lib, but when you are reduced to the expedient of "making bricks without straw" it is, to say the least, "hard going".

It was hard going for Cardiff City during the 1913-14 season. They lost their first five Southern League games by the odd goal and were still bottom when their arch-rivals Swansea knocked them out of the F.A.Cup by winning 2-0 at the Vetch Field in late November.

At times, 'Fels Naptha' could be moved to verse: the last stanza of his poem written in the aftermath of the Swansea defeat, urged the fans to keep faith:

We've got a good team and we know it,
There's nothing in fitness they lack;
Let's hope that their form will soon show it,
Don't look back!

He wasn't averse to a little homespun philosophy – "Worry is interest paid on trouble before it is due. Don't worry" – and would quite often offer what turned out to be accurate assessments of most of the players – "Keenor is another player who has shown great promise, and I believe he will go far." All the way to a historic F.A.Cup win at Wembley, as it happened.

The signing of full-back Charlie Brittan from Spurs for a then Cardiff record of £1,000 in November 1913 met with the approval of 'Fels Naptha'. Having recovered from their disastrous start, Cardiff City reached mid-table in February and his match report on a 0-0 draw with Brighton contained this brief accolade: "I am reluctant to pick out any of our side for special mention but I feel compelled to pay a special tribute to the Captain, Charlie Brittan. He played like – Charlie Brittan. 'Nuf said."

That report also contained the first of what was to become a regular feature of the programmes – the promotion of players in their outside occupations. In this case, Billy Hardy was the beneficiary:

> The halves, as they always do, played a great game. That reminds me. Hardy has just commenced business as a coal merchant. If the measure of his success is to be gauged by his popularity, then he will do well. His many friends are anxious that he shall have a good send-off, and as we can all help to achieve this, let me appeal to my readers to send their orders for coal to:-
> Wm. HARDY, 28, Tewkesbury Street, Cathays, Cardiff.

Frequent mentions were made of Hardy's new business and when Charlie Brittan later became a newsagent and tobacconist in Cowbridge Road, he received the same supportive treatment.

At the end of the season, Cardiff City finished a creditable tenth in the table and 'Fels Naptha' felt it was time to pay tribute – not with "long, and sometimes wearisome, statistics of the doings of the club" but with open letters to everyone involved – from the chairman to the players to the press and his readers.

Everyone was congratulated and there were some especially kind words for Bart Wilson, assistant secretary and reserve team manager:

> The growth and success of Cardiff City A.F.C. must, I am sure, give to you immense satisfaction, as you have been with it from the embryo stage, and followed its fortunes keenly. You seem to have pursued the policy that:-
> Nothing is achieved before it be thoroughly attempted, as all your efforts on behalf of the club have been thorough, and undertaken with that enthusiasm which goes a long way towards success.

In summary, 'Fels Naptha' declared his "absolute confidence" in both the way the club was being run and his ability to maintain the programme's standard next season. His last column ended on a sad note:

> To everything there is a season, and a time to every purpose under the sun. The season for football has ended, and, like Othello, my occupation's gone. It is at such moments as these one realises the truth of Dickens' lament: How cold the comfort in "good-bye".

There was to be little more than cold comfort for Cardiff during the 1914-15 season and, in fact, for the next four years. The First World War had begun in August and, although they just missed out on promotion by finishing 3rd in the Second Division of the Southern League, football was inevitably overshadowed by the hostilities in Belgium. Fred Stewart signed winger George Beare from Everton and full-back Arthur Layton from Middlesbrough and when the goals dried up as City dropped to 17th place in the table, he brought in Liverpool's Arthur Goddard to form a right-wing partnership with Beare.

The opening programme and journal of the new season contained a rare photograph of the club's president, the Earl of Plymouth. He had accepted the position through his friendship with one of the club's directors. There was also a report of a final club trial and an appeal for certain Ninian Parkites to stop criticising the players:

> Barracking serves no purpose but that of evil. It brings out the worst propensities of those who indulge in it, and it engenders a spirit of rebellion in the heart of the player barracked, who soon asks himself

"What's the use of trying?" Many a promising player has been spoiled for his club through this practice. Don't let us have it in Cardiff.

It was a different type of criticism which was to preoccupy the programme editor for the rest of the season. Although the Football Association had decided that matches would continue, there was a growing feeling – particularly among the press – that the game should be suspended until the war was over. Those men who attended matches were derided as "loafers".

In September, the editor denounced opposition to the playing of football matches as both "humorous and contemptible" and focused his anger on two papers, the *Western Mail* and the *Cardiff Evening Express*, for setting football against rugby to gain "a little cheap popularity" during the crisis:

> Last week they published a photograph taken at Ninian Park and another at Cardiff Arms Park to show the comparison between events taking place on each ground in order to belittle and intimidate the club.
>
> They have shown an utter disregard of the legal and moral responsibility of the club towards the players, and have ignored as not worth considering, the fact that nearly all the players are married men with families to support, and that in many instances, if a footballer gets injured his career as a player is finished.

The editor revealed that all the players had volunteered for home defence duty and were subscribing weekly to the War Fund which would also benefit by £60 in practice match proceeds. Seven signed players had enlisted, Ninian Park had been offered for drilling use and manager Fred Stewart had told the principal military officers that "every man was anxious to show that they are animated by a loyal and patriotic spirit, and desirous of helping all in their power."

It was a theme to which the programme would frequently return as the war continued. In early November, the *Western Mail* was in the dock again for having "stopped issuing their football edition and reporting football to any extent". Both barrels were then turned on the paper's decision to withdraw coverage:

> On the face of it, this appears to be taking a very high and patriotic stand. But is it? They have not yet stopped the supply of horse-racing

reports, or attempted to discourage those who support the Turf by eliminating tips from their columns.

They have not yet denounced the thousands of eligible young men who nightly flock to the various places of amusement in our town, nor have they suggested that these places should be closed. Why not? What is the distinction? Football only occupies two hours per week, whilst places of amusement are opened nightly.

After enlisting the support of writer H.G. Wells through a letter he had written to *The Times*, the programme editor suggested a possible solution to the problem:

It seems to us that the only way to stop the opposition of this paper is to turn the ground into a racecourse, and thus provide opportunities for the publication of tips to its readers.

Later that month, the club directors – in a simple advert with the headline 'Your King and Country Need You' – appealed to all their supporters to offer their services "at this most momentous period in the history of the British Empire". The team had certainly set a good example. The number of enlisted players rose to nine when Fred Keenor and John Stephenson joined the Middlesex Regiment in February.

A month later, it was time for the directors to make what the programme described as a "special and earnest appeal" to their supporters. Under the headline 'For the Good of the Club', 'Fels Naptha' outlined the financial problems facing football. Many players had been signed on but with the war producing depleted gates, directors had been forced to reduce wages. As a result, the players needed to find summer work. It was time for some care in the community:

It is unthinkable that in a great industrial centre such as Cardiff, the services of such men such as Cassidy, Goddard, Layton, Kneeshaw, Hardy and many others, should be lost to the club for the want of about four months' work!

It behoves us all therefore to do something towards that end. It is not someone else's business. If you care an atom for the future of the club you are asked to interest yourself earnestly in this project. Maybe you are working in a fitting shop, or some other place, where the services of a healthy, able-bodied man is required. If so, drop a line to Mr Stewart (Secretary-Manager), 2 Pentre Street, Grange, and he will use his judgement to choose a player best fitted for the work.

Let us all help. If we do so earnestly, the difficulty will be easily overcome. The position in which the players find themselves demands our ungrudging sympathy and help. It can best be described by Shakespeare:

> You take my house when you take the prop
> That doth sustain my house: you take my life
> When you do take the means by which I live.

No mention was made of the results of this appeal but throughout March, 'Fels Naptha' reminded readers of the problems caused by the war – such as the withdrawal of cheap rail tickets for football clubs – before announcing that admission prices were being put up.

Then it was the turn of the players to be hit in their pockets. The football authorities decided to limit their earnings to £156 a year compared with £208 under the old conditions. Their summer wage of £4 a week would disappear – effectively a twenty-five per cent pay cut. To protect the weaker clubs from the more wealthy, it was agreed that breaking this rule would constitute an illegal payment.

As the season wound down and the war went on longer than anticipated, 'Fels Naptha' singled out the players for special praise in his review of the season:

> In a few weeks, most of the players will have returned to their homes, there to await events which must decide whether their services will be needed next season. So far as my informant goes, unless the war takes a more serious turn, football will be again resumed next season.
>
> As they will not be in receipt of summer wages, I trust they will be able to find employment until August. In any case, idleness is only the refuge of weak minds and the holiday of fools.

When the war did take a more serious turn, the Government stepped up its recruitment drive in the summer of 1915 and formal football fixtures were suspended. With the generous financial support of the club's directors, Fred Stewart managed to cobble together enough players for Cardiff City to take part in the newly-formed South-West Regional League and a few friendlies over the next three years. The ceasefire in November 1918 paved the way for competitive football to re-start the following August.

Unlike some clubs, Cardiff City escaped relatively lightly from the carnage of the First World War. Only two players, Tom Witts and James McKenzie, failed to return but the club also lost the man who gave his name to their new ground. Lord Ninian Crichton-Stuart was killed in action in Belgium in October 1915 and in a match programme tribute, 'Fels Naptha' declared "he died the death of a brave soldier and a gallant gentleman."

Bart Wilson had been in mourning again in 1917. His son John became a victim of the Great War while serving with the 17th Welsh Regiment in France.

# The Bluebirds Take Flight

Fred Keenor was among the lucky ones. Hundreds of British footballers went off to fight for their country. Seventy-five of them did not come back. Keenor, born and bred in Cardiff, returned to his home city after seeing active service, and despite his wartime experience – or perhaps because of it – he was able to pick up the threads of a career which culminated in the club's greatest moment.

There was simply no holding Cardiff City in the roaring Twenties. Election to the Football League was followed by promotion to the First Division. Two years later, they came within a whisker of winning the championship – a missed penalty in their last game costing them the title. In 1925, they reached the F.A.Cup Final for the first time before losing 1-0 to Sheffield United but beat Arsenal at Wembley by the same score two years later to create history. Cardiff City were the first – and probably the last – team to take the F.A.Cup out of England.

Throughout these seven magnificent years, Fred was a colossus. No player could have been keener. Good luck may have contributed to his surviving the Battle of the Somme, but it was sheer hard work which enabled Cardiff's most famous half-back to play a part in the club's heyday. War wounds to his shoulder and knees while at the front were simply shrugged off as he applied himself to the job in hand. Fred served his football apprenticeship first under Charlie Brittan and then Jimmy Blair during the transition to the Football League before becoming skipper himself and driving the club forward to even greater glory in 1927.

Fred Keenor was to be a captain of industry who led from the front, a hard-tackling half-back who never shirked a tackle or a challenge. He may have played fewer Football League games than Tom Farquharson and Phil Dwyer, but in all he made more than 500 appearances for the club over nearly two decades. If Bart Wilson was 'Mr Cardiff City' off the field, Fred Keenor was his equivalent on it.

One of eleven children, Fred was born in Cardiff on July 31st 1894. From an early age, it was obvious that football would play an important part in his life. He captained the Stacey Road School in Roath for three seasons – leading them to the championship without losing a game – and joined City as an amateur soon after his eighteenth birthday from local side Roath Wednesdays. He later signed as a professional for 10 shillings a week.

After appearing in a friendly against Mid-Rhondda on April 30th 1913, Fred made his first-class debut against Exeter in the First Division of the Southern League a fortnight before Christmas. A handful of appearances during that season were followed by 22 in 1914-15 as he found himself being mainly used as a replacement for injured players. Harvey, Cassidy and Hardy were recognized as the best half-back line in the Southern League so Fred's chances were limited. In February 1915, he enlisted in the 17th Middlesex Regiment which became known as the Footballers' Battalion because players, officials and supporters were urged to join up soon after the War began.

In early October 1915, the battalion came to Ninian Park but, at Fred Stewart's request, Private Keenor turned out for Cardiff City. As usual, 'Fels Naptha' was swift to praise the players in the club's programme and journal. After noting the absence of the regimental band because of the cost of travelling to Cardiff, he banged the drum for those men who had answered the call to arms by joining the Footballers' Battalion:

> I trust they will be given a rousing reception, representing, as they do, the national game's contribution to the Army. They have followed the gleam which points the way to duty, and duty has no place for fear. May their example be followed by those who are able to take it, for duty inspired by patriotism is a path which all may tread.

In the event, bad weather restricted the crowd for what 'Fels Naptha' described as "a brilliant exhibition of soccer by some of the stars of the football world". His kind words were later supported by positive action when on the day after Boxing Day in 1915, a collection was made during the game against Barnsley at Ninian Park for Keenor and John Stephenson, the other Cardiff player in the Footballers' Battalion. "It is hoped to send each of these old City favourites," wrote the columnist, "a parcel of 'comforts' from time to time, and if the response is sufficiently generous, to provide refreshments for the wounded soldiers who visit Ninian Park during the season."

In late January 1916, 'Fels Naptha' explained that a "substantial parcel" had been sent to the two men who had written to thank the club:

> I have seen the letters and am able to vouch for the depth of feeling contained in their expression of thanks. By the way, the optimistic note struck by both of them on the result and duration of the war was most prominently expressed. They both believe the war will end this year, whilst Keenor can see himself cakewalking to Berlin!

Fred's confidence proved badly misplaced because he was wounded in the knee at Delville Wood in the summer of 1916 as the war dragged on. After being invalided home, Fred convalesced before rejoining the battalion. While stationed near London, he helped Brentford to win the London Combination Championship before being demobbed and re-signing for Cardiff City in May 1919. His son Graham, who was to join the club as player and then administrator in the 1950s, says his father was always reluctant to talk about his experience at the front:

> He never liked to discuss anything to do with the war. The only reference I can ever remember him making was to Delville Wood in the Battle of the Somme which was being held by the South Africans. It came under a terrific barrage and went up like a massive bonfire.
>
> There was a relic of the war because I noticed Dad had an indentation in his right shoulder – as if someone had gouged out a piece from underneath his right shoulder blade. I don't know if they left the shrapnel in there or not. He wouldn't be drawn on it. I found him most reluctant to discuss it. The impression I got was that the war was so horrendous that, along with a great many other soldiers, Dad blotted it out. He had lost too many friends. He often said that he was one of the lucky ones who came back.
>
> As well as his shoulder, he also damaged his knees but none of the

injuries seemed to affect him. He was very fit and as strong as an ox. He obviously sustained that right through his career.

Fred Keenor was one of a number of players who returned to Ninian Park after the war as Fred Stewart once again rang the changes in preparation for the resumption of competitive football. The secretary-manager had stayed in the city during the war to build up his corn seed and coal merchants business and was soon involved in a different kind of bartering. Money was still short and despite subsidising the club during the war, the directors realised that new signings were necessary.

Inside forward Billy Grimshaw arrived from Bradford City while other new recruits included full-back Alex Stewart (Watford), Billy Williams and Tom Dalton (both from Pontypridd). Centre-half Ernest 'Bert' Smith was given a trial after being demobbed and was finally signed on the recommendation of Bart Wilson. Local boy Len Davies made his City debut – and only appearance of the season – at Luton in September, while Billy Hardy was released by the Army in November as City made a mediocre start to the new season.

The second week in October saw Ninian Park stage two celebratory matches. Cardiff City's long-serving trainer George Latham was awarded a benefit against Swansea and then the Grand Victory International, England versus Wales, was played five days later. Latham was an all-action hero, an all-round good egg who spent 23 years in two spells at Ninian Park after playing for Newtown, Liverpool and Southport. Between 1905 and 1913 he made 10 appearances for Wales for whom he also acted as trainer.

After being decorated during an eighteen month spell fighting in the Boer War, Latham was commissioned as lieutenant when the First World War broke out and was later promoted to captain. He won the Military Cross on the recommendation of officers from another battalion for leading an attack which captured an important Turkish position in the first Battle of Gaza in Palestine. 'Fels Naptha' paid this fulsome tribute to 'Gentleman George':

> Whilst we admire him for his football achievements, and still more for his lofty patriotism, we find still more to attract us in his smiling

and genial disposition, in his unfailing courtesy, and in his self-sacrificing and sympathetic heart.

It is men like Latham whose example has been a beacon to the race, whose conduct has fulfilled the highest aspirations of human endeavour, whose deeds will echo through the corridor of time.

As well as the gate receipts, Latham received a cheque from the directors and a clock from the players "as a token of their regard for one of the finest men who ever donned a jersey". In 1924, he was appointed masseur to the Great Britain Olympic team. He was also to play a key role in Cardiff City's preparations for the 1925 and 1927 F.A.Cup Finals.

Not only did Wales beat England in the Victory International but the secretary of the Welsh F.A. Ted Robbins was very impressed with the way the club had organised the match. With Scotland due to play at Ninian Park the following February, the next club programme revealed that Mr Robbins "considers Cardiff an ideal centre for Welsh football and Ninian Park a credit to the club".

The same programme contained evidence of the return to normality following the end of the war. With the hostilities over, football became fun again... especially within the Cardiff City dressing room. Readers heard about a beauty contest being conducted amongst the players:

It is not generally known that the City players pride themselves on their good looks. Wherever they got the idea from Heaven only knows but there it is.

Somebody suggested that a match should be played by the eleven best-looking players versus the rest. Then the trouble started. 'Kidder' Harvey asserted that he ought to head the list of the Beauties! And was deeply hurt when Jack Evans suggested that he looked like the Wreck of the Hesperous.

But when Pat Cassidy claimed the right to appear in the Adonis class, the comments on his facial appearance were most rude. George West said he wasn't much to look at ("Hear hear") but whatever happened, he didn't want to appear in the same class as Kneeshaw, who replied that he wasn't a candidate for the dogs home. In his opinion, Nature had perpetrated one of her worst jokes when she turned out West. (They don't speak now)

When George Beare claimed a right to appear in the same side as Charlie Brittan (who, by general consent, was given his place in the side), Layton told him in the most forceful manner that whatever side Beare was in, he wished to be on the other, as he wasn't risking his reputation for good looks by playing with the outside right.

The voting is expected to be interesting and exciting. The only certainties appear to be Brittan and Smith. The lavish offers of cigarettes, one to the other, bears somewhat the semblance of bribery and there seems no other way to account for their humility and apparent courtesy to each other.

It appears that Fred Keenor facial qualities didn't merit a mention either way and that, judging by the modern-day footballer's obsession with his looks and appearance, not a great deal has changed in the last eighty years!

Two weeks later, after a 2-1 win at Millwall, 'Fels Naptha' identified the quality on which Cardiff City's success in the Twenties would be based. He described the victory as "the result of dogged perseverance and good play" before reporting on the match and then highlighting the strong team spirit in the City side:

> The reception afforded Charlie Brittan on the arrival of the team at Cardiff Station was a fitting climax to a memorable day, his election to the City Council giving as much pleasure to the players as those more directly concerned.
>
> The good feeling existing among the men is one of the most pleasing features of the club and it speaks much for their general character that their loyalty towards each other is able to withstand the severest test.
>
> Let us hope this feeling may continue. To be capable of respect is well-nigh as rare at the present day as to be worthy of it; it is a serious thing in him who feels it and the height of honour for him who inspires the feeling.

Mutual respect and affection throughout the club became the cornerstone on which Fred Stewart was able to build successive and successful Cardiff City teams. He brought together men who knew their limitations to form sides which played to their strengths. Flair and imagination were not discouraged but they had to co-exist alongside hard work. Cardiff's players were tough, uncompromising but fair and proud of it – but they could also play the game as it should be played – with style on the ground. When his team were top of the First Division in January 1924, Fred Stewart took the opportunity to explain the reasons behind their success. In an interview in the *Athletic News*, he said there was no secret beyond a simple policy:

> We get players of decent ability, and each man does his best, with unity of feeling and purpose. The big point is that we are all such good friends – not only the players but the directors also. We take each other's opinion. We never make a change in the team without consulting with the players. Their opinion is worth having.

'Fels Naptha' wasn't too interested in the views of some of Cardiff's supporters during the 1919-20 season. After a 1-1 draw at Southend, he launched, not for the last time during the season, a strong attack on the unrealistic expectations of a section of the Ninian Park regulars:

> There are 21 other clubs in the Southern League all striving to win and if we expect our club to keep on beating the lot, we are asking for an impossibility.
> I hope to see the followers of Cardiff City cultivate a loyalty to the club which will be proof against all the setbacks that may come to us – and we are bound to have them some day.

The season turned on the signing of 26-year-old Arthur Cashmore, the former Oldham Athletic centre forward who Stewart bought from Darlaston in December after seeing him score a hat-trick. He was off the mark on his debut in a 2-1 home win over Crystal Palace – the start of a 15-match unbeaten run. In the F.A.Cup, Cardiff beat Oldham Athletic of the Football League's First Division and then Wolves of the Second before losing 2-1 at Bristol City.

In early January 1920, 'Fels Naptha' was on the warpath again. Southampton's supporters were his target following their behaviour during a match at the Dell a week after the Oldham win:

> Apparently disappointed at the result of the game up to half-time, and the utter inability of the Saints team to avert defeat, the spectators took a hand in the proceedings, and from booing and hurling insulting epithets at our men, resorted to other methods.
> This took the form of stone slinging and, ultimately, bottle throwing. Jack Evans, in the act of taking a corner kick, received a portion of a brick in the back.

Who said that football violence was a product of the late twentieth century? Southampton escaped with a point – thanks to a dubious penalty – but their board received a solemn warning from the outspoken Cardiff programme columnist:

> If the directors of a club do not use all the influence and power they possess to curb the passions of their followers, they will have themselves to blame if one day they find their ground closed and a source of revenue cut off.
>
> I hope the record we possess at Ninian Park for sportsmanship will be cherished by all as something we must cling to, for our love of sport and the reputation of the club.

In fact, Cardiff's standing in the game could hardly have been higher. In a programme article by a 'special correspondent' under the headlines 'A Straight Talk to Spectators' and 'Unruly Conduct of Football Crowds Getting Far Too Common', they were singled out for praise:

> In the dressing rooms of the Cardiff City club, I have seen a notice signed by the management... [it] says, in effect, that the management expect every player in the team to "play the game" and to respect the decisions of the referees appointed... it is no part of the duty of the players to quarrel with the referee... I am told further that this notice has had a good effect on the conduct of the games in which Cardiff City have taken part this season. Other clubs might follow suit, and spectators, too, might take the lesson to heart. Nobody wants milk-and-water football, but neither do we want mere rowdyism ever in the ascendant.

Cardiff City were banking on their good name when they applied to join the Football League from the Southern League in February 1920. Relations between the two organisations were not good and there were plans to create a Third Division consisting mainly of Southern League clubs. But Cardiff's directors had set their sights higher. They wanted to enter the Second Division and, according to 'Fels Naptha', their "progressive policy" had been well received in and outside the city – even though it later cost them a £500 fine for insufficient notice of withdrawal from the Southern League:

> The decision they have arrived at has not been come to without the

most searching and thorough debate on the pros and cons of the question. Much spade work has yet to be done before the voting which takes place in May but... Cardiff's chances of inclusion are very rosy indeed.

They weren't helped by a disastrous run from mid-March when the team didn't win for six matches and failed to score in five of them. This slump undoubtedly cost Cardiff City the title – they eventually finished fourth – but not their place in the Football League. 'Fels Naptha' had been confident all along and his optimism proved well-founded when Cardiff City received twenty-five votes behind Leeds United's thirty-one and were elected to a reconstituted Second Division on May 31st.

All the lobbying by Fred Stewart and the club's directors had paid off: after just twenty years – and only ten as a professional club – Cardiff City had become the first Welsh team to gain admission to the English League. In fact, they achieved the feat only by half an hour because their Welsh colleagues in the Southern League, Merthyr Town, Newport County and Swansea Town, were then elected members of the new Third Division. Bart Wilson's dream had been realised; history had been made.

In his review of the season, 'Fels Naptha' was his usual complimentary self. It had been a wonderful effort in the circumstances. No championship but a 2-1 win over Wrexham in the Welsh Cup and the club in the black. Everyone was congratulated including Bart. There was even a special word for the fairer sex:

> I cannot close without paying a tribute to the ladies (especially Mrs Stewart and Mrs Wilson) who have assisted in entertaining visiting directors and friends, and done so much to brighten the proceedings in the tea room. Otway was a man after my own heart when he wrote:–
> O woman! Lovely woman! Nature made thee
> To temper man; we had been brutes without you.
> Angels were painted fair to look like you.

During the summer of 1920, Cardiff City took a number of steps to prepare for what promised to be a memorable season. A higher grade of football meant bigger gates so the Canton Stand, with its unique bench seating, was begun and eventually completed a year later. With the directors deciding that money was no object, both before and after the club's election to the league, Fred Stewart was busy assembling a squad which would do justice to Cardiff's newly-acquired status. Harvey and Cassidy were not re-signed as thirteen new players were brought in – including Jimmy Gill from Sheffield Wednesday and the Cardiff Corinthians inside forward Herbie Evans.

After revealing the squad to his readers, 'Fels Naptha' was remarkably upbeat and accurate about Cardiff's chances in the Second Division:

> There should be no doubt of the club's ability to hold its own in its new sphere. That it will do this, I have the fullest confidence. Indeed, I see no reason why Cardiff City should not be reckoned with in the struggle for promotion.

And so it proved. What began with a 5-2 thrashing of Stockport County – Fred Stewart's former club – ended with the double being completed over Wolves – sweet revenge for a 3-1 defeat in a F.A.Cup semi-final replay by the Molineux club. The race for the title went down to the wire as Cardiff finished second to Birmingham City on goal average. After 25,000 had crowded into the still primitive Ninian Park for the first Football League game against Clapton (now Leyton) Orient, the average home gate rose to 28,000. A crowd of 50,000 saw Chelsea knocked out of the F.A.Cup in the fourth round and in the first semi-final at Anfield, Cardiff were involved in another historic occasion. When King George V and Queen Mary took their seats after the interval, it was the first time that reigning monarchs had attended a semi-final in Britain.

Cardiff City had well and truly arrived. They had made their mark on English football and 'Fels Naptha' was in seventh heaven. With promotion beckoning, he again paid tribute to the team spirit amongst the players which had brought the club to the brink of the First Division: "That they have accomplished so much is due to a great extent to the joyous life they live together and to the perfect understanding existing between them."

The directors, Fred Stewart and Bart Wilson were then all praised as "men, who, by their enterprise, courage, foresight and 'vision' have steered the club from comparatively recent obscurity to its present position."

With promotion secured, 'Fels Naptha' reflected on the most memorable season in the club's history so far:

> The same question is being asked today as was put twelve months ago: "Are we good enough for the class we are entering?" We unhesitatingly believe we are. We think that it will be found that our team will be able to adapt itself far better to the more skillful interpretation of the game in the First Division than the robust displays associated with the Second.
>
> We think it will be found that whilst the play in the Premier Division will demand the almost perfect condition of players, it will be a test of brains more than muscle.

Fred Stewart had been planning from the moment Cardiff gained promotion. He was only too aware that new players were needed for the new division and, once again, the directors backed his judgment as, among others, Tommy Brown (Brighton) and Willie Page (Stoke) arrived at Ninian Park. The ground was improved by the re-turfing of the pitch and spectators being urged through the programme notes for the opening game against Spurs not to invade the playing area because of the remedial work:

> This has been done with sea-washed turf by expert men, the pitch now being equal to the best in the country. An appeal is therefore made to all not to run over the field after the match.
>
> Thousands of tons of ashes, etc, have been utilised to improve the banks, especially at the Grangetown end of the ground, whilst the new stand has been covered and many other improvements executed at a cost involving thousands of pounds.

Despite this expense, Ninian Park was still not capable of dealing with a large crowd. Fifty thousand people officially paid and another ten thosand broke into the ground for Cardiff's First Division debut against Spurs and there were a number of 'unfortunate incidents' including the hijacking of the Score Board by spectators for use as a vantage point. The directors were forced to seek advice from the police about crowd control, they complained about the sale of pirated programmes at the ground and through the official programme and journal, they refused to entertain "unwarrantable attacks" from "unreasonable critics" of the club":

> One of the chief causes of complaint is the charge of 3s for the New [Canton] Stand. We believe that at Liverpool a charge of 6s is made for similar accommodation.
>
> In any case, we are sure the directors, who have secured for the club the position it now holds, will not accept dictation in the policy they have adopted, whether it be in the charge to the ground or the selection of players."

Fred Stewart knew the step up to England's top division on the field would not be easy. Cardiff City found the going tough straight from the kick-off. They lost 1-0 to Spurs and were beaten in their next five games. A month after their debut, 40,000 turned up for Cardiff's first win – 3-1 against top-of-the-table Middlesbrough. 'Fels Naptha' was a relieved man:

> To many, the match was a revelation and confounded and, I hope, silenced the critics who have been unsparing in their attacks on players and directors alike. The whole side played with so much determination and skill that the Middlesbrough directors were unstinted in their eulogy, expressing the opinion that our defence was probably the best in the league.

Fred Keenor was now an established member of that defence and, as he prepared for his testimonial in October, the half-back found himself the subject of 'Football Confidences', a feature unashamedly stolen from the Spurs programme in which a well-known player or supporter answered a dozen questions. These were some of Fred's replies:

> Favourite position? *Any old where.*
> Favourite motto? *Live and learn.*
> When do you feel at your best? *When everything goes right.*
> Greatest ambition? *To play as long as Billy Meredith.*
> Pet aversion? *Unfair critics.*
> Favourite hobby? *Gardening.*
> Which is your lucky day? *Pay day.*

In mid-November, George Latham, Cardiff's trainer, was the subject of 'Football Confidences'. He revealed that his favourite motto was never to trust a bookie and his greatest ambition to win another Welsh cap. He had last turned out for Wales in 1913 when they were a man short and a recall now seemed unlikely. But in January 1922, he achieved the next best thing. At the advanced age of forty-two, 'Gentleman George' was pressed into action when overnight illness deprived Cardiff of Jack Evans and Jimmy Gill at Blackburn and he became the club's oldest Football League debutant, in a 3-1 victory. With the game won, the Cardiff players decided it was time for a bit of fun: "When we were three up, I was moved to outside right," George recalled later, "and then the lads had a game with me. They sent long forward passes to my side of the field and shouted to me to go after the ball, just to see if I had any wind left – I hadn't much!"

Illness also cost Cardiff the services of Fred Keenor from mid-November to mid-January. He was initially absent through injury before being hit by a bad dose of the flu: "It is a matter of regret that Keenor is still unable to play," said the programme notes. "He has contracted a severe cold which has laid him so low that he may not be able to turn out for a few weeks."

An attempted comeback in early January was aborted when a flu epidemic swept through the club and it wasn't until the home game against Birmingham a week later that Keenor returned. By that time, Len Davies had scored his 10th goal for City in their 4-1 F.A.Cup win over Manchester United at Old Trafford and he then hit the club's first hat-trick in the Football League in a 6-3 hammering of Bradford City at Ninian Park. Another defeat of Manchester United – this time 3-1 at home with goalkeeper Tom Farquharson making his debut – in their last game meant Cardiff finished fourth in the table.

After beating United, Southampton and Nottingham Forest, they reached the quarter-finals of the F.A.Cup before losing 2-1 to Spurs in a replay but won the Welsh Cup with a 2-0 win over Ton Pentre. Not a bad return for the first season in the top flight of English football. Sid Nicholls would certainly have good reason to remember Cardiff City's debut. As the 1920-21 season drew to a close, a matchday programme revealed details of an incident involving the chairman:

The brutal and unwarrantable attack on Mr. S.H. Nicholls on Wednesday night has caused considerable indignation especially amongst his co-directors on the Cardiff City board. Mr. Nicholls was on his way home at about 11 p.m. after attending a meeting of the directors, when he was set upon by half-a-dozen roughs. But though considerably outnumbered, we learn that the blackguards had 'reckoned without their host', for a few of them received as much as they gave. The police were informed of the incident and may yet locate the assailants.

Cardiff City's inaugural season in the Football League had been quite a baptism and once again 'Fels Naptha' offered bouquets to all concerned. He assured supporters of the board's determination to hang on to their best players and praised the travelling support the team was receiving. "Wherever we go, the most conspicuous feature of the afternoon's proceedings has been the enthusiasm of the Welsh element. There is little doubt that their patriotic fervour does much to inspirit and hearten our men."

With their debut season behind them, 'Fels Naptha' claimed Cardiff had earned "the striking compliment of 'the wonder team of the league' " after their opening six defeats.

To the chairman, his co-directors, Fred Stewart and Bart Wilson, the columnist extended his

hearty felicitations on a most successful season, a season which we hope and believe will be associated with pleasant memories by all of them and as one setting up another landmark in the history of Association football in the Principality. Most of us will look back without regret to days of great if transient joy and feel at this moment that we can truly say:
> Happy the man, and happy he alone,
> He who can call to-day his own:
> He who, secure within, can say,
> To-morrow do thy worst, for I have lived to-day!

The immediate future did indeed turn out to be rather disappointing: the following season, City slipped to ninth place in the First Division and were knocked out of the F.A.Cup – again by Spurs – in the third round while retaining the Welsh Cup by beating Aberdare Athletic 3-2 in the final.

But it was the day after tomorrow – and the rest of the week – that would provide the club with their halcyon days. During the 1922-23 season, there were signs that Cardiff City were on the verge of something big. They scored 73 league goals – the highest in the First Division – and their growing reputation as one of the strongest teams in English football was enhanced when six players were selected for international duty on Saturday April 23rd 1923.

Fred Keenor, Len Davies and Jack Evans played for Wales against Ireland who had Bert Smith and Tom Farquharson in their side while Jimmy Blair turned out at left-back for Scotland against England. A makeshift City side beat Sheffield United by the game's only goal at Ninian Park in setting a record for the number of players which a club had on international duty while still winning a First Division match.

The following season saw Cardiff City enter the history books again with a record which remains intact today. Their first three seasons as a Football League club had gone remarkably well but the best was yet to come.

# Always the Bridesmaids

A gruelling football season is almost over. There's just one game to go. A three-horse race has gradually been reduced to two and is about to reach its climax. With the finishing line in sight, there's nothing to choose between the two teams save a single point and a handful of goals. At stake is the First Division championship which neither club has won before.

Huddersfield, under the former mining engineer Herbert Chapman, lie second in the table to Cardiff City, managed by part-time coal merchant Fred Stewart. Fourteen years of Football League experience against just four. The championship race could hardly be closer. Everything rests on the outcome of their last games on Saturday May 3rd 1924.

The mathematics are simple: if Cardiff City beat Birmingham City, they collect two points and the title. If they draw, and Huddersfield put three goals past Nottingham Forest, then the Yorkshire side become champions by way of a superior goal average.

The drama of Cardiff City's failure to win the championship has been matched since only by Arsenal's achievement at Anfield in 1989 when their 2-0 win snatched the title from an incredulous Liverpool on goal difference. The 1995 Premiership race wasn't settled until the last game when Manchester United faltered at West Ham and Blackburn stole the title despite losing at Liverpool. The 1924 result retains its place in the record books because of the wafer-thin margin of Huddersfield's success – 0.024 of a goal.

Before the season began, and despite announcing a profit for the year of nearly £2,500, Cardiff City's directors had to scale down an ambitious plan to redevelop Ninian Park. The project was postponed because of the cost of building dressing rooms and offices in a new stand but there could be no delay in improving the increasingly troublesome playing surface. In the programme for Cardiff's opening home fixture against Bolton Wanderers in August 1923, the directors explained why the pitch had been given top priority: "Tons of dressing has been used to induce a better growth of grass and to remove the treacherous surface caused by the sea-washed turf with which the pitch was laid a couple of years ago."

The close climax to the 1923-24 season came as no surprise to Cardiff City's supporters who had seen their team top the table for long periods. Fred Stewart hed strengthened his squad by signing inside-forward Alfie Hagan and wing-half Harry Wake from Newcastle's reserves and goalkeeper William Robb from Wallsend but relied heavily on the players who had performed so well in Cardiff's first two seasons in the First Division.

The team swept all before them as they embarked on an 11-match unbeaten run. A 3-0 win at Sunderland in early September was particularly impressive – according to the next home programme, Fred Stewart thought the game was "the greatest he has ever witnessed and he has never seen our lads play such wonderful football".

Not surprisingly, crowds were flocking to Ninian Park to see their side and the club had to warn supporters about a couple of unwanted practices. Season ticket holders were told not to bring their children into the stand without paying:

> As they know the seats all around them are booked, they should realise that this cannot be allowed – a season ticket admits one individual, not a family.
>
> A Centre Stand season ticket holder has asked us to appeal to the public not to walk on the stand seats especially on wet days. The gentleman referred to assures us he has had a pair of light pants ruined through this practice.

A more general inconvenience was surfacing on the Bob Bank opposite the main stand – so called because it cost a shilling to enter. The club were aware that action was needed:

> Our friends on the Shilling Bank will be pleased to note that the directors are serious in their anxiety to do something for the comfort of spectators, the stepping at the end of the new stand being an earnest of their intentions. This will be continued as soon as funds permit.

Another concern was the persistent refusal of the England selectors to pick Billy Hardy, Cardiff's Bedlington-born half back. The club pulled no punches:

PREJUDICE!

Discussing the composition of the probable English International Eleven in the *Athletic News* last Monday, 'Tityrus', than whom there is no more competent judge in the British Isles, says:-

"For the left flank Hardy, of Cardiff City, is the best of the season, *but as he is attached to a Welsh club*, although in the League, he may not be considered."

The italics are our own and explain the line at the head of this article. Surely it is time those who are responsible for the choosing of the best English side put aside this unreasonable prejudice and went in for the best men who are qualified, without regard to the club to which they are attached!

In early November, Cardiff City received support from across the border when the *Liverpool Echo* delivered its verdict on the Football Association's 'unjust' treatment of Hardy:

The present policy of the F.A. in depriving a Cardiff City player English international honours, however high his abilities, to our mind savours of ultra-conservatism, red-tapism, narrow-mindedness, or call it what you will, as C.B. Fry would say.

On a lighter note, the Cardiff programme editor noted the recent proliferation of club histories – the latest being a book about Glasgow Rangers – and provided an intriguing snapshot of the club's assistant secretary: "If this stunt is carried on, one can see Mr. Bart Wilson dictating the notes to his grandson of the City's history, the while he rolls his own fags of 'Birds-eye' and clenching his fists when reciting the episode of the rifling of the contents of 'our first bar' in the chalet off Mark Street Lane."

The unbeaten run came to an end in late October when, after being held to a 1-1 draw at home by Preston, City lost the return game 3-1. At that stage of the season, Cardiff were the only team not to have lost in the whole Football League and, according to the programme editor, were unhappy with the way they lost their record:

Up to twelve minutes before half-time the City appeared to have the better of the play, despite the fact that they were playing against a high wind. Then Roberts got a good goal, which was quickly followed by two others which were obtained through glaringly off-side play.

It is a pity the referee or linesmen did not detect this, as it might have put a new aspect on the succeeding play, which was greatly in favour of Cardiff City.

The griping over, the editor did have the good grace to congratulate Preston North End before noting that, with the record gone, "perhaps we shall get more enjoyable games now the tension ceases to exist".

City were soon back on track with Len Davies setting a new record by scoring all four goals in their 4-2 at West Bromwich Albion to become the League's leading marksman. With the Scottish international winger Dennis Lawson recruited from St. Mirren, they didn't lose again until their last match of 1923 – 2-1 at Villa in front of a 70,000 crowd. "It was a bitter pill to give them the two points," said the programme's match report, "but that's the glorious uncertainty of the game, and the spice that makes it so gripping as a pastime."

As well as regularly picking up points to stay top of the league, Cardiff City were winning friends and influencing people – including referees. One of them wrote to former chairman and now director Sid Nicholls to pay his own personal compliment after taking charge of two City games:

> I may say you have got together a most gentlemanly lot of players who never quibble over decisions, although, perhaps, there may have been some they did not agree with, but they took them smiling, and I do sincerely trust it may fall to my lot to have charge of your team on many occasions, when I feel sure they will always endeavour to play the game as clean in future games as they have done in the two games I have just had.

After a good start to 1924, City's championship hopes foundered during March when their return of one point from five matches effectively set up the cliffhanger with Huddersfield. It began, ironically, on St. David's Day when City lost 2-0 at Huddersfield. Defeats by Notts County (twice) – when five players were on international duty – and Blackburn followed before City recovered with a 0-0 draw with Everton at Ninian Park.

March also saw Cardiff knocked out of the F.A.Cup by Manchester City in a quarter-final replay. A crowd of 76,166 – the biggest crowd to ever attend a match involving the club – witnessed a goal-less game at Maine Road before a piece of magic from Manchester City's Welsh Wizard, fifty-year-old Billy Meredith, set up the winner at Ninian Park.

Sunderland took over the First Division leadership during March and Cardiff also lost Herbie Evans with a broken leg during the 2-1 defeat at Blackburn. Veteran defender Charlie Brittan retired to go into business in Birmingham having played a crucial part in the club's development before losing his place to Jimmy Nelson.

During April, City remained unbeaten, dropping just two points out of fourteen. Sunderland fell by the wayside and everything depended on the last Saturday of the season, with Cardiff meeting Birmingham at St. Andrews while Huddersfield were at home to Nottingham Forest.

In the match programme for their last home game – also against Birmingham – 'Fels Naptha' cast his eye over the previous nine months:

> This season will probably be remembered for our bid for the championship of the League, a task which has been rendered doubly difficult owing to the demands made on the club for players to take part in international contests. It will be no surprise if the few points lost through being compelled to field weak teams may prove our undoing.

In the event, just one more point would have been enough to avoid the excruciatingly tense conclusion to the championship race. Huddersfield had scored five goals fewer than Cardiff but, crucially, had conceded one less. In an interview in the *Athletic News* in January 1924, Fred Stewart had gazed into his crystal ball with remarkable accuracy:

> We shall be there, or thereabouts, at the end of the season. Our players are determined to succeed on behalf of the wonderful support they receive in South Wales.
>
> In conclusion, may I quote from Shakespeare:–
> I profess not talking only this – let each man do his best.

Sadly, their best was not good enough. Nearly 50,000 people witnessed Cardiff City falling at the final hurdle – effectively the first of what turned out to be three Cup Finals in four years. Seventy minutes had gone when a header by Jimmy Gill from a Jack Evans corner was fisted away by the Birmingham half-back Percy Barton. Ron Crump, the London referee, pointed to the spot and Cardiff were given a golden opportunity to take the title. But who would they call upon? Their normal penalty-taker, Jack Evans, had started to miss, Gill was reluctant to accept the responsibility so it was top scorer Len Davies, with 23 goals, who stepped forward.

The normally reliable centre-forward hit the ball straight at keeper Dan Tremelling, the chance was gone and with it went the championship. There was no further score while at Leeds Road, Huddersfield beat Nottingham Forest 3-0 after being a goal up at the break and so took the title by the narrowest of margins. At the end of the Huddersfield match, thousands waited for news from Birmingham and eventually manager Herbert Chapman came out of the telephone room under the stand to declare: "We've won it!" Never again were Cardiff City – or indeed any team – to be so close to winning English football's premier prize. A few minutes after the final whistle, all the Cardiff players signed a congratulatory telegram to the Yorkshire club.

Herbert Chapman became the architect of Huddersfield's hat-trick of titles between 1924 and 1926 and when he moved on to Arsenal, he almost repeated the feat. His death from pneumonia in January 1934 occurred midway through the season which would bring the second of three successive First Division championships to Highbury. The Birmingham penalty miss haunted Davies until his death, also from pneumonia, at the age of forty-five in Liverpool. He holds the record of being the only Cardiff City player to score more than 100 league goals for the club.

Despite the disappointment, the first team squad were still given a heroes' welcome when they arrived back at Cardiff General Station from Birmingham. The blow of missing out on the championship was softened by the club's first overseas tour immediately afterwards. Cardiff won four out of five matches played in Czechoslovakia, Austria and Germany with their new signing from Liverpool, Harry Beadles, making his first appearance for the club.

There was the usual flurry of transfer activity in the close season as Fred Stewart moved players in and out of Ninian Park. Jack Nicholls, the son of director Sid, was signed from Newport County while the recruitment of Welsh international winger Willie Davies from Swansea Town kept the Vetch Field club in business with a £2,500 cheque.

Little mention was made of the previous May's near-miss when Cardiff met Sheffield United in their first home game of the new season in August 1924. In the match programme, "Fels Naptha" sounded an optimistic note in a brief observation on the rule which forced clubs to fulfill league fixtures without those players required for Home International fixtures:

> To lose the championship of the Second Division in 1920-21, and the championship of the First Division last season by goal average alone, was a circumstance calling for exceptional philosophical resignation.
>
> Yet we cannot help feeling that in the losing of that much-coveted distinction, we gained a far more lasting tribute in the admiration of the sporting world for the great sportsmanship displayed by the directors in acceding to the demands made upon them for players to represent their countries.

So the club vs. country repercussions still rankled – as did the state of the Ninian Park pitch which once again had received 'special attention' as part of general ground improvements during the summer:

> Tons of virgin soil and sand, together with large quantities of special grass seed, have been strewn over it to bring about its present state. The pitch is better to-day than it has ever been in the history of the club.
>
> The shilling bank has been properly raked, the depressions filled in, and other work done for the comfort and convenience of spectators. Much also has been done in other directions, such as painting, maintaining and making good, a great deal of this not visible to the majority of spectators.

There was so much interest from supporters that season ticket sales reached a record level. The match programme and journal explained the benefits of such booming business:

Every seat in the Canton and Grange Inner Stands have been allotted whilst but a few remain in the Centre Stand. If the whole of the tickets are taken up, it will probably prove a boon to the holders, as it may be possible then to grant Season Ticket holders the privilege they have been urgently demanding of admittance to Cup-tie matches in preference to others.

The timing could hardly have been better in view of City's cup run. Despite the programme's belief that it might "even approach the brilliance of 1923-24", the new championship season never rose above the mediocre and Cardiff finished 11th Early injuries to key players such as Len Davies, Harry Wake and Jimmy Nelson and Jack Evans's absence through flu produced a poor start from which City never recovered.

It was a different story in the F.A.Cup where the club were developing quite a reputation. Having reached the semi-finals in 1921 and the last eight in 1922 and 1924, they made it all the way to Wembley in 1925 after being quoted as joint favourites with Aston Villa and Huddersfield.

Darlington, the eventual winners of the Third Division, proved a formidable stumbling block with City needing two replays to overcome them. In the first game at Ninian Park, the programme revealed that the long-running pitch saga showed no signs of ending:

The City directors have invited Messrs Sutton & Co, the great seed specialists, to send an expert to Cardiff to advise them. An interview has been arranged for next week and it is highly probable that in the near future some drastic measures will be taken for the improvement of the ground.

The state of the pitch was mentioned as a possible reason for the 0-0 draw with Darlington at Ninian Park – its 'deadness' making accurate passing almost impossible. 'Fels Naptha' also blamed the playing surface at Darlington for the second 0-0 stalemate when more than 18,000 people paid £1,190 to watch the match – a club record. "It was a hard, gruelling game on a ground which was described by our players as worse than Ninian Park has ever been."

A less partisan view was offered elsewhere in the programme where it was noted that Cardiff had failed to beat a Third

Division club at home in the first round for the third successive year. Len and Willie Davies scored the goals in City's 2-0 win in the second replay at neutral Anfield – "the first decent pitch they had played on since September" – to set up a second round home tie with Fulham.

In the light of supporters' reaction to the three Darlington games, the programme editor offered a few tips to the crowd at Ninian Park for the Fulham match. "A few cheers for our lads will not be out of place (The most surprised will be the players). Don't boo the referee. He'll be doing his best. Angels can do no more." As it happened, the referee had a key role in the game because he suspended play in the monsoon-like conditions. After a ten-minute delay, the teams agreed to continue and Len Davies scored the Cardiff winner.

As City prepared for a trip to Notts County in the third round, the directors revealed that the Ninian Park pitch would be relaid in the close season with a more suitable turf. City won 2-0 at Meadow Lane in front of a 39,000 crowd as Joe Nicholson, replacing the injured Len Davies, scored the first and Jimmy Gill sealed the result. 'Fels Naptha' waxed lyrical about the Cardiff performance:

> The goal by Gill was the finest exhibition of artistry ever seen. With the ball at his feet, he eluded opponent after opponent, all after him like terriers and when he placed the ball in the net he gave Iremonger no chance.
>
> The spirit of the lads on the field emphasized the value of the excellent advice of Captain Blair to the men before they left the dressing room. "Now boys," he said, "let's all play the game. If the other side resort to fouls, don't imitate them. Play the ball and not the man and keep going to the end of the game."

Leicester City were Cardiff's next opponents and the match programme contained a neat reversal of the popular saying about the future for teams knocked out of the F.A.Cup. Readers were told that the recent defeat by Swansea Town meant that The Citizens – as Cardiff were sometimes called – were now free of the Welsh Cup and the S.W.&M.F.A. Cup. "This is by no means to be deplored, as the Citizens, being safe from relegation, are now able to concentrate on winning the F.A.Cup."

They certainly had to remain focused in a sensational game against Leicester City at Ninian Park in early March 1925. Cardiff had beaten the eventual Second Division champions 1-0 in the second round two years earlier and they triumphed again – thanks to a change in the law. Until the 1924-25 season, players couldn't score direct from a corner but when Law 11 was amended, it was now possible and Cardiff took full, if fortunate, advantage.

Harold Beadles gave City the lead before Leicester equalised and a replay looked on the cards. There were just eight seconds left when Willie Davies swung over a corner kick from the left at the Grangetown End:

> I took it in a hurry with my right foot. The swerve on the ball beat everybody and it went into the net! I had forgotten, in the excitement, that a goal could now be scored direct from the corner-flag, but the next minute I was being mobbed by thousands of spectators!

It took an announcement by Jimmy Blair and Davies to convince many of the crowd that City had in fact won. In the absence of a tannoy, the two players were summoned from the dressing room to impart the good news to supporters. Under the headline 'Some Reflections on the Leicester Match', the following Saturday's programme explained what happened:

> The corner kick, whilst admittedly lucky in finding the net direct, was the result of great pressure, leaving our opponents with no other alternative but to take a risk – a risk which cost them the game.
> To sum up. Cardiff City scored a good goal and a lucky one. Leicester scored a lucky one. Balance in favour of Cardiff City – a good goal.

Cardiff returned to Meadow Lane in Nottingham for the semi-final against Blackburn Rovers, semi-finalists eleven times and winners on five occasions. Like Cardiff, Blackburn were mid-table at the time so a tight game was predicted. Nobody expected the eventual 3-1 scoreline or the ease with which City won – least of all 'Fels Naptha', as he explained in the next match programme:

> Never shall I forget the almost magical scoring which took place at Meadow Lane. Three goals in 17 minutes and that in a semi-final!

It was a match won by a brilliant side through skill and determination, and those of us who had the privilege of witnessing it will ever remember the loyalty of the men who wrought, who gave of their best for the club and the town of their adoption and who gained by their efforts imperishable fame.

City's goals were scored by Nicholson, Gill and Beadles and after all the favourable press comment, the programme also contained the following observation:

It is regrettable that owing to a slight injury to Nicholson (caused through the exuberance of Saturday night's reception) and the necessity to rest Blair, the team which did so well in the semi-final will not be able to receive as a whole the reception to which they are entitled to at Ninian Park today.

Nicholson had cut his knee after falling through the canvas roof of a taxi while trying to escape from enthusiastic fans. Sadly, Cardiff's wonderful form completely deserted them against Sheffield United in the fiftieth – and their first – F.A.Cup Final. City's fame might have been imperishable but they were not. They had a busy April – playing six First Division games – but that was no excuse. They just didn't perform on the day.

The understandably enormous demand for tickets in South Wales was not appreciated by the Football Association. Only 1,750 out of the 92,000 capacity were initially allocated to each club but after Cardiff lodged a protest, a few more were grudgingly provided. Despite the shortage, some 40,000 Welsh supporters eventually managed to obtain tickets for the match. The match programme editor was unhappy about their price: "A guinea seems a lot to pay for a football match, but we would remind those who are hesitating that the main object of a trip to Wembley will be to see the first Cup Final in which a Welsh club is engaged."

As the final approached, the club announced that everyone directly involved with Cardiff City – directors, players, groundstaff and their families – would have a day out at Wembley. Details of the arrangements were printed in the programme and those supporters who weren't able to go to the final, were informed that a film of the match was being flown from London to Cardiff for showing on the same evening.

A regular contributor to Cardiff's match programme was 'The Wanderer' who, a week before Wembley, wrote a long article entitled 'Can Cardiff City Win? A Final Tie Full Of Promise and Possibilities.' He confirmed the right of Welsh clubs to take part in the competition because it was the Football Association and not the English Cup:

> The fact that the entry of Cardiff City, as well as of other Welsh clubs, was accepted a few months back, means that the authorities must surely have been prepared to see one of these Welsh sides win the Cup. And why worry if they do?

He then declared Sheffield United and Cardiff City to be very well-matched teams before pointing out that only one of the twenty-two players – the Sheffield United right-back Cook – had appeared at Wembley before. He discussed the different training methods employed – Sheffield United had practically lived at Scarborough during their cup run while Cardiff had trained at Ninian Park and wouldn't leave for London until the day before the final. 'The Wanderer' thought there was nothing between the teams in terms of fitness but he predicted a Sheffield United win – perhaps after extra time – in "a fine, full-blooded and stirring encounter" which he hoped would be played "in the sporting spirit".

Unfortunately, the Jubilee Cup Final proved a tedious anti-climax – for everyone apart from Sheffield United who won with a Fred Tunstall goal in the thirtieth minute. Harry Wake, the Cardiff right-half, had cut out a pass from Billy Gillespie but was caught in possession just outside the area by Tunstall. The England winger then ran on to beat Tom Farquharson from about eight yards for the only goal of the game.

There was more evidence of Cardiff's renowned sportsmanship after the players had collected their medals from the Duke of York in the Royal Box. The Lord Mayor of Cardiff, W.H. Pethybridge, went into the Sheffield United dressing room to offer his congratulations before speaking to the losers, as the next home programme revealed:

> Our lads, far from being downhearted at the result, were quite merry. The Lord Mayor said he was glad to see they had taken their defeat

like sportsmen and congratulated them on having reached the final. He was confident that day was not far distant when they would bring the cup to Cardiff.

In fact, it was to be another two years before Cardiff triumphed at Wembley. After the Sheffield United defeat, Fred Keenor, later to become captain, vowed that they would return to the Twin Towers to win the F.A.Cup. He apologised for their poor performance and absolved Harry Wake of any blame for their defeat. On arriving back in Cardiff on the following Monday, the players received a rapturous reception from the public and a civic welcome from the Mayor including a prestigious dinner at City Hall.

By becoming the first Welsh club to reach Wembley, Cardiff City had created history. The following season, the club again found themselves in the record books but for less laudable reasons. Scottish international full-back Jimmy Nelson became the first City player to be sent off in a League match when he was involved in a last-minute flare-up at Manchester City in the opening game of the season; in early November 1925, Cardiff paid Motherwell a record £5,000 for centre-forward Hughie Ferguson and the club suffered their worst-ever league defeat when they lost 11-2 to, of all teams, Sheffield United. Fred Tunstall was again on target as City fell to pieces on New Year's Day 1926. They recovered to finish 16th – thanks to Ferguson's 19 goals in 26 games – and were beaten 2-0 in the fourth round of the F.A.Cup by Newcastle United.

The 1925-26 campaign may have been largely forgettable but the following season will be remembered for as long as Cardiff City exist. After two near-misses – with the championship in 1924 and the F.A.Cup in 1925 – Cardiff cast off their bridesmaid gown to at last become the bride. The vanquished became victors and, in doing so, made football history.

Once again, Fred Stewart had bought and sold during the summer and City bade farewell to Jack Evans, their first professional who left for Bristol Rovers after sixteen years at Ninian Park. Once again, Cardiff made a poor start to their league campaign with just one win in their first nine games – a 3-1 home victory over Leeds.

In the aftermath of the 1926 General Strike, poor form was compounded by poor attendances. Many of Cardiff's regular supporters from the South Wales Valleys simply couldn't afford to watch football. As the world coal market collapsed, the Government held an inquiry into the state of the British mining industry. The report, while acknowledging that the men's conditions of work could be improved, also recommended a cut in wages. The 'Nine Days' – from the 3rd to 12th May – represented the official duration of the strike which inevitably followed but the miners of South Wales were the last to return. When they finally did go back in November, they were forced to work an eight-hour day for ten shillings – half the pay they had received for one hour less in 1921. At the time it cost one shilling for a standing spectator at a Cardiff City home match.

Even so, as the first home programme reported, early season-ticket sales had gone better than expected "in view of the serious times" and the club was delighted when Cardiff City Council decided to run the tramways to Ninian Park. "It is impossible to over-estimate the benefit which is bound to accrue to the club in increased gates when this extension is accomplished," wrote the programme editor, "for tramcars will be able to run spectators from all parts of the city to the ground. This advantage will doubtless be made us of by many who now consider the ground too far from home, especially during severe weather, and the club will benefit accordingly."

But as the 1926-27 season progressed, the gates on a few occasions slumped to fewer than 8,000 as City failed to make an impression in the league. Despite bringing in players such as the former England international George Blackburn from Aston Villa and Tom Pirie from Aberdeen, Fred Stewart struggled to find the right blend. In desperation, he gave Pirie, James Baillie from Wishaw and local teenager Ernie Curtis their debuts in a 2-0 defeat by Manchester United at the end of September. A run of four wins out of five games in October and November enabled City to reach half-way in the table but was followed by four successive defeats.

New signings Frank Matson, Fred Castle and goalkeeper Tom Hampson were later given league debuts as injuries and indifferent performances meant Stewart was continually forced to shuffle his pack. They lost Willie Davies with pleurisy after 15 games, an illness which kept the Welsh international out of the game for a year.

It was City's F.A.Cup form which kickstarted their season and helped keep them in Division One. After Cardiff had beaten and lost to Arsenal over Christmas and the New Year, their campaign began with a third round tie against Aston Villa at Ninian Park. With Tom Sloan replacing the injured Fred Keenor, Cardiff went 2-0 up through Len Davies and Ernie Curtis, playing only his 14th first-team game, before Villa grabbed a late consolation goal.

The following Saturday, Cardiff drew with Burnley and then lost only one league game in ten before the end of March. According to programme notes for the Burnley game, City's chairman Walter Parker had had a prophetic conversation with an opposition dignitary:

> One of the Villa vice presidents told the City chairman that during an experience extending over thirty years with the Villa, he has found that invariably the team which beat the Villa won the Cup!

Cardiff locked horns with Darlington again in the fourth round. Unlike 1924-25 though, the tie was away from Ninian Park and City needed just one game to see off their spirited opponents with winger George McLachan – recalled for the match – and Hughie Ferguson scoring the goals. The draw was not kind: Cardiff would have to travel to Bolton, a successful First Division side and clear favourites to reach the sixth round.

Around this time, the Cardiff directors rejected the idea of broadcasting certain matches at Ninian Park because of the effect the country's economic problems were having on attendances. The proposed radio coverage was very primitive with listeners kept in touch by way of a plan of the pitch divided into squares. The programme editor explained why the club were against broadcasting games:

> Obviously, if people interested can sit in their homes and follow the games by means of a chart, the finance of the club must suffer, and in view of the crisis through which the country has gone owing to the recent strikes, clubs can ill afford to take the risk of depleted gates.

After its enthusiastic reception at the fourth round tie at Darlington, the club gave the go-ahead to community singing at Ninian Park. This new form of entertainment and live broadcasting of matches would both feature for the first time in an F.A.Cup Final when Cardiff City met Arsenal at Wembley in the following April. 'The Wanderer', in his programme column, was soon to come out in favour of radio being used to cover football:

> It is my opinion that interest in the game will be increased, that through the medium of wireless, the sport will gain new clients. Even in any case, there are limitations to broadcasting, because a man can only listen in to one game on any one Saturday.

Details of what was to become the team's pre-cup tie preparations were revealed by 'Fels Naptha' in the middle of February. After drawing 1-1 with Manchester United at Old Trafford, the players spent the week at Southport being put through their paces by trainer George Latham.

> It is pleasing to record that every man is fit and well, the training they are undergoing suiting them admirably. On Tuesday morning, they indulged in ball practice, afterwards proceeding to the baths, where they had a hot salt water bath, followed by a swim in the swimming baths, where, by the way, they enjoyed themselves to their hearts' content. In the afternoon, some went golfing while others indulged in tennis.
>
> On Wednesday, similar training took place, minus the baths, and on Thursday they repeated Tuesday's training again, indulging in a hot sea water bath. They are all very confident that they can beat Bolton and their physical condition is excellent.

It was during the trip to Southport that the players began to think that Cardiff City's name might well be on the Cup. One day after training, some of them noticed that a small black cat was following them around on the Royal Birkdale golf course. At first, nobody took much notice but when it was still on their trail a few holes later, the players decided that it must be an omen. It was left to Hughie Ferguson to pick up the cat and track down its owner. Luckily, he found the right house alongside the course and managed to persuade the owner to let the animal be adopted. A deal was done: if Cardiff reached

Wembley, then a match ticket would be supplied to the cat's owner.

The cat, named Trixie by the players, became the official club mascot and travelled in style in its own wicker basket to all Cardiff's away games. Its photograph frequently appeared in the national press over the coming months. Trixie enjoyed a long association with City and even survived the fire which destroyed the club's main stand in 1937; she died two years later.

A visit to Southport was a ritual City would follow twice again on their way to Wembley because it worked so well against Bolton. Nearly 50,000 people packed into Burnden Park to witness Cardiff's best performance of the season. Fred Keenor, with injury problems and contract differences with the club behind him, was recalled for the fifth round tie and led City to a wonderful win. Cardiff were denied a clear-cut penalty and then Bolton's David Jack thought he had scored when his shot hit the post and appeared to cross the line. Thankfully, the referee played on and City survived.

Inspired by Keenor, Cardiff defended for long periods and ten minutes after half-time were awarded a penalty when McLachlan's cross was handled by the Bolton full-back Finney. Hughie Ferguson, playing at the time on the right wing, displayed a centre-forward's coolness in putting away the spot-kick and as Cardiff grew in confidence, twenty minutes from time a Ferguson cross was met by Len Davies to seal a memorable victory.

Two weeks later, Cardiff were in London to take on the Second Division leaders Chelsea. A crowd of more than 70,000 – including some 12,000 City supporters – paid nearly £5,000 to watch a scoreless draw played out in muddy conditions. The midweek replay attracted another 48,000 spectators for one of the most dramatic games ever to be played at Ninian Park.

On a heavy ground, Cardiff changed tactics by replacing their short passing ground game with a series of long balls. The policy paid off almost immediately when, after ten minutes, Sammy Irving put City ahead after a shot by Len Davies had rebounded from the bar. Davies doubled the lead ten minutes later by scoring with an opportunist shot and Cardiff looked on their way to Wembley.

Ten minutes before half-time, a bizarre piece of goalkeeping by Tom Farquharson changed both the course of the match and the laws of the game. Chelsea were awarded a penalty when Tom Sloan fouled centre-forward Turnbull at the Canton End. As Andy Wilson prepared to take the kick, Farquharson withdrew to the back of the net before rushing forward so quickly that he saved Wilson's shot from inside the six yard box rather than the goal-line.

"I thought I was seeing things when I looked at Tom Farquharson in the Cardiff goal," Wilson recalled later. "As I placed the ball, he was standing with his back against the net, outstretched hands gripping the meshes. I shot and he dashed forward and made a wonder save."

When he was later interviewed in the Cardiff match programme, Farquharson explained his rather unorthodox approach to dealing with penalty kicks by standing in the back of the net:

> I can move forward before the kick is actually taken, a course I cannot take if I stood on my goal-line. By advancing forward I can leap to either side far more quickly than from a standing position. Of course, I size up the kicker, and can tell before he takes the spot kick whether he is a right or left foot shot. This fact invariably indicates which side of me the ball is likely to travel. I have said likely to travel as, of course, the kicker on many occasions will attempt the unorthodox and succeed, and very often, too, the fact that he has attempted the unorthodox has been the means of his undoing.
>
> The successful goalkeeper is he who is ever on his toes and has anticipation born of experience.

Two years after the Chelsea game, the laws were changed to make sure goalkeepers didn't move before the ball was kicked.

As the referee prepared to blow for half-time, Chelsea pulled a goal back – again in very controversial circumstances. A shot by Priestly appeared to have skimmed the far post and gone for a goal-kick but the referee had other ideas. He awarded a goal and as Cardiff protested, the referee showed the players that net pegs behind the upright had been tugged free by the ball passing through. When a nearby policeman confirmed that the ball had indeed gone through the netting, the referee allowed the goal to stand.

Five minutes after the break, the home side were level when Turnbull headed home Pearson's free-kick. Cardiff were on the ropes. Chelsea then hit the bar and City were temporarily reduced to ten men when Ernie Curtis had to leave the field with a badly bruised knee and ankle. On his return, he set up the winner when his cross from the right wing was handled by half-back Wilding and Ferguson scored from the spot with just seven minutes to go.

Only Reading now stood between Cardiff and their second Wembley appearance in three years. The club's directors weren't happy with the choice of Wolverhampton's Molineux as the semi-final venue – especially as Birmingham City's ground was not being used and held almost twice as many spectators – or the perception that a good F.A.Cup run was good for the club coffers. The programme notes put the record straight by adding up the cost to Cardiff of postponing league matches as a result of their cup-ties with Darlington, Bolton Wanderers, Chelsea and Reading:

> Thus we find that our losses in payment of compensation up to and including the semi-final will amount to not less than £2,500, probably more, information which will be a revelation to those who think the gates from cup-ties are all 'extras'.
>
> If we are fortunate enough to win our way to the final at Wembley, we shall probably have to pay Leicester City another £500.

The price of success was not the only thing on the directors' minds. Cardiff had to play four games in eight days before the semi-final and they weren't completely clear of relegation. There was growing unrest among spectators about the small number of available tickets at Molineux. Secretary-manager Fred Stewart had only received 580 and not the reported 2,500.

The programme editor tried to pacify the supporters on the Monday before the semi-final:

> It will be utterly impossible to satisfy all season ticket holders who are applying for tickets, as they number 2,000. Everything possible will be done, however, to see the few tickets at the disposal of the club, are distributed fairly.

Second Division Reading had done well to reach the last four by beating Weymouth, Southend, Manchester United – 2-1 in a second replay at Villa Park – Portsmouth, Brentford and Swansea Town. Any hopes of them completing a Welsh 'double' were dashed by a professional Cardiff performance. City had just completed three successive home wins to secure their First Division place and having spent the week at Southport again – taking brine baths and healthy walks – they simply swept Reading aside.

First-half goals by Ferguson, who had survived a late scare over a stiff neck, and Harry Wake – both set up by George McLachan – set City on their way and the McLachan-Ferguson combination led to City's top scorer netting the third after the interval.

For the second time in three years, Cardiff City were back at Wembley. They prayed that this time there would be no slip-up.

# Third Time Lucky

Some said it was Trixie the black kitten which the team adopted in Southport as they prepared for their fifth round tie at Bolton. Others claimed it was Fred Keenor's decision to kick a ball out onto the Wembley pitch for his players to run after so they could relax before the Cup Final started. Some mischievously – and rather cruelly – suggested that Arsenal's Welsh goalkeeper Dan Lewis had deliberately conceded the only goal of the game. Only the skipper himself knew the real reason behind Cardiff City's 1927 F.A.Cup win.

A new interview feature was started in the following season's match programme "with the object of bringing the player a little nearer the spectator". After likening football celebrities to those who served in the British Navy – they were all strong silent men – the interviewer noted that the Cardiff captain had actually proved most helpful. In reply to the question: "We hear a lot about the black kitten, is that your lucky charm?" Fred finally revealed the secret of City's Wembley success:

> I've got a pair of football boots which are the nightmare of our trainer George Latham and which weigh just about four times the weight of any other pair. When I wear these boots, everything goes right – yes I did wear them at the Cup Final – and I pin my luck to them.

Of course, there was an element of luck – or good fortune – about Cardiff's 1-0 win over Arsenal but, in truth, their appearance at Wembley was the culmination of a determined battle against relegation which became inextricably entwined with a glorious progression towards the Twin Towers. Cardiff City were concentrating on the league *and* the cup.

The Gunners were managed by Herbert Chapman, whose Huddersfield side had thwarted City in the First Division three years earlier. Cardiff's preparations, to be executed with military precision, were outlined in the Easter Monday match programme.

After today's game at Ninian Park, the players will have a short period of rest in a congenial environment prior to the great event of Saturday next. Tomorrow at 12.30 they leave for Southport where they will undergo a preparation which has always been beneficial to them.

On Friday, they will travel to a place about six miles from Wembley, where they will remain until Saturday, leaving shortly after one o'clock direct for the stadium. By this means, they will avoid the distracting attentions of well-meaning but tactless friends.

Supporters were told that the former Prime Minister David Lloyd George would be travelling from his home in Criccieth for the match and "every seat and every inch of standing room" had been sold.

Readers of the Liverpool programme were also treated to the thoughts of the great Charles Buchan, Arsenal's legendary England international inside forward and skipper. He paid tribute to Cardiff's defence but without knowing the make-up of their forward line, he declined to pass judgement on the City attack:

> I only hope that it will prove to be the weak link in the chain, otherwise we seem to be up against an impassable barrier. I do not anticipate that the Arsenal will be beaten but I do hope that the better team will win.

Two years on, 'The Wanderer' had switched sides. Having rightly predicted a win for Sheffield United in 1925, this time he opted for Cardiff City. They had one of the strongest defences in the Football League, "if not the strongest", and had conceded just three goals in their F.A.Cup run. "I don't think the Cardiff forwards are quite equal to the rest of the side but they have men who can snap up opportunities as they arise."

Arsenal's recent poor league form meant their best hope lay in rising to the big occasion and 'The Wanderer' noted that four of the Cardiff team had played at Wembley in 1925 while no Arsenal player had appeared in a final. City would feel less like strangers in the stadium. "My tip, then, is the Cup for Wales by a narrow margin, always provided of course, that the luck runs anything like evenly."

In the event, 'The Wanderer' was spot on. After Harry Wake's mistake against Sheffield United in 1925, this time

Cardiff had the rub of the green when Hughie Ferguson's shot squirmed out of Dan Lewis's grasp and over the line. They say you make your own luck in sport and Cardiff certainly had worked hard for the crucial break which won the match. The Welsh dragon could hardly have chosen a more appropriate date to slay England's finest: April 23rd, St. George's Day. The timing – not to mention the result – was perfect, even if the game itself was not. The general consensus was that neither team had reproduced their best form but, in the end, Cardiff had done just enough to win.

Before the game, everything went strictly according to plan. After another successful stay at Southport, the team, complete with Trixie in her wicker basket, arrived at Wembley in good spirits. Nineteen-year-old Ernie Curtis was about to become the youngest player to take part in a Cup Final. He had replaced the unfortunate Harry Wake, injured against Sheffield Wednesday a week before the final and thus losing the chance to make amends for his mistake against Sheffield United two years earlier. In *Wembley 1927* by Derrick Jenkins and Ceri Stennett, Curtis recalled the most famous day in Cardiff City's history:

> I remember I had no pre-match nerves at all. We had no fear of Arsenal, as our records that season were very similar. We had been to Wembley in 1925 but it was their first visit. We arrived around an hour before kick-off. Apparently in 1925, the team had got to the stadium too early and nerves had affected everyone during the long wait. This time it was different – a sing-song on the journey there and then straight into the dressing rooms.

More than 91,000 people – the lucky ones from the 300,000 who had originally applied for tickets – had gathered for the third successive sell-out final. As they started to prepare themselves for the match, City's players felt quite at home in North West London. It looked as if Cardiff, if not the whole of Wales, had decamped to Wembley for the day. The team listened to both sets of supporters sing 'Abide With Me' and 'Mae Hen Wlad Fy Nhadau' among other songs before the British national anthem.

A shrewd piece of captaincy by Fred Keenor then made the

Cardiff players feel even more relaxed. It wasn't until 1930 that the two teams walked out together when a suggestion by Herbert Chapman before Arsenal played Huddersfield was acted upon by the Football Association. The dressing rooms were situated underneath the stadium's offices at the West End rather than in their present position at the opposite end of Wembley. Cardiff were instructed to take to the field first but instead of walking, Fred Keenor ran out – and then broke with protocol again: "I did not mention a word to our manager, Fred Stewart," Keenor recalled later, "but I told the lads: 'as soon as I get on that pitch I'm going to kick the ball to the halfway line!' I gave it a mighty thump and four or five of us chased after it."

Moments later, Buchan led out his Arsenal side and, after marching onto the turf, the two teams lined up for the pre-match presentations near the half-way line. The assembled F.A. officials were not amused but Fred Keenor's move did the trick by defusing the inevitable tension. Ernie Curtis recalled: "For any of our lads who had been feeling apprehensive, it was now just like any other game."

When he recalled the game on the following Monday, the *South Wales News* reporter, 'Arthurian' (Arthur Stevens), had noticed the more relaxed atmosphere in the Cardiff team:

> Spectators of Saturday's game who had witnessed the final two years ago were agreeably surprised to find that the City on the present occasion, when taking the field, betrayed not the slightest sign of nerves. They galloped on in sprightly fashion, and in contrast to the almost military-like stride of the Gunners, whose progress on to the field was in measured tread and slow.

It was proving an eventful couple of days for King George V. Two days earlier, he had opened the National Museum of Wales in Cardiff and here he was being introduced by the captain of the city's football team to the men who, in just under a couple of hours, would create history for the Welsh club.

"When Fred Keenor introduced me to the King," recalled Ernie Curtis, "he shook my hand and mumbled something indecipherable. When people asked me later what he said, I told them: 'Hello Ernie, how are you?' 'Fine George, see you after the game!' "

Once the final got underway, Arsenal made little progress against a determined Cardiff side who adopted an ultra-cautious approach. As the *Westminster Gazette* reporter succinctly put it: "The City forwards worked upon the theory which had taken them to Wembley – eight men to keep 'em out and three to snatch a goal."

Arsenal dominated the first twenty minutes without making a breakthrough as Billy Hardy's tight marking of Charles Buchan restricted their opportunities. The Cardiff half-back was later described as the best player on the field by the English press – another irony in view of his rejection by the England selectors. Full-back Jimmy Nelson also excelled by keeping Arsenal's winger Joe Hulme quiet. With defences on top, the 1927 F.A.Cup Final will not be remembered as a classic but it will never be forgotten for the bizarre goal which brought the trophy back to Wales.

Seventeen minutes were left of what had been a disappointingly dour match when fate took a hand – or rather an elbow. From a Keenor throw-in on the left, McLachan passed the ball inside to Ferguson. The Scotsman was known for his sharp shooting from the edge of the box so he let fly – this time from just inside the area. The Arsenal goalkeeper Lewis, from Maerdy in Rhondda, crouched down to collect the shot as Davies moved in on him. Unnerved perhaps, Lewis allowed to the ball to escape from his grasp and it rolled slowly over the line into the net – it was suggested off the keeper's elbow.

Initially, there was widespread confusion about the scorer. Who would be credited with the goal – Ferguson, Davies or even poor Lewis? By Monday morning, it was official. After speaking to Ferguson during the celebrations at Cardiff's hotel in Bloomsbury on the Saturday night, 'Arthurian' quoted the Scottish international's account:

> I know that I shot but I did not know whether the ball was touched by anyone else. As we were returning to the centre from the goal area, I spoke to Len Davies and I asked him if he had touched the ball and he replied 'No'.

At that moment in the game, it didn't really matter. City were ahead and it was a lead they were not to surrender. In fact, two minutes before full-time, Curtis almost snatched a second. After cutting in from the wing, the baby of the Cardiff team was faced by a virtual open goal but contrived to shoot wide. When the final whistle blew, thousands of supporters ran onto the famous turf to celebrate the historic victory.

Back in Cardiff, the crowds who had gathered in Cathays Park to listen to radio commentary of the game on loudspeakers fixed to trees and lamp-posts around City Hall could barely contain their excitement. There were similar scenes outside the offices of the *South Wales News* and *South Wales Echo* in St. Mary Street. In homes throughout the city, copies of the *Radio Times* were hurled into the air by supporters who had followed the game on radio via a plan of the pitch divided up into numbered squares printed in the magazine. The phrase 'back to square one' meaning 'back to the beginning' is said to have originated from this first broadcast of an F.A.Cup Final.

The BBC's first specialist radio football commentator George Allison must have had difficulty in controlling his emotions as he described the action – he was an Arsenal director who became their manager from 1934 to 1947. But there was no getting away from it. Cardiff City had the won the F.A.Cup! As the *South Wales News* observed: "Cardiff became a city of rejoicing".

If by no means a classic final, the game had been played in the right way – hard and fair. The sportsmanship displayed by both teams was best illustrated by Buchan's action at the final whistle. As the teams walked up to the Royal Box to receive their medals from the King, the Arsenal captain ran up to Fred Keenor and grasped him warmly by the hand. Other Arsenal players then followed his example by congratulating the rest of the Cardiff team.

Unlike today, the winners were first to climb the famous steps in 1927. Keenor and his team-mates had to push their way through a throng of Cardiff supporters as the police struggled to keep the path to the Royal Box clear. But when finally made it, Fred Keenor received the trophy from King George V under the admiring gaze of past and future Prime Ministers David Lloyd George and Winston Churchill plus the Lord Mayor of Cardiff, Alderman William Grey.

Not surprisingly, David Lloyd George was delighted with the result. "This is the first Cup-tie I have attended," he told the London correspondent of the *South Wales News*, "and I was thrilled. It was a splendid game. Both teams fought with British pluck and sportsmanship. I am very pleased that my fellow-countrymen have, for the first time, taken the Cup to Wales."

Alderman Grey seemed intent on indulging in a spot of name-dropping when he returned to Cardiff, having been given a seat in the Royal Box at the final:

His Majesty appeared extremely interested in the match and followed the game closely. I was seated next to his Majesty for the greater part of the time, thanks to the courtesy of Lord Derby, who very generously offered me the place of honour. On one occasion, I ventured to express the hope that my enthusiasm would not interfere with his Majesty's enjoyment of the game. "No, no" was the reply, "cheer as much as you like". And I did, especially when the City scored!

Back in the dressing room, the two captains faced the press with refreshing honesty. "I think we were very lucky to win," said Fred Keenor, "because to be candid, I think the Arsenal deserved to do so. It was a rather poor game for a final but we do not expect these matches to provide the most skilful display. So much depends on the result that we get anxious, and I am sure we all were today. I am very glad we have won, if only because we were taking the Cup to Wales for the first time."

Ever the gentleman, Charles Buchan offered congratulations to City for their historic achievement. "Cardiff played an honest, clean game, each member of the team obviously striving to do his utmost, and my final words are 'Good luck to the City and good luck to Wales and its Association football now that they have the Cup'."

When the dressing room celebrations were over, the Cardiff players made their way to the Palace Hotel in Bloomsbury where they had a meal with the directors and their wives. To make the team feel at home, the dining room was decked out in blue and white and the floor was covered with an artificial grass carpet – a replica of the Wembley pitch. To the victors, the spoils – a sumptuous meal in a plush hotel; to the vanquished, a pint of beer at a local pub bought by their captain before going home.

In the beginning. The only known photograph of Riverside Cricket Club, taken in 1899, the year the football section was formed. Bart Wilson is seated in the centre of the middle row.

Where there's muck there's brass. Ninian Park, created on the site of a former corporation rubbish tip, in December 1910 as Cardiff take on Ton Pentre in the Welsh Cup.

One of the early Cardiff City line-ups towards the end of their first professional season 1910-11. Player-manager Davy McDougall (behind the boy with the ball) is sitting next to bowler-hatted Sid Nicholls, a former rugby international.

Billy Hardy – full-time wing-half, part-time coal merchant but never an England international – in action against Spurs at Ninian Park in March 1922.

So near yet so far. Most of the City team who lost the title by 0.024 of a goal, pictured on the club's first foreign tour in the summer of 1924. Len Davies, second from the right in the back row, looks decidedly drawn after missing the vital penalty in Cardiff's last league game of the season. The five match tour took in Czechoslovakia, Austria and Germany.

Wales in the West End. Cardiff City supporters on their way to Wembley for the 1927 F.A.Cup Final.

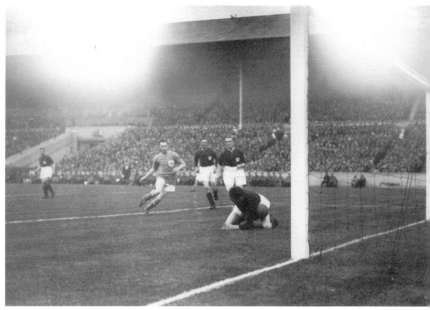

Desperate Dan. Welshman Lewis makes the mistake to gift City their historic goal as Len Davies prepares to celebrate.

From cat to cup. Skipper Fred Keenor swaps lucky mascot Trixie for his familiar cigarette and the famous trophy. Billy Hardy's cup runneth over.

Back at Ninian Park, the official F.A. Cup-winning team photograph sees the directors looking for some limelight. Chairman Walter Parker, seated on the right, is in front of Bart Wilson with trainer George Latham, in bow tie, right at the back.

A proud Walter Parker with eight-month-old grandson Sidney 'Bill' Lewis and the coveted cup.

City's longest-serving and most successful manager, Fred Stewart.

Eddie Jenkins, second from the right in the back row, takes his place in the 1933-34 side which finished bottom of Division Three South. Goalkeeper Tommy Farquharson and Ernie Curtis (seated with ball) represent the last link with the F.A.Cup winners.

Bouquets but then brickbats. Secretary-manager Cyril Spiers introduces the Moscow Dynamo captain to post-war skipper Fred Stansfield before the Russians painted Ninian Park red in a 10-1 wipeout.

Happy days *are* here again: the triumphant Division Three South side are crowned champions before their last league match against Leyton Orient at Ninian Park in June 1947.

Happy Birthday, Bart. Cardiff City's founder is presented with a gold propelling pencil after reaching the age of 80 by secretary Trevor Morris and a few first-team players in January 1950.

Quick off the mark. Welsh international winger George Edwards sets City on their way in the fifth minute with the opening goal of the 1951-52 promotion season in the 4-0 defeat of Leicester City at Ninian Park.

Winger-turned-centre-forward Wilf Grant settles Cardiff nerves with the first of their three goals against Leeds in May 1952 as City return to the First Division after an absence of twenty-three years.

After the following day's sightseeing at Windsor, during which they also visited Runnymede and Kempton Racecourse, it was time for the Cardiff City entourage to return home. Their Wembley reception was as nothing compared with the one which greeted them in Wales on the Monday. When they boarded their train at Paddington just before half-past three, the players had no idea that so many people at Reading, Swindon and Newport would want to see the team and their trophy. If they had looked out of their compartment windows as they headed west they would have seen three aeroplanes from the Surrey Flying Services overhead. This 'guard of honour' picked up the train en route and escorted it to Cardiff General Station where it finally arrived in the early evening.

Harry 'H' Parsons was among the crowd waiting to greet the players as the train headed towards Cardiff General. He later became Cardiff City's kit man after being recruited by Jimmy Scoular in the mid-Sixties to look after the youngsters. For the next thirty years, Harry would become the life and soul of every club party, the confidant of the players and the link between them and successive managers. Back in 1927, 'H' was a starry-eyed nine-year-old boy from Grangetown who was loving every minute of the homecoming:

> My father took me up to the old monument on Custom House Street near the Glamorganshire Canal to watch the team arrive from London. I can remember seeing Fred Keenor holding the Cup out of the window as the train crossed the bridge near the top of Bute Street before pulling into the station. There were so many people around that we didn't go to Cathays Park.

The players rode from the station in an open charabanc, complete with a police escort of nearly fifty constables and a superintendent leading the way. Their families were travelling in buses behind them. As the procession made its way along St. Mary's Street, High Street, Duke Street, Greyfriars Road and Park Place, an estimated 150,000 people were anxiously awaiting their arrival in the civic centre. It was a staggering sight. Cathays Park was awash with well-wishers.

Fred Keenor, familiar cigarette in mouth and unfamiliar F.A.Cup firmly in hand, jumped from the car and disappeared into City Hall, swiftly emerging with the rest of the Cardiff City party onto the balcony. They were all there: chairman Walter Parker and his fellow directors, trainer George Latham and the players. Even Trixie the cat was allowed to milk the occasion, lovingly bedecked in blue and white ribbons in the arms of a beaming Hughie Ferguson. The biggest cheer was reserved for Fred Keenor as he held up the trophy to the crowd. The bunting was up, it was time to celebrate. Winning the F.A.Cup only seven years after joining the Football League had been beyond most people's wildest dreams but it had happened. The players had seen nothing like it. Irishman Tom Sloan summed up their reaction to the welcome: "St. Patrick's Day in Ireland wasn't in it. The reception! The cheering!"

When they were finally allowed to leave the balcony, the players and officials moved inside for a dinner and dance given by the Lord Mayor. The meal began with Consommé à l'Arsenal and ended with Welsh rarebit and toasts to the King and Cardiff City Association Football Club.

The dance was scheduled to finish at 2 o'clock in the morning but the celebrations continued throughout the week. They had to end at some stage because Cardiff were playing Everton in a league match at Ninian Park on the Saturday. The match programme provided 'Fels Naptha' with the opportunity to pay this unrestrained tribute:

> Cardiff City, winners of the F.A. Challenge Cup 1927!
> Who can ever forget this magnificent feat by a club which has been in existence but a comparatively short space of time?
> This climax to a season which no one expected to finish in such glorious fashion has put the coping stone on the work of men who have had to do with the conduct of the club and the fostering of the game in the Principality.
> Of the first directorate, only three now remain – Mr. S.H. Nicholls, Mr Walter Riden and Dr. A. Brownlee. Add to these Mr. Bartley Wilson, who will always be remembered as the real founder of the club, and you have a quartet who are bound to feel a pardonable pride in the club's accomplishment.

'Fels Naptha' then congratulated the chairman Walter Parker, Fred Stewart and George Latham but saved his most fulsome praise for the team:

Of the players, it is impossible to say too much. They have fought every game in a clean and sportsmanlike spirit, bringing honour to themselves, to their club and to the Principality.

Time will pass, new men will appear and those who have managed the club will pass away, but we venture to believe that it will be long before they will be forgotten, for they have carved themselves a niche in the history of sport in Wales which can never be erased.

Long after the 1927 final, the game's main talking point continued to fascinate football aficionados – just how did Cardiff manage to score the decisive goal? Fred Keenor was always keen to shift the blame away from Dan Lewis. In *The Cardiff City Story*, the City captain explained to Peter Jackson, the *South Wales Echo*'s football reporter, what had actually happened:

What a lot of people haven't taken into account was how Ferguson had hit the ball. He put such a spin on it that it would have been difficult for the keeper to have saved cleanly. The ball twisted in his hands, bounced onto his chest and curled back into the net. Len Davies was challenging and I think Lewis took his eye off the ball for a fatal second as he went down for it near the post.

Ernie Curtis, who was standing in line with the edge of the penalty area on the right when Ferguson took aim, had a similar recollection.

Dan Lewis crouched down a little early. The ball spun as it travelled towards him, having taken a slight deflection, so he was now slightly out of line with it. Len Davies was following the shot in and I think Dan must have had one eye on him. The result was that he didn't take the ball cleanly and it squirmed under him and over the line.

Repeated viewing of film of the goal reveals that the Arsenal keeper did well to make the initial save as Davies moved in, on the lookout for any rebound. In fact, Ferguson's shot was deflected off the boot of Butler, the Arsenal defender, and was spinning like a top when it landed in front of Lewis. As the keeper crouched down to collect the ball, it bounced off his chest as he continued falling to his left, parallel to the goal-line. The impact of his body hitting the ground caused the ball to squirm out of his grasp and under his left armpit. Lewis realised what was happening but as he frantically tried to do something about it, he only succeeded in making matters worse. In a split second, the ball hit his left thigh before being knocked goalwards by his left elbow as he turned around in a vain attempt to collect it. It then rolled gently over the line before nestling comfortably in the corner of the net. Davies, following up, merely had to jump over Lewis's legs before turning away in celebration.

Lewis's subsequent explanation suggested that the ball might have picked up a shine from the Wembley turf and slipped from his grasp when it came into contact with his new jersey. Some Arsenal supporters weren't satisfied and letters arrived at Highbury claiming that Lewis, as a Welshman, had thrown the game.

The frustration of those few fans was as nothing compared with that of Hughie Ferguson. At the end of that season, Ferguson had scored a remarkable 271 goals in 281 matches and fell just four short of his personal target of 300 by the following May. His record of five goals in Cardiff's 7-0 win over Burnley on September 1st 1928 still stands but the man who scored the vital F.A.Cup Final winner – one of 91 goals in 138 games for City – was plagued by injury during his final season at Ninian Park.

In 1929, he returned to his native Scotland with Dundee where, largely because of the same series of niggling injuries, the goals dried up altogether. On December 14th 1929, Ferguson was dropped. A month later, he was dead. Relentless barracking from certain supporters became too much and on January 9th 1930, after a training session at Dens Park, Ferguson committed suicide by gassing himself. The once prolific marksman could not cope with life when his goalscoring touch deserted him. In a match programme interview in November 1927, Ferguson had reflected on the reason behind Cardiff's Wembley win. "We were not a great side, but we were bubbling over with determination – aye, that's the word, determination, and that quality covers a multitude of defects." As always, the interview ended with the standard question 'what is your message to the spectators today?' Ferguson replied that the players were greatly encouraged by the crowd's appreciation before making a poignant reference to the other side of the coin of support:

> Be assured that we players are impressed on the field both by your cheers and jeers. Of the former, never tire, the latter – well, sportsmen never resort to it, and they are the only people who matter in sport.

Sadly, his view was not shared by some of the Dundee regulars at Dens Park. Hughie Ferguson was thirty-three years old and left a widow and two young children.

News of his death reached the Cardiff City players as they were about to leave for Southport to prepare for an F.A.Cup third round tie at Liverpool. The programme was quick to pay tribute to their former player. Ferguson was a "clean sport, a good comrade and a gentleman" who first helped the club stay in Division One and then won the F.A.Cup for Cardiff.

> No one was more conscious of his decline as a player than he and none could have tried harder to rehabilitate himself with the directors and spectators. But, like many others, he had at last to realise that his day was done and this doubtless had the effect of hastening his end, accentuated by those despicable critics who find pleasure in 'barracking'.

A less harsh appreciation – and a reminder of Ferguson's immense talent – appeared in *Motherwell FC: The History of the Steelmen* by John Swinbourne.

> He would hang about like a knotless thread, usually on the edge of the arc outside the penalty box. It was beneath his dignity to run about chasing the ball and he demanded that it should be played directly to him. He had a phenomenal shot and with unerring accuracy he would shoot the ball venomously into the net – usually from outside the box."

Ferguson's shot in the 1927 Cup Final may have lacked his usual venom but it created a phenomenon. After the failures of Scotland's Queens Park in 1884 and 1885 and their own defeat in the 1925 Final, Cardiff City had managed to take the F.A.Cup out of England for the first and only time.

Although the team comprised three Welshmen, one English-man, three Scots and four Irishmen, the *South Wales News* observed that the victory would be greeted with delight, not just in Cardiff but throughout the country:

The sentiment of Wales – and sentiment is more often right that it gets credit for – hailed the final as in the nature of an international struggle. To the people it was more than a struggle between two teams; it was a struggle between the two nations. This may not be exactly logical but sentiment transcends logic. So this year's Cup Final will remain in consideration a Welsh victory.

In conclusion, we can express on behalf of all our readers our pride and satisfaction in the whole Cardiff City team, whose success has given an added prestige to Welsh sport by their clever, clean and incisive football.

Despite such fine sentiments and the presence of the Mayors of both Swansea and Newport at the team's civic reception, not everyone in Wales appreciated the first Welsh win at Wembley. The oval ball brigade still found it hard to accept that Association football had made such stunning progress in the seventeen years since Cardiff City had become a professional club. The day after the reception, the *Western Mail* published a letter from a reader from Cymmer bemoaning the absence of home-grown players in the Cardiff side. His sentiments strike a familiar chord seventy-two years later as the debate over foreign players in English football intensifies and rugby continues to grapple with professionalism.

Out of the team of eleven who played for Cardiff City there were, I believe, only three who could qualify to play for Wales in an international match, or who had any native connection with Cardiff.

It is, of course, a matter of money. If you have a rich city and a big gate, you can hire a fine team. But where is it going to end?

Let us consider the possibilities of Cardiff City in the future. From South Africa, it may import a huge long-limbed Zulu whose arms span half-way between the posts for goal. From China may come a couple of imperturbable, hard-working backs. From India, quick and cunning Gurkhas could be brought in as half-backs. And the forwards might be big, swift and versatile Maoris who are already in the front rank of Rugby football. And logically, this multi-coloured team would represent Cardiff just as much as a team composed of men imported from England and Scotland, and for just as little!

Long may Rugby football flourish, where we can take a personal interest in, and enjoy a reflected glory of the prowess of our own townsmen and fellow nationals, and tell the world with some show of truth that "that's the stuff we are made of!"

Blatant racism and prejudice aside, Cardiff City had put Welsh football on the map. The proverb *Tri chynnig i Gymro* – three tries for a Welshman – had proved true. Cardiff's third tilt at the top in three years had been successful. Heartbreaking failure in the First Division and despair in defeat at Wembley could now be consigned to the record books. Cardiff City had won the F.A.Cup, their place in history was assured and the 'English' trophy would have to be renamed – without its accompanying adjective.

Sadly, the win marked the end of an era for Cardiff City. From then on, it was downhill virtually all the way as the Bluebirds went into free-fall.

# Happy Days Are Here Again?

Dannie Abse was three years old when Cardiff City made history by winning the F.A.Cup.

By the time he went to see them in action for the first time six years later, City were on Skid Row. Playing in Division Three South under the managership of Bart Wilson, they were about to reach the bottom of the slippery slope. All but one of the Wembley winners had left and poor old Tom Farquharson was working overtime as City's defence conceded a century of goals.

At the end of the 1933-34 season, Cardiff suffered the humiliation of having to apply for re-election after finishing at the foot of the whole Football League. The club's golden age was over. They had tumbled from the First to the Third Division basement in just four years. Incongruous though it now seems, the players used to run out at Ninian Park with the sound of 'Happy Days Are Here Again' ringing in their ears. It is one of Dannie Abse's abiding memories of his time spent watching Cardiff City from behind the goalposts at the Grangetown End:

> Just before kick-off the brass band would assemble outside the players' tunnel. When the team spurted on to the turf, the band would strike up Cardiff's inappropriate, inanely optimistic, signature tune.

Music had become a regular part of the match day entertainment during the Twenties with the St. Saviour's Silver Band running through an ever-expanding repertoire as the decade progressed. The crowd were treated to rousing renditions of popular songs such as 'One Summer Night', 'Just like Darby and Joan', 'You were meant for me', 'On the Sunny Side of the Street' and 'My Wife is on a Diet' before the game and during the half-time interval.

At the start of the 1929-30 season, readers of the match programme were informed of a 'New Attraction at Ninian

Park'. From now on, the choruses to the band's songs would be printed for the crowd and "the number shown by the band will indicate the song they are playing. Now let's all be happy, and join in the choruses!"

For some reason, 'Happy Days Are Here Again' had secured its special place in the band's pre-match ritual by the time Dannie Abse's obsession with Cardiff City had taken hold in the Thirties. As their voices floated on the Ninian Park air, did many – if any – of the supporters ever stop to consider the meaning of the song they were singing? The by now wafer-thin match programme and journal they held in their hands perfectly symbolised Cardiff City's decline and the words of their strange signature tune could hardly have been more unsuitable:

> Your cares and troubles are gone,
> There'll be no more from now on;
> Happy days are here again,
> The skies are clear again,
> Let us sing a song of cheer again,
> Happy days are here again.

There was precious little to cheer about when on August 16th 1933 Dannie's elder brother Leo took him to see the club play for the first time against Torquay:

> I think it was the only time I ever went with him and he never went again as far as I know! I was hooked after that game – a 1-0 defeat in front of 18,000 at Ninian Park – and from then on, I went on my own. I can't remember why I enjoyed it. I didn't go every week they were at home but I went a number of times.

While Leo became a solicitor and then entered politics, his younger brother chose medicine, writing and, of course, a life-long passion for Cardiff City. First published as a student, Dannie combined a career as practising doctor with that of poet, novelist and playwright:

> Football is wonderful theatre where you don't know the outcome. It's so exciting! Sometimes it's bad theatre, sometimes it's great theatre and, if one's involved, even if it's mediocre theatre, one's still engaged. I would rather watch a mediocre game between Cardiff and some other Third Division side than I would say a Premiership game.

Twice in my life, I've been given a season ticket to watch a team other than Cardiff. Once it was Arsenal and the other time Spurs. I didn't have the same feeling as I did for Cardiff and I watched them in a more academic way – I wanted them to win but I didn't feel committed.

That commitment to Cardiff City involves Dannie being a season-ticket holder at Ninian Park – Block D Row M in the Grandstand – and, over the years, he has quite consciously arranged his frequent trips to South Wales around the club's fixture list:

I used to come and visit my mother Kate in her flat in Cathedral Road to take in home games and if I'm invited to give a poetry reading at Hartlepool or Scunthorpe or some other Third Division town, I look to see when Cardiff are playing there. If they were in London and I'd been asked to be somewhere else, then I'd say 'no' – you have to get your priorities right!

It's the game and the fact that I have one particular team which has fascinated me for so long. It's silly and juvenile in that I have made it into an obsession up to a point but, on the other hand, it enriches my life – like playing chess once a week, going to the cinema and reading books. If you write about football, you can rationalise your juvenile interest – it has economic impetus behind it but I haven't got that. In fact, the last thing I would like to be is a football writer. I was once a theatre critic and had to go along and see all these awful plays. I'd rather just watch football rather than write about it.

The explosion in football literature, as opposed to the reporting of matches, over the last decade has left one of Britain's leading poets completely cold. Autobiographical novels like Nick Hornby's *Fever Pitch*, Gary Nelson's account of life in the lower leagues, *Left Foot Forward*, and magazines such as *FourFourTwo* and *Total Football* are the direct result of the beautiful game becoming fashionable. Without the stigma of hooliganism, it is now perfectly acceptable to flaunt your fanaticism in public. It's cool to drool over foreign footballers and to forever be putting together fantasy teams. Closet football supporters now regularly 'out' themselves, no longer ashamed of their secret passion. Far from being a dirty word, football is now all the rage – for publishers, radio and television executives and especially the chattering classes. Dannie Abse seems to be an exception to the rule:

> I find talking about the game – unless it's contemporary Cardiff City
> – boring. It's become very popular among intellectuals, especially in
> London, to go on and on about it. I remember when my wife Joan and
> I were invited round to one of my editors' houses. He'd also asked
> Nick Hornby and the men spent the whole evening talking about foot-
> ball – in the end, they were making up teams. I found it excruciatingly
> boring so I was left on one side talking to the women – but not about
> Cardiff City!
>
> I must admit that I didn't finish *Fever Pitch*. I bought it for my son
> for Xmas and before I passed it over, I read the first chapter. It wasn't
> for me. As a doctor, I used to find it quite useful to talk about foot-
> ball. I would make some conversation about a team and establish some
> sort of rapport with patients because sometimes their interests were so
> far away from mine. But in latter years, you find that all kinds of liter-
> ary people seem to be interested in football.

As a boy, Dannie always felt more comfortable with the
round ball but like many youngsters in Cardiff, he played rugby
in the morning for his school, St. Illtyd's, and football in the
afternoon – for a Llanishen Sunday School team:

> When I played rugby I'd always be nervous before a game although,
> once it started, I was all right. I never felt like that with football. I used
> to play inside forward and I just wanted to get on and enjoy it.
>
> When I began watching Cardiff City in the Thirties, I didn't know
> any better. They were in Division Three South and they didn't get any
> better! I was aware that Cardiff City were good when they'd won the
> Cup and that Farquharson was the only player from that period still in
> the team.

City's sad, embarrassing decline had begun almost immediately
after their Wembley success. Complacency set in and the directors appeared content to bask in the glory of their historic win.
They started to believe their own publicity as tributes were paid
to the club throughout the summer of 1927. In the programme
for the opening match of the new season against Bolton
Wanderers at Ninian Park, the editor outlined the team's
prospects for the next nine months:

> We have no hesitation in expressing the belief that the coming season
> will prove an even better one than last, for never in the history of the

club has it been so well placed for players as at present.

In former years, we have signed on a number of new men to strengthen the club's resources. This season, not a single new player of note has been added to the playing strength, a testimony in itself of the satisfaction of the directors with the men at their disposal.

In fact, secretary-manager Fred Stewart signed goalkeeper Joe Hillier from Bridgend and John Ridgeway from local football in Sheffield but otherwise did seem happy enough with his squad. The board or Stewart or probably both had made a serious error of judgment. Apart from Ernie Curtis, all the F.A.Cup-winning side were approaching their sell-by date. Whilst not quite in the twilight of their careers, it was pretty obvious that players such as Billy Hardy, aged thirty-five, Fred Keenor and Sam Irving, both thirty-three, could not go on for ever.

In their shortsightedness, the directors wrongly opted for improving the ground rather than the team. Instead of spending the proceeds of the Wembley win on strengthening their squad, they chose to build a cover for 18,000 supporters at the Grangetown End of Ninian Park. When it was decided to sell some of their quality players – Irving to Chelsea, Curtis to Birmingham and Willie Davies, when recovered from pleurisy, to Notts County – they were traded in for inferior models such as Bill Roberts, Matthew Robinson and Frank Harris, all of whom came from non-league football.

To be fair to the board, the post-Wembley season didn't go too badly. Cardiff City created history again by beating the famous amateur side Corinthians in the Charity Shield in October 1927 to become the only team to ever hold the Shield and the Welsh and English F.A.Cups at the same time. A fifth round 2-1 defeat by Nottingham Forest meant there would be no return to Wembley while sixth place in the First Division and another Welsh Cup win represented a reasonable return. In truth, it masked a dangerous lurch towards mediocrity.

In the end-of-season review in their last home programme, the directors acknowledged that all was not well. The Depression was really starting to bite. Low gates – mainly because of "the bad state of trade and consequent poverty of those from whom we get chief support" – had not helped but the new shelter at the Grangetown End would "greatly nullify the inclement weather which endured for no less than nine consecutive Saturdays" badly hitting attendances.

Despite these setbacks, the directors were happy with the financial state of the club and appeared almost blissfully unaware of the problems mounting up on the field – "our playing strength is very good, needing only the addition of one or two players to make it really first-class."

As well as so blatantly deluding themselves, the directors were becoming more and more sensitive to criticism. 'Fels Naptha' launched a scathing attack on the fickleness of fans as he thanked the board, management and players for all their efforts:

> When we are carrying all before us, there are not wanting plenty of enthusiastic admirers who cheer till they are hoarse. But, when adversity comes, and encouragement is wanted most – when, in fact, our so-called supporters have an opportunity of proving their real value to the club, then, alas, they have been found wanting.

The close season saw Bart Wilson going back to his roots by running an unbeaten City cricket team while Walter Parker, after taking a year's break, returned to the chair when the new season got underway. The Grangetown Stand was duly opened on 1st September 1928 before the home game against Burnley in which Hughie Ferguson put five past City's hapless opponents. Things appeared to be looking up, but, in fact, Cardiff were on their way down.

Fred Stewart's signing of Welsh international inside-forward Stan Davies from Birmingham City proved a disaster and injuries to key players – international full-backs Tom Watson and Jimmy Nelson and then half-back Tom Sloan – were compounded by Ferguson's injury problems. He played only 20 games – scoring a creditable 14 goals – and it was City's lightweight attack which sent them into Division Two.

As 1929 drew to a close, Fred Keenor was interviewed in the match programme under the headline 'What's Wrong with Cardiff City?' After mentioning the injuries to Nelson and Ferguson – Ninian Park was like "a casualty station" – the skipper suggested that the good fortune City had enjoyed had been transformed into bad luck:

> We are not bemoaning our fate and complaining at Ninian Park... just
> that little bit of luck which is needed will assuredly come along and our
> star will then be in its ascendancy.
>
> To our supporters I would say: This is the testing time of true
> support, both morally and financially. Don't be found wanting!

In fact, it was the players who were found wanting as wing-half Frank Moss from Aston Villa and St. Johnstone's Jim Munro – Scotland's top scorer – proved ineffectual signings and City managed only one win in their last 16 games. They scored 43 goals in 42 league matches – failing to find the net in seventeen of them – yet their defence only conceded 59 – the lowest in the First Division. After suffering their heaviest F.A.Cup defeat by losing 6-1 to Aston Villa, City were relegated along with Bury before being beaten 3-0 in the Welsh Cup Final by Connah's Quay Nomads.

As he surveyed the wreckage of a disastrous season, 'Fels Naptha' listed the reasons for Cardiff's relegation – injuries, low gates, a new stand and thus no money for new players – but remained remarkably upbeat:

> So much for the past. What of the future? We have the fullest confi-
> dence that the directors,
>> Men of cheerful yesterdays
>> And confident tomorrows
> will prove equal to the task of providing good football at Ninian Park
> and, with an eye to the future, will steadily build up a team which will
> once again find its way back to the First Division.

For once, the columnist's confidence was badly misplaced. Veterans such as Fred Keenor and Len Davies were now the mainstays of a struggling side as Fred Stewart tried to buy his way out of trouble in the 1929-30 season. Another Wembley winner, George McLachan, returned to the top flight with Manchester United and City finished eighth in the Second Division and only reached the fourth round of the F.A.Cup where they were beaten 2-0 by Sunderland.

The following season, 1930-31, saw Cardiff complete their journey down the divisions. Injuries again played a part as did age and loss of form. Billy Hardy, now approaching forty, was appointed player-coach in his twentieth season at Ninian Park and Fred Keenor's best days were clearly behind him. The skipper's judgment wasn't what it used to be either. In a programme article, he looked forward to City's prospects for the new season and spoke enthusiastically about the young players in the squad:

> We have a wealth of exceptionally good talent which with careful coaching and a smattering of experience will prove the basis of a brilliant side ere long.
>
> I have been honoured with the captaincy of the club this season. No captain in the English League has a better lot of boys than I have, and we are going to have a great season.

Fred Keenor could hardly have been more wrong. Cardiff lost their first five games and Fred Stewart gave league debuts to fifteen players – including a local lad called Eddie Jenkins. In all, he used more than twice as many in a vain attempt to stop the rot. City won only once from mid-January until the end of the season and were resigned to relegation long before May.

Now aged ninety, Eddie Jenkins is Cardiff City's oldest surviving player. Another Eddie Jenkins had made 12 appearances for the club in the early part of the golden era between 1921 and 1924 but Eddie J. Jenkins was a regular in the side which suffered the ignominy of seeking re-election after finishing bottom of the Football League.

Born in Splott, his father worked as a blacksmith at the local steelworks before becoming the owner of a milk business. Eddie soon found himself involved in the family firm:

> I left school at fourteen to help during the Depression. I delivered milk in Splott, first from Farmville Road opposite St. Illtyd's College. I was always kicking a ball around and played for Howard Gardens School before turning out for Splott Labour Amateurs in the Cardiff and District League. I remember being invited along to Ninian Park for a trial before joining the groundstaff for the 1930-31 season.
>
> Fred Keenor was a big shot at the time. He was an experienced Welsh international who inspired everybody around him – a bit like Wilf Wooller was later on with Wales and Glamorgan Cricket Club.

Eddie's first involvement with Fred Stewart had come three years earlier during Cardiff's F.A.Cup winning season. He was probably the first person in the city to apply for a ticket for the final.

On the afternoon that Cardiff beat Reading to reach Wembley I went to Clifton Street Post Office and bought a 2s postal order which I put in an envelope with my application form. The club's registered office at that time was Fred Stewart's house in Newport Road not Ninian Park, and within an hour of the result, I had delivered my application to him.

The final wasn't a good game to watch but I remember Dan Lewis parrying the ball and then letting it slip over the line and into the net.

Wembley 1927 must have seemed a world away when Eddie made his debut for his home town club at Bradford City on 4th February 1931. Not only were City struggling to stay in the Second Division but the young twenty-one-year-old had the unenviable task of trying to fill a legend's boots by replacing Fred Keenor. Rumours were rife that Cardiff were about to strengthen their squad so the directors put the record straight via their programme notes in late January: "The management is still searching for good 'ready-made' players and expect in the near future to get what they require. Beyond this, all newspaper statements are mere moonshine."

The skipper was injured for the postponed match in Bradford on the Wednesday and the following game at Barnsley three days later. Eddie's trip to Yorkshire was not a happy one. After putting up a good fight, Cardiff lost 2-1 to Bradford and were then on the end of a 4-0 thrashing at Barnsley. Eddie was immediately dropped and replaced by a more than 'ready-made' player in John Galbraith. Although approaching the veteran stage himself, Fred Stewart's latest signing from Clapton Orient was seen as Keenor's successor and became a City regular for the next three years. Eddie just had to be patient:

I was versatile. I played in five different positions while with Cardiff – right and left-back and the three half-back positions. Fred Keenor was on his way out and I was his possible replacement but it was very difficult to follow such a great player. He took me under his wing and showed me the ropes and in fact, I played six games with Fred. I remember he told me I'd done very well in my first match at Bradford – but next time I shouldn't hang too far back! He gave me some useful tips about marking.

Eddie played another eight games as City descended into Division Three. In the match programme, 'Fels Naptha' explained why Cardiff were being relegated – again lack of money because of poor gates – but refused to be downhearted:

> We have to start again from the bottom, but if we can repeat the triumphs of former days then we shall all feel it was worth it. Let us therefore not be despondent but look forward to the days when we shall again be a potent factor in football history, for whatever has happened, nothing can rob us of the reputation we enjoyed and still enjoy as one of the best sporting clubs in the world.
>
> May we not hope that Fame, that idol to which the finest spirits have in all ages burnt their incense, may again prove the spur to our ambition, the inspiration to heroic deeds, the incentive to greatness.

Poor 'Fels Naptha' had disappeared into dreamland. Back in the real world, one indisputable fact remained. Four years after lifting the F.A.Cup at Wembley, City were in Division Three South. And worse was to come.

In the summer of 1931, City finally said goodbye to Fred Keenor. In view of his huge contribution to Cardiff's success during the Twenties, it was strange that the former skipper received no formal farewell tribute in the City programme. In fact, his departure was noted in a single paragraph in a preview of the new season by an anonymous club director. The board were praised for "heroically bearing a heavy financial burden to keep the club going" and their belated team re-building programme was touched upon. "They decided on parting with many of the players, some of whom had been with us many years and given long and faithful service – notably Keenor and Len Davies."

And that was it. The inspirational skipper who had led Cardiff to their greatest triumph was now worth a mere two lines of appreciation. Keenor played his 369th and last league game in a 0-0 draw against Spurs at Ninian Park in front of nearly 7,000 spectators on 6th April 1931. It really was the end of an era. Len Davies, after scoring 178 goals in 369 games for City, also made his farewell appearance against Spurs. While Davies went to play for Thames F.C., an East London club who disbanded in 1932 to be replaced by Newport County in Division Three South, Keenor joined Crewe Alexandra. After making a further 116 league appearances, he then spent a season with Oswestry before moving south to Kent where he combined the job of player-manager at Tunbridge Wells Rangers in the Southern League with poultry farming. His son Graham, the youngest, remembers his father's new life in Kent:

> My first recollections were of Dad actually playing for Tunbridge Wells Rangers. He did everything there – including tending to the pitch!
>
> I remember him once coming off the field and going into the dressing room with quite a stud mark on the front of his shin. He went to a little box where he kept a bottle of iodine and just poured it all over the cut! As a young boy, I had a fear of iodine and that made an impression on me – Dad was pretty hard! He was still a good footballer but his age meant he couldn't do as much work on the park as he wanted.
>
> He received one or two warnings about taking it easy and then in 1936 he went down with diabetes. After spending some time in hospital, we moved to a small village between Tunbridge Wells and Hastings where we ran a corner shop.

Fred Keenor eventually returned to his home city in 1958 to work as a storekeeper for a building firm. He died in 1972 at the age of seventy-eight and seems likely to be remembered as the greatest Bluebird of all.

While Keenor was enjoying an Indian summer at Crewe, Eddie Jenkins spent a frustrating season on the sidelines at Ninian Park. With Galbraith assuming Keenor's position, the local lad had to make do with reserve football. He played just six times in the Second Division and found himself involved in a wages dispute as Cardiff's financial crisis worsened.

In March 1932, Eddie was offered retained terms of £1 a week in the summer, £2.10 shillings when in the reserves and £4 if playing for the first team. Both Tom Farquharson and John Galbraith's corresponding wages were £5, £5 and £6. A week later, Eddie had won an extra ten shillings per category and three weeks later, his first team wage had risen to £5. At a board meeting in late April, it was resolved "not to reconsider Jenkins if the present offer is not accepted." But by late June, Eddie had been offered even more money – he would receive £4 a week in the reserves and £6 if he made the first team.

Fred Stewart and his assistant Bart Wilson were not so lucky – or perhaps not such determined negotiators. In late April, the board decided to cut their wages by twenty per cent – and Bart would have to help out at the club's registered office at least two half-days a week. Stewart's treatment seems a little harsh, not to say untimely. He was about to be presented with a Football League long service medal after twenty-one years with the club. He had actually managed to improve the club's performances in the second half of the season and City finished ninth in Division Two. They made history with a record 8-0 win over Enfield in the first round of the F.A.Cup as Albert Keating became the first City player to score a hat-trick in the competition.

As a result of City's growing financial problems, the directors decided to increase the company's capital by £8,000 in March 1932. The public were offered but overwhelmingly rejected the chance to buy shares at ten shillings each – much to the disgust of the board who vented their feelings in an April match programme:

> In spite of personal canvass and appeals through the Press, the total number applied for amounts to 517 – £258-10-0! Where are the thousands, we are told, waiting eagerly to take up shares? One cannot help a feeling of disappointment, for the response has by no means justified the legal expense incurred.
>
> However, it may have done some good, if only to convince those well-meaning shareholders who wanted to help the club, that the solution of the club's difficulties was not to be so easily overcome.

A more successful venture was the Cardiff Sports Carnival held at Ninian Park during the city's Civic Week in June "for the benefit of Cardiff City A.F.C." Prize money of £150 was available to the winners of a number of events including a twelve mile road race which finished with three laps around the ground. Boxing and greyhound racing were later to feature at Ninian Park as the directors desperately sought new sources of income.

That summer was notable for two other events – the departures of two of the most influential members of staff. Billy Hardy left to take up a coaching position with Bradford Park Avenue while George Latham joined Chester City in a similar capacity. Since becoming Fred Stewart's first signing in 1911, Hardy had been instrumental in Cardiff's rise to the top, making a total of 582 first-team appearances including the man-of-the-match performance in the 1927 F.A.Cup Final win over Arsenal. With his bald pate and prodigious heading ability for a man of 5 feet 6 inches, Hardy had become almost as synonymous with Cardiff City as Keenor. His time at Ninian Park ended on a sour note when the directors felt unable to award him a richly-deserved benefit.

George Latham had also joined Cardiff in 1911 and played a crucial role in their development either side of the First World War – first as player and then as trainer – as City became one of the fittest teams in the Football League. Unlike the decision to dispense with Hardy's services, Latham's departure did merit a mention in the programme:

> It was a very gloomy gathering of directors which met on Wednesday last to discuss the ground staff, and the decision to part with Latham, who has put in over 20 years with the club, was come to with the greatest reluctance and the deepest regret, for he has endeared himself to all management and players alike.

There was no improvement in the club's financial position during the 1932-33 season. Fred Stewart and the players all accepted pay cuts but at least Eddie Jenkins was making progress. The trouble was that he established himself – first at full-back and then half-back – at the heart of a City defence which couldn't stop leaking goals.

An 8-1 thrashing at Luton was followed by a 6-2 defeat at Swindon and then a 7-3 drubbing at Brentford on 1st April. Cardiff were playing like fools but it was no joke. They were heading towards re-election before two wins in their last three games saw them finish in nineteenth place. A stay of execution masquerading as a close-run thing. "I was very happy to be in the team," recalls Eddie, "but nobody likes playing in a losing side. There was no joy in that but we all stuck together – you had to do your best."

Sadly, City's best was not good enough. – and neither was Fred Stewart's. At the end of the 1932-33 season, the sixty-year-old secretary-manager realised his time was up and resigned, having indicated in March that he would be leaving. The directors held an emergency board meeting at Ninian Park on 14th May where the end of his twenty-two-year tenure as manager was officially confirmed – quite literally in black and white – in the minutes of the meeting:

> It was resolved that Barclays Bank Ltd be informed that the signature of Mr. Fred Stewart as secretary of the Cardiff City Association Football Club be withdrawn and that of W. Bartley Wilson substituted in its place.

So, after two decades of faithful service behind the scenes running the reserves and then the A team, Bart was given his big managerial break. At the age of sixty-three, Cardiff City's founder would be signing the cheques and, with the directors at their weekly board meeting, choosing the team. It was a sad way for Fred Stewart to end his association with Cardiff City but something had to be done to arrest the decline of the club he had proudly taken from the Southern League to Wembley.

Stewart had probably overstayed his welcome. Since the F.A.Cup win, his judgment – and that of the directors – had been decidedly dubious and City were paying the price. As Stewart retired to his coal merchant's business, the board were left to deal with a rare mistake by the master wheeler-dealer.

The directors had been expecting to receive an extra £250 once Joe Hillier and John 'Jack' Jennings had played twenty matches for Middlesbrough after their transfer in 1930. They were incensed when they received just £50 from the Teeside club and the former secretary-manager was summoned to a board meeting to sort out the discrepancy. The minutes revealed what had happened:

> Mr. Fred Stewart explained that he had made an unaccountable error in his letter to the Middlesbrough club in writing £50 instead of £250 as intended but was prepared to swear on oath that he mentioned the sum of £250 when speaking over the phone to their secretary.

When Middlesbrough refused to pay up, Bart wrote with an offer of a "further opportunity of settling the matter amicably" before Cardiff City referred the dispute to the authorities. It was to prove a costly error by Stewart because two months later, the Football League sided with Middlesbrough and Cardiff waved goodbye to £200.

It was money City badly needed. They had to pay off some of the rent and rates owed to Cardiff Corporation, the local tax collector had been in touch and their bank manager was expressing more concern about the size of the club's overdraft. Cardiff City were in dire straits and although Bart had undoubtedly taken possession of a poisoned chalice, he set about his task, as always, with great enthusiasm and with the support of former captain, Jimmy Blair, as coach. Walter Parker returned for a third spell as chairman and between them, three of the most influential figures in Cardiff City's history set out to turn the ship around.

It was into these troubled waters that Dannie Abse innocently sailed in September 1933, completely oblivious to the problems bedevilling the club he would loyally support for the next sixty-six years. As a ten-year-old boy, all he cared about was his heroes on the pitch – and Eddie Jenkins wasn't one of them. He failed to make an impression on the young Abse – despite making 32 league appearances during the season.

It all began quite brightly with a 2-1 victory at Watford – the first of four wins in City's opening seven league games in which Eddie featured. But after trouncing Crystal Palace 4-0 at Ninian Park in early October, the team began to struggle, not winning again until the last game of the year when they completed the double over Watford.

All the while, Bart Wilson was finding his combined roles more and more demanding. There was so much more work to do – especially for a disabled man of his age. The minutes of board meetings during the season paint a picture of a club – and a secretary-manager – under stress.

As well as withstanding constant pressure from the bank, Walter Parker also tried to sell advertising space around Ninian Park. In October, the number of directors was increased from seven to nine. The two new board members had to satisfy Barclays Bank "with a guarantee of not less than £750".

Bart had never been busier. No job was too small for him not to be involved. Along with Jimmy Blair, he was instructed to go scouting for fresh talent, to travel to sign new players and to obtain quotations for the renewal of steps from the boardroom to the stand which were "reported to be unsafe". There was also the problem of heating arrangements in the boardroom which were "condemned as unhealthy" and the non-payment of season tickets. Bart was also instructed to investigate the cost of buying some scales and "measuring apparatus so that an accurate record of players weights and heights could be kept" before being authorised to buy a Remington typewriter for nine guineas.

In early November, the beleaguered Bart was given a pay rise of £1 a week. In his expanded role as chief cook and bottle-washer, he certainly deserved it. Later that month, the secretary-manager was instrumental in the return of Ernie Curtis to Ninian Park through a £1,250 deal which showed just how hard-up City had become. Birmingham were paid £250 immediately with the rest of the fee being made in three payments over the next six months. After negotiating the transfer, Walter Parker told his fellow directors that "the Birmingham chairman stated that an extension of time for repayment would be given if necessary". He was true to his word because when City were unable to come up with the last £500, Birmingham agreed that the payments could be delayed until the end of October.

As well as four-figure transfer deals for tried and tested players, Cardiff City were also looking to the future – however uncertain it may have appeared. In early January 1934, they agreed to pay Ebbw Vale F.C. £5 a week to become a nursery club. But they weren't able to pay up-and-coming young amateurs enough to turn professional.

Tommy Forse was a seventeen-year-old full back who began playing for the reserves during Bart's time in charge. He remembers being approached by the new manager about going full-time:

> I was earning about £4 or £5 a week – a lot of money in the Thirties – from my milk round and I knew that my mate Louis Ford, an out-of-work ship's carpenter, had signed pro for about thirty bob a week.
>
> I went in and told Bart I wanted to go full-time and he asked me how much I wanted. When I told him at least £5 a week, he nearly fell of his chair. 'My first team's not getting that!' he said, so I stayed as an amateur.

At the beginning of 1933, an open appeal to Cardiff tradesmen to buy shares netted more than £500 with David Morgan, James Howell and the Park Hotel all helping out but the board minutes showed that the position was still pretty desperate at the end of January: "It was resolved to travel to Exeter on February 3rd by the train leaving Cardiff at 11.25 a.m. to take advantage of the cheap tickets issued on this train."

City's budget – not to mention their schedule – were both pretty tight. Later that month, the board refused to support a move to allow the unemployed into their matches at half-price because "such a privilege would be open to abuse". For Cardiff City, charity began at home – the club, followed by organisations like Cardiff Royal Infirmary and the Blind Institute who received regular donations, were deserving causes – not so the unemployed.

Walter Parker's negotiating skills – or perhaps his masonic contacts – were instrumental in persuading the income tax authorities to accept £400 in settlement of their outstanding claim for £1,000 in late-February but City continued to lurch from crisis to crisis.

By the beginning of March, Bart was ready to step down as secretary-manager. Cardiff had been bottom of Division Three South since early January and although five successive defeats – including a 5-1 hammering by Bristol Rovers at Ninian Park – were followed by a good 3-1 home win over Queens Park Rangers, Bart and the directors had had enough. At a board meeting in the Grand Hotel on Wednesday 7th March, he officially resigned to be replaced by Ben Watts-Jones, a former chairman of Swansea Town and a committee member of the Football Association of Wales. Having faithfully recorded the minutes of the meeting, Bart later added the following observation: "Mr Watts-Jones attended and after discussion, it was decided to accept his services as Honorary Secretary."

Bart returned to his role as administrator with the blessing of the board and 'Citizen', the reporter who covered City for the *Western Mail*. 'Citizen' claimed it was "more or less a mutual arrangement" between Bart and the directors that he should resign because the board felt the work of secretary and manager was "too heavy a burden to be shouldered by one individual."

Under the headline, 'Hint to Directors', 'Citizen' then

expressed his view that Bart had received a rather raw deal:

> I regret exceedingly that Mr. Wilson's first experience of football managership should have ended so soon. Those of us who have been in intimate touch with the affairs of Cardiff City have felt for a very long time that the manager has been unduly handicapped in his duties because the directors have taken too strong a grip on the managerial side instead of allowing the manager to manage.
>
> I have been in almost constant touch with Mr. Wilson throughout the season, and the more I have come into contact with him the more I have appreciated his many sterling qualities as a judge of a footballer, which, after all, is the prime essential of a manager.
>
> It is certain that if Cardiff City directors hope for better results from Mr. Wilson's successor, it will be necessary for them to repose the fullest confidence in him and allow him to manage.

Within a week of stepping down, Bart was having to placate the Deputy Chief Constable because of an unpaid bill of £143 for police services at Ninian Park. After being warned that "no further assistance would be rendered until the amount was paid", Bart and Walter Parker both sent off cheques for £5.

Cardiff City were living from hand to mouth. The directors were frequently digging deep into their own pockets to keep the club going and on the field, the position was just as precarious. Ben Watts-Jones fared scarcely any better than Bart with a dispirited team winning just one of their last twelve games and finishing rock bottom. During that run, Eddie Jenkins only missed the 3-0 defeat at Bristol City, where he would soon be continuing his career.

When the retained list for the 1934-35 season was drawn up in mid-April, Eddie was offered a first team wage of £5 a week and £3.10 shillings should he play for the reserves. There was no mention made of any payment during the summer. Tom Farquharson was offered £6, £4.10 shillings and £3 during the close season. Two years earlier, Eddie's wages had been £6 and £4 for first and reserve team football. The directors were determined to take a hard line with the players so a week later, they laid down the law to one individual: "It was resolved that should E. Jenkins decline to accept the terms offered him he be put upon the open to transfer list at a fee of £250."

This time, there was to be no reconciliation. After eighty-three league appearances for his home town club, Eddie joined Bristol City. After a short spell at Ashton Gate, he returned to South Wales to play thirty-three times for Newport County:

> I was obviously disappointed when they told me I wasn't wanted anymore. I finished my career at Newport and went full-time into the milk business. Spurs did make an inquiry about me just before the war when I was at Newport but my father said there was more security in the milk business so it came to nothing.

After seeing service in the Mediterranean and the Far East in the Royal Navy during the Second Word War, Eddie returned to Cardiff to run the family business and become a Football League referee. In 1955, he exchanged the milk business for a small credit drapery firm, became president of the Cardiff and District Chamber of Commerce and retired in 1982. He still lives in Cardiff and apart from arthritis in his feet, is in reasonable health. Eddie, who celebrated his ninetieth birthday in July 1999, has few regrets:

> I had no bad feelings towards Cardiff, you just have to take it as it comes. If you're wanted, you're wanted and if you're not, you're not. Even though we were going through a bad patch, I was very proud to play for the club and I take great pride in being their oldest surviving player. There's only one who can be the oldest – one at a time.

Next in line is eighty-seven-year-old Enoch Mort, who now lives in Gilfach Goch. He played in the last thirteen games of the 1933-34 season. The club's dismal performance could have spelt the end of Cardiff City in the Football League as well as calling time on Eddie's career at Ninian Park. Fortunately, the club had enough friends in low places to be re-elected. Ben Watts-Jones decided drastic surgery was needed so, putting Fred Stewart in the shade, the secretary-manager bought and sold as best he could and a flood of new faces arrived at Ninian Park – along with an old hand, George Latham having returned as trainer in place of Jimmy Blair.

The directors spent the summer propping up a club teetering on the edge of extinction. On August 1st 1934, they were told that the bank overdraft stood at £7,123.19s.7d so five of them, led as usual by Walter Parker, chipped in with £50 loans. Bart

Wilson received mixed news at that particular board meeting: his weekly expense sheets were examined and accepted but the contract for the phone at his home in De Burgh Street was cancelled. So much for the perks of the job!

With so many newcomers – eight players were making their debuts in Cardiff's first game at home to Charlton Athletic – the team took time to settle and lacked consistency. They finished nineteenth in the league and fell at the first hurdle when Reading knocked them out of the F.A.Cup at Ninian Park in front of nearly 17,000 – including Dannie Abse:

> I remember we lost 2-1 to a late goal scored by a chap called Tait. He must have been ten yards offside and he tapped the ball twice with his hand before shooting home but it was given. I was at the Grangetown End standing up in the front and the whole crowd got pushed onto the field. I never felt frightened going to watch football. Kids were looked after and there were cripples all around the touchline so there was no danger.
>
> Afterwards, as the players were leaving the field, I remember hearing abuse at a football game for the first time. I think it must have been Tait calling Jock Leckie, our goalkeeper, a 'Welsh bastard' – he wasn't Welsh but a Scot – but as a relatively small boy, I was just taken aback by people swearing so much.

Leckie had replaced the legendary Tom Farquharson, the last link with the 1927 F.A.Cup-winning side, who had finally bowed out on May 4th 1935 after a 4-0 defeat at Bristol City. He had made an incredible 519 appearances for Cardiff – 445 of them in the league. On retirement, he returned to his original trade as a painter and decorator in Cardiff and later ran a tobacconist's kiosk in Queen Street. He then emigrated to join his children in Canada where he died in 1971. Farquharson was capped by both Northern and Southern Ireland and will be fondly remembered as a loyal one-club man.

The six-foot Irishman was rumoured to have Republican sympathies and always carried a gun with him. Eddie Jenkins recalls an incident involving full-back George Russell who had joined City from Bristol Rovers in 1932: "George was showing off in the dressing room one day, and Tom brought out this revolver and threatened to shoot him if he didn't behave!"

City flirted with re-election again during the 1935-36 season but a four-match unbeaten run in March enabled them to finish in 20th place. Non-league Dartford had earlier created huge embarrassment by beating Cardiff 3-0 at Ninian Park in the first round of the F.A.Cup. George Latham finally severed his ties with the club in May 1936 after an accident in Sloper Road as he cycled to the ground from his home in Clive Street. The incident left him badly shaken and he retired through ill-health before returning to his native Newtown. The town's football ground, Latham Park, was named after him when he died three years later.

During the summer, Ben Watts-Jones again decided the team needed an overhaul but another disappointing season saw them narrowly escape re-election by finishing eighteenth in Division Three South. Tommy Forse, now aged twenty, came close to making the first team in December 1936 but when two ageing full backs, Bob MacAulay and Jack Mellor, were drafted in from Chelsea and Manchester United for their debuts at Luton, Tommy stayed in the reserves. In retrospect, he was quite pleased not to have been given his big chance – the team received an 8-1 drubbing.

"The directors were bringing in old players who were here today and gone tomorrow," recalls the man who would later become president of the Welsh F.A. "Several of us youngsters were pretty disgruntled because we were winning most of our games, seven of us won Welsh amateur caps and yet we weren't being given a chance. I think today we would have been pushed in."

Two weeks after the Luton result, First Division Grimsby Town knocked Cardiff out of the F.A.Cup in the third round by winning 3-1 at Ninian Park. It was to prove a particularly costly defeat. Encouraged by City's biggest crowd of the season – more than 36,000 turned up – burglars broke in on the Sunday night and tried to steal the gate money but only succeeded in burning down the wooden grandstand which had been built in 1910. Until the centre section of the current stand was completed in the 1937-38 season, the players had to change under the Canton Stand.

On April 1st 1937, Ben Watts-Jones returned to his previous life as a football club director and joined Cardiff City's board.

Coach Bill Jennings, the former Bolton and Wales international, took over and spent the summer assembling a new squad of players. It proved a turning point: the club's revival was underway. With experience provided by former Bolton goalkeeper Bob Jones – who conceded just 54 goals in the 42 league games – and a cutting edge courtesy of Jimmy Collins, signed from Liverpool, City set off at a cracking pace.

Collins became a firm favourite with the fans. He scored in his first game at Clapton Orient and then bagged a hat-trick on his home debut in a 5-2 win over Torquay. In all, he scored 40 goals in 75 games for Cardiff. The destruction of the main stand may have inconvenienced spectators but the crowds flocked to see revitalised City. Average gates at Ninian Park topped 20,000 as the team lost only once during the season.

Jimmy Collins was a cheeky chappy from London who, along with Bert Turner and George Walton, was responsible for most of Cardiff's goals. In fact, he finished top scorer in his two seasons at Ninian Park.

"Collins was a pretty stocky fellow," recalls Dannie Abse. "I remember being very excited on one Christmas Eve when I was downstairs in a tram car. Collins came in and sat opposite me and I remember thinking: 'Gosh! There's Collins!' It was such a thrill to see one of my heroes in close-up."

Another player to leave his mark on the teenage Abse was Ernie Blenkinsop, a former England and Sheffield Wednesday captain who arrived in November 1937. He only played 10 league games before becoming coach in the 1938-39 season:

> Blenkinsop was a left back who had come from Liverpool and I just realised the total difference in class between him and the players who were hoofing the ball all over the place. I didn't know how bad the football was but I did notice the difference when I saw Blenkinsop. Later on, I became more critical and aware, having seen better teams.

Blenkinsop's elegant style of play appeared a little out of place in a team which specialised in thundering tackles and thumped clearances. "He was a very cultured player," recalls Tommy Forse. "He taught me a lot about positional play – the importance of not diving in and committing yourself. He was a brilliant footballer and a perfect gentleman."

The 1937-38 ended in disappointment with City having to settle for 10th place when the goals dried up. They went down to one of their heaviest F.A.Cup defeats when First Division Charlton Athletic beat them 5-0. Things didn't get much better in the following season despite several new signings as City finished 13th in Division Three South when inconsistency hampered their promotion challenge.

But in the F.A.Cup, Cardiff enjoyed their best run in the competition for eleven years. After beating non-league Cheltenham Town in a replay, they then put out Crewe Alexandra and Charlton Athletic before meeting Newcastle United in the fourth round. More than 42,000 turned out to see Cardiff draw 0-0 at Ninian Park – they lost 4-1 in the replay.

As the season drew to a close, the club righted a wrong by staging a benefit for Billy Hardy against Fulham at Ninian Park with Wilf Wooller and Freddie Hill scoring for City in a 3-2 defeat. Wooller was in the process of making his name as probably the best all-round sportsman ever produced by Wales. In April 1939, he had captained Cardiff Rugby Club to victory in the prestigious Middlesex Sevens in London and in May he scored his maiden first-class century for Glamorgan against the West Indies at the Arms Park before taking 5-69 on the final day.

Wooller's brief involvement with Cardiff City was the result of his relationship with Herbert Merrett, the managing director of a docks coal-exporting company, Gueret, Llewellyn and Merrett. After graduating from Cambridge, Wooller had been taken on by Merrett who joined Cardiff City's board in March 1939 after targeting the club for more than a year.

The directors were considering selling some shares when Merrett first wrote to them in January 1938. Bart Wilson had produced a list of the club's debt to individual directors and the number of shares they each held. Walter Parker had lent the club the most – £338 – and owned the most shares – 776. The board, with about half of the 7,000 shares in their possession, decided to hold a special meeting on a Sunday morning to discuss Merrett's plans for their club.

Five days later, a three-man deputation came face to face with Merrett in the Park Hotel. Minutes of the meeting reveal that he offered £14,000 to clear the club's debts. Before laying

126

down his conditions for the takeover, Merrett remarked to the directors "that the man who pays the piper should be the one to call the tune".

The man who would be owner drove a hard bargain. He wasn't prepared to join the board on the same conditions as the present directors but agreed to the £750 guarantee as long as he was issued with 1500 shares. He denied having offered to buy Cardiff City for £25,000 and maintained the board was much too large. According to Merrett, his move to buy Cardiff City was for the good of the club and football – he didn't expect to make money out of it.

Not surprisingly, the board declined his offer. But Herbert Merrett had not risen from a lowly junior clerk's position to become one of the leading industrialists in South Wales without possessing a strong streak of determination. By 1939, he held directorships with nearly thirty companies and, knowing City's parlous financial state, he was prepared to bide his time. Over the next six months, Merrett acquired a stake in the club – 10 shares in April and then 162 in August. In November 1938, he tried again and wrote to the board. Walter Parker agreed to meet with him to 'ascertain his proposals'.

A month later, during a normal board meeting in the Park Hotel, Walter Parker informed the directors that "Mr Merrett was in the building and wished to interview the members on matters arising out of his letter."

Merrett again offered to buy the club, repay any loans, buy shares and allow all the directors to become life-members. He denied agreeing to spend anything between £20,000 and £40,000 on strengthening the team and said that "what he did when he assumed control was his business".

When Walter Parker's proposal to accept Merrett's offer was defeated by five votes to two – with two abstentions – Parker immediately resigned and agreed to sell his shares to another director Dr. William Nicholson. Parker had been instrumental in setting up Cardiff City A.F.C. in 1910; through his largesse, he had helped the club win the F.A.Cup and then survive, but now he had decided to call it a day after nearly thirty years. He realised that Cardiff City needed some fresh impetus and felt that Herbert Merrett could provide it. After being assured that his complimentary tickets for the directors box were still in order, Walter Parker formally severed his links with the club to concentrate on local politics. He became Lord Mayor of Cardiff in 1944.

If the directors thought their latest rejection would mean the end of Herbert Merrett's interest in Cardiff City, they were badly mistaken. He was a businessman who wanted to do business. As their bank manager asked to meet a deputation of directors to arrange a £10,000 overdraft, Merrett moved in for the kill by buying 765 shares at the end of January 1939 and another hundred in early February. After receiving a lukewarm response to his offer to present the club with a billiard table, furniture and some redundant timber from his Cwrt-y-Ala estate in Dinas Powys, Merrett was finally invited to take Walter Parker's place as a director towards the end of March.

By the middle of April, Herbert Merrett knew he would soon be in control of Cardiff City Football Club. Everything was going his way – he even came out top of the directors' annual ballot for F.A. Cup Final tickets by landing the best seat priced at 10s.6d!

On April 19th 1939, at a board meeting in the Park Hotel, three very important decisions were made. The directors agreed that the chairman should be appointed for three years rather than elected annually, Herbert Merrett was selected as that chairman and Cyril Spiers became manager – an appointment which would eventually enable Cardiff City's incongruous signature tune to ring true.

Having bought his way into the club, Merrett wasted no time in getting to work. Cardiff City's bank account was switched from Barclays to National Provincial and the overdraft accordingly rose to £15,000. Despite doing much to restore the club's credibility in his two years as secretary-manager, Bill Jennings was rapidly, and rather unfairly, replaced by Birmingham-born Spiers, the former Aston Villa, Spurs and Wolves goalkeeper who had joined the coaching staff at Molineux just before the end of his playing career. Spiers was given a three-year contract at an annual salary of £750 plus points bonuses. Promotion to the Second Division would net him an extra £250 while if City returned to the First Division, he would receive a £1,000 bonus.

With the outbreak of the Second World War in September 1939, all Football League fixtures were suspended after three games. Spiers decided to put the break to good use by developing the club's youth programme. As well as maintaining the first team through the use of several guest players – including the late Bill Shankly – he set up a nursery side and persuaded much of the local talent to come to Ninian Park – including a young man from Cardiff called Abse.

During the war, Dannie studied at medical school in London and after appearing in the King's College first team, he was chosen to play for London University. As a result of his selection, he met Wyn Griffiths, a Blaengwynfi-born veterinary student and goalkeeper based in Reading. Wyn turned out for Arsenal against the celebrated Moscow Dynamo side after the war before playing one league game for Cardiff City three years later.

"Around Easter 1944," recalls Dannie, "Wyn suggested that I train during the holiday break with Cyril Spiers who apparently welcomed guest players at Ninian Park. Afterwards, the manager asked if I could play for the reserves in a Welsh League match against Oswestry the following Saturday. But on that afternoon, he took me aside in the dressing room and explained that only ten of the Oswestry team had turned up."

So Dannie found himself making his debut at Ninian Park against, rather than for, his beloved Cardiff City in front of fifty people. The highlight of his match was a spurned opportunity midway through the second half. Fifteen minutes of fame beckoned as Dannie bore down on the Cardiff goal some thirty yards out with the ball at his feet. With just the keeper to beat, he contrived to collide with him and shoot wide, via a post, with the voice of Cyril Spiers – "Now's your chance, son!" – floating across from the touchline.

Often when I sit in Block D Row M of the Grand Stand at Ninian Park my eyes stray towards the Grangetown End goalposts. Or rather, to the left upright. To be exact, to the foot of the left upright where an invisible X marks the spot where a ghost ball once scraped its outer side.

To be honest, I was never good enough to become a professional. Even when I was kicking the ball around beforehand, I realised I wasn't up to their standard. During the game, I would be waiting for the ball instead of going towards it and a player would be getting in front of me even before it arrived. They were much better than me.

I didn't want to be a professional footballer. My ambition was to write the next poem and the one after that and to carry on with my medical studies. Football was a hobby which I enjoyed playing – like cricket, it was part of one's life but I didn't think about earning a living at it.

As a former doctor, I wouldn't like my son to become a professional footballer. The game has changed so much since the Thirties – there's more shirt-pulling, you see more professional fouls and I often think it's more dangerous.

When I first went to football, there weren't any substitutes and occasionally people would be so badly hurt that they had to be put out to hobble on the wing, but there were fewer injuries then because the game was slower. Now it's faster, there are more injuries so clubs have bigger squads. They're like gladiators today and I worry that more and more players will suffer from arthritis in later life. With so much money involved, the stakes are higher.

Despite all the changes, I still get the same buzz when I go to Ninian Park as I did in the Thirties and I still enjoy the game as much as ever. I think my interest will stay with me until I die.

As Cardiff City celebrate their centenary, has Dannie Abse the poet perhaps been moved to pen an appropriate verse or two to mark the event? Although he has written the occasional poem about his favourite club – 'The Game' is probably the best known – football has featured little in his work. "In terms of my writing, it has always been on the periphery – unlike medicine, which has been much more important from the point of view of subject matter. I'm afraid I can't write to order!"

But Dannie's support of Cardiff City during the fallow Thirties was later put to good use during his career as a writer. "In my novel, *Some Corner of an English Field*, some of the names of the characters were Cardiff City players of this time. I borrowed Eli Postin and Albert and Reg Keating although I didn't follow Cardiff then with the same commitment as I did later."

During the last three score years and six, Dannie has lost count of the number of times he's watched Cardiff City but it must run into thousands. From his homes in North London and Ogmore-by-Sea, he tries to see as many games as possible. And when not able to watch City in the flesh, he has bought club videos, listened to the Clubcall line and read about their exploits in the *Football Echo* which he still receives every week.

When I was writer-in residence at Princeton University in New Jersey for the 1973-74 academic year, I made sure the pink paper regularly reached our rented home. I didn't take the *Times Literary Supplement,* the *New Statesman,* the *Listener* or the *Spectator* – I needed to keep in touch with vital news!

It was the same Cardiff paper which would prove the catalyst in the career of another local writer when he joined the throng to marvel at the team created by Cyril Spiers immediately after the Second World War.

The secretary-manager's appointment turned out to be one of the most significant in Cardiff City's history. His tireless work during the war years was to bear fruit in spectacular style when peace-time league games resumed in 1946. Happy days were not quite here again, but they were just around the corner.

# The Yo-yo Years

Cardiff City 1 Moscow Dynamo 10. It still ranks as one of the worst defeats in the club's history but because it was a friendly thrashing, you won't find any mention of the result in the official record books.

The Second World War had ended earlier in the summer of 1945 and on a dank, autumnal Saturday afternoon in November, a makeshift Cardiff City team was systematically taken apart by the crack Russian side in front of an incredulous 31,000 crowd.

Ten-year-old Peter Corrigan had a wonderful view of the game from his father Arthur's shoulders. The *Independent on Sunday* columnist was to become a regular at Ninian Park before graduating from supporter to reporter in the Fifties at the start of his career in journalism. The Russians were the first team to make an impression on him:

> I can remember the disbelief because we all thought Cardiff City were a good side – even though they were only in the Third Division. With typical British insularity, we knew nothing about the Russians but they came here and annihilated us. My memories of the game are very vague but I can remember 'Tiger' Khomich, their goalkeeper, a very acrobatic character.
>
> I then started to go to Ninian Park regularly – my father dropped me in the Grange End boys enclosure where I often used to meet my cousin Brian Madeley, who's now a journalist on *The People*. We would watch the games and then get the players' autographs. Before they built a boys' enclosure, I would go on my father's shoulders or sometimes we would be passed down to the front to sit near the St. John's Ambulance men down by the wall.

Moscow Dynamo were on a short British tour playing Arsenal, Chelsea, Glasgow Rangers and Cardiff, the leading club in Wales. According to the board minutes, the directors were delighted to receive the Russians – despite the "fairly heavy" expense of accommodation and entertainment.

As it turned out, Cardiff made a profit of just over £1,000 – a fifth of their then overdraft – after controversially putting up ticket prices for this one-off match. But the crowd certainly got their money's worth. After exchanging bouquets for miniature miners' lamps during the presentation, the Russians simply ran rings around Cardiff with three players, Bobrov, Beskov and Archangelsky, all scoring hat-tricks. Terry Wood missed a penalty for Cardiff before Beriah Moore's consolation goal. A crowd of 85,000 had already seen Moscow Dynamo draw 3-3 with Chelsea at Stamford Bridge – even though one blinkered critic had observed that "they are not nearly good enough to play our professionals" – and, after demolishing Cardiff, they went on to beat Arsenal 4-3.

The Second World War had led to four City players being captured by the Japanese. Billy James and Bobby Tobin were unable to re-establish their careers because of injuries sustained while in captivity, Jackie Pritchard, a reserve goalkeeper, was drowned at sea in November 1943 but Billy Baker returned to make 293 league appearances for the club. During the war, Cardiff City had been playing in various regionalised leagues and when peace returned to Europe, the football authorities decided to give clubs the 1945-46 season to reassemble their playing staffs.

According to Ken Hollyman, one of five City players who faced the Russians and then became regulars in the team which went on to win the Division Three South championship. The Dynamo Moscow result was not as disastrous as the scoreline might suggest. After being demobbed from the Royal Navy, Hollyman had hitch-hiked back to Cardiff from his Oxford training depot for the game:

We were no match for the Russians whose technique and support play had us chasing shadows but we learned from that lesson. They were three times fitter than us, they could control the ball better and they used man-for-man marking.

Once league fixtures began again, we thoroughly enjoyed ourselves. I don't recall any of us having our names taken, we were a young and very fit side built on good defence. We would stop the opposition playing and then give the ball to our forwards who had a field day.

We didn't have much coaching in those days because there wasn't the time. A lot of the players had outside jobs – I was a sheet metal worker – and we had to train in the evenings. We played so many five-a-sides that we were a yard ahead of the opposition – we were so fit.

Many of the team which stormed to the title in the 1946-7 season were local lads recruited by Cyril Spiers to fulfill Cardiff's war-time commitments. Apart from Hollyman, Fred Stansfield (Grange Albion), Arthur 'Buller' Lever (Machine Products), Colin Gibson (Penarth Pontoons) and Roy Clarke (not quite local – he came from Newport) all played against Moscow Dynamo before forming the backbone of the championship-winning side along with Alf Sherwood (Aberaman Athletic). When Cardiff-born Stan Richards joined from Tufnell Park in London after an earlier spell with Cardiff Corries, City were all ready for the resumption of Division Three South football. Spiers, the architect of the side, sadly would not be with them, having resigned following a contractual disagreement.

The appointment of Cyril Spiers as secretary-manager marked a sea change in the way the club was run. He was, in effect, the team manager, responsible for the signing and selection of players – albeit with the approval of the board. Having serving as coach under the legendary Major Frank Buckley at Wolves in the Thirties, Spiers demanded and gained immediate respect. At a meeting in May 1946, chairman Herbert Merrett asked his fellow directors for their views on the re-signed squad of players. When Tudor Steer, a Cardiff estate agent who later became club chairman, explained that he was "not altogether satisfied" with the centre-forward and full-back positions, Spiers recorded his reply in the minutes:

> The Secretary-Manager said that he considered we had all positions well covered with the exception of that of goalkeeper and he would like to have another good goalkeeper. He suggested strengthening the full-back position by moving Stansfield back, leaving the centre-half positions to be filled by Lever, Booth and Williams. He thought we had the centre-forward position well covered by Richards and Rees.

The manager's response showed that interest but not interference from directors would be tolerated. Later on in the same meeting, the reason behind his imminent departure surfaced for the first time. Spiers had apparently taken a pay cut to help out City during the war years when times were hard. He now wanted his original contract to be honoured:

> After a lengthy discussion, the Manager was informed that no alteration be made to his salary at the moment but the board had agreed to increase the bonus fee for promotion to the Second Division to £500. The Manager expressed great disappointment with the board's decision.

The promise of an extra £250 was not enough to keep Spiers happy and a fortnight later, he resigned to become manager of Norwich City. Merrett wasted no time in finding a replacement. Within days, Newport County's recently-departed manager Billy McCandless was appointed. Having taken Newport County to the Third Division South championship in 1939, he repeated the feat with Cardiff in 1947 and then completed a unique treble by winning the same title with Swansea Town two years later.

The first post-war fixture list followed that of the 1939-40 season when Football League games were suspended. As fate would have it, Cardiff travelled to Norwich for their first match. Cyril Spiers made good use of his intimate knowledge of the City side as his new team beat his former charges 2-1. Stan Richards scored the first of a record 30 goals in just 34 games for Cardiff during the season.

Another defeat followed – 3-2 at Swindon – before City hit the winning trail by beating Notts County and Bournemouth at Ninian Park. After losing at Bournemouth on 18th September, they then embarked on a remarkable 21-match unbeaten league run – 19 of them victories. Nobody could live with this young, rampant side as records tumbled and 30,000 crowds became the norm at Ninian Park. Ten Welshmen and an Englishman were unbeatable at home while the team established the existing record of eight successive away wins.

After two matches, goalkeeper Danny Canning replaced George Poland, who had been re-engaged after the war, Arthur Lever and Alf Sherwood played at full-back with skipper Fred Stansfield, Ken Hollyman and Billy Baker the half-backs. Bryn

Allen and Billy Rees were the inventive inside-forwards while wingers Roy Clarke and Colin Gibson (the lone Englishman) supplied the service to Stan 'Open the Score' Richards. The centre-forward's nickname stemmed from a popular song of the time, 'Open the Door Richard', which was duly adapted by home supporters during games. "Stan was a big, strong fellow with a fleshy face," recalls Peter Corrigan. "He was not at all athletic-looking but when he swung his leg or jumped to head a ball, he knew where the goal was. When there were no goals and the crowd were bored, they would sing 'Open the Score Richards' and very often he did!"

Harry Parsons wasn't at all surprised to see Richards firing Cardiff City to the Third Division South Championship. They had been classmates at school and as he watched the 1946-47 team from the Bob Bank, Harry remembered the commitment shown by Stan when he was growing up in Grangetown: "You would seem him night and day kicking a tennis ball by himself against a big green door near our homes," recalls Harry whose son John later played for Cardiff City. "Stan looked as if he had something about him at school and he practised so much that he had to make it in football."

Like most supporters, Peter Corrigan can reel off the names of the side he grew up watching. He later became very friendly with Arthur Lever, Ken Hollyman and Alf Sherwood when they moved to Newport County who were previously managed by Fred Stansfield, their former Cardiff captain. "Fred was a very hard player, very tough-looking and I'll never forget the day he broke his leg. Cardiff were playing Barnsley at Ninian Park in January 1949 and I can see him now, sitting up, pointing to his leg and calling for the stretchers. He knew he had broken it. That was his last game for Cardiff and Cyril Spiers immediately replaced him with Stan Montgomery who had arrived a couple of months earlier from Southend."

The Cardiff City team rarely changed during the championship-winning season with eleven of the players making 34 or more league appearances out of a possible 42. Peter Corrigan explains their success:

They were a good passing side. They were all good footballers. From

Lever and Sherwood at full-back, right through to the wingers Gibson and Clarke. Sherwood was a super player at a time when full-backs weren't called upon to do much more than kick the ball into Row G – taking the winger with it if possible! Ken Hollyman, at right-half, was the archetypal midfield dynamo and how he didn't play for Wales, I'll never know! That was one of the crimes of the Millennium as far as I'm concerned. Billy Baker covered so much ground and he could finish too.

It was party time at Ninian Park and with so many people wanting to see their local heroes, the celebrations sometimes got a little out of hand. On 7th April 1947, with the finishing line in sight, a staggering 51,626 supporters packed into the ground for Cardiff's league game against Bristol City – with near-disastrous results. Peter Corrigan was there:

I was in the Canton Stand with my father when we saw two men clamber up onto the roof of the Grangetown End Stand. They were on the bottom left-hand corner and one of them suddenly fell through! The man, and the people he fell onto, survived but I'll never forget that. I remember that incident more than the game which ended in a 1-1 draw.

Everyone went to Ninian Park in those days. You hear people talk about Wales being a great rugby nation but you scarcely heard Cardiff Rugby Club's name mentioned then. There was obviously great relief that the war was over – we'd come out of a long, dark tunnel – and although there had been some war-time games, suddenly there was this excellent team which everyone wanted to watch.

Supporters used to stream out of trains from the Valleys at Ninian Park Halt. We would be walking up from town along Ninian Park Road under the Taff Railway Bridge when we would meet them. There was never any trouble. If there was a big crowd, I was instructed to put my fists up under my chin and keep my elbows tucked in! I used to get carried along for fifty yards by this great crush but I was never worried. It's frightening now when you think of all the disasters that have happened since. After the games, the trains would be queuing up to take everyone home in a masterpiece of transportation – if only they had the same expertise today! Inside the ground, there were very few away supporters because, so soon after the war, people didn't have much money and they used to work on a Saturday morning. It was absolutely riveting – I would spend all week looking forward to the Saturday afternoon. I'm sure they used to down the mines and in the steelworks as well. When I was at Ninian Park, there was nowhere else I wanted to be – it was marvellous.

Meanwhile, the boys in the backroom – Trevor Morris and Bart Wilson – were working overtime to cope with the huge surge of interest in the team. Morris had been on Ipswich Town's books but his career ended when he broke a leg playing in a war-time game for Cardiff City. During the war, he served with the R.A.F. Bomber Command and was awarded the Distinguished Flying Medal. Before going into the forces, he had combined playing with football administration by working in the football club's office after training:

> I would go back in the afternoon and do any jobs which needed doing – like selling season tickets. Bart had his system going which I took on. That's how I later became secretary. Bart had been through the mill, he had been to the F.A. Cup Final and he was very proud of the club's achievements. He taught me a lot about football and about life. He used to talk about the characters like Keenor and Farquharson and people would come into the office just to chat about the old days.

When Trevor Morris returned to Ninian Park in May 1946, he was employed as assistant to manager Cyril Spiers at £5 a week. According to the minutes, the board wanted to see how he would shape up and resolved that "should he prove satisfactory in every way, his salary to be reconsidered in three months time."

Trevor passed the audition and renewed his relationship with 'the Grand Old Man' of Cardiff City. Now seventy-five, Bart was being paid half as much as Morris to be office dogsbody. Every day, he would either walk or be taken by taxi to Ninian Park. The Wilsons had been bombed out of their home in De Burgh Street during the war and, after staying with their daughter May in Fairwater, Bart and Sarah had settled in Llanfair Road near the Penhill crossroads.

As well as their administrative work, the pair had more pressing duties at home games. Minutes of a board meeting reveal that three months after joining as assistant, Trevor, along with Bart, found himself involved in crowd supervision by "the checking of stiles and gates on match days".

Over the next eight years, Trevor Morris got to know the founder of Cardiff City very well:

I would rate Bart Wilson as probably the straightest, the whitest man I ever met in football. A spade was a bloody shovel to Bart and he said so. I had a lot of respect for him. He didn't cut any corners and he said what he thought without being abusive – he was a character, a mixture of Wales and the West Country.

Bart put me on the right lines because I became a disciple of his view that Cardiff City didn't belong to one individual like Herbert Merrett, it belonged to the people of the city. He was right and I have used that argument all my sporting life. We had a good cross-section of the community on the board. There was Dr. Alex Brownlee, a surgeon at Llandough Hospital and Tudor Steer was an estate agent. We had Chris Page from Page and Stibbs, the number one electrical people in Cardiff and Walter Riden who had been Fred Keenor's teacher in Roath.

When I came back from the war I told Herbert Merrett that he needed somebody in the office apart from Bart who was almost in his dotage. All of a sudden, there were 30-40,000 people coming to watch Cardiff and there was only the two of us.

With such big crowds pouring into Ninian Park, success on the field was matched by an equally impressive transformation of the club's finances. By the end of September 1946, Cardiff City had started to make money for the first time since the Merrett takeover. After the worst winter for years when coal stocks were frozen and many football matches postponed, the team weren't crowned champions until early in June 1947 after a 1-0 home win over Leyton Orient. Cardiff City were nine points in the clear and £18,500 in the black.

The directors were keen to pass on the praise for the club's promotion to the people who had brought it about – the captain, manager and trainers (in that order). Minutes of a board meeting after the championship title had been won reveal the 'deep appreciation' felt by the directors to everyone involved:

Whilst it is not intended to single out any individual members of a fine fighting side, it is considered worthy of record that this success was achieved by a team, which included a greater number of local or district players than has ever before represented the club in league football and that a larger percentage of the team were part-time players with limited opportunity for training.

With so many of the post-war players coming from the local area, Cardiff City's younger supporters felt a particular attachment to their idols. After watching them at Ninian Park, they would later pass them in the street. Peter Corrigan remembers his involvement with his heroes:

Ken Hollyman used to live in Moy Road in Roath not far from my home in Alfred Street and there was always a little queue of people outside his door wanting autographs. His nephew, Alan Dart, was in my gang so sometimes we were privileged to be taken into the house just to gawp at Ken. We used to see Billy Baker and Dan Canning around the place but just because they were part of the community, it didn't take away the magic – their icon status wasn't affected at all.

Nowadays, footballers are remote, they live in the leafy suburbs with high walls around their houses. Then, they were still stars but accessible stars, gods even. There was an aura about that side – they kept winning and the crowds were so large.

During the 1947 close season, the players and their wives or friends were treated to a promotion dinner at the Angel Hotel and their wages rose to a maximum of £12 in the winter, £10 in the summer and £9 in the reserves. Nearly £9,000 was spent on re-building and extending the enclosure with concrete terracing in front of the Grandstand and ticket prices went up – it would now cost 3s rather than 2s.3d to watch the team from the Canton Stand.

In August 1947, Trevor Morris and Bart were rewarded with a £5 bonus each for all their hard work – Bart's weekly wage had been raised to £2.10s straight after the war. The annual general meeting at Ninian Park the following month heard that Cardiff City were nearly £11,000 in the black. The minutes reveal that, in response to a vote of thanks, the chairman hailed the club's performance on the field as "very successful". Although Sir Herbert Merrett had claimed that his takeover was not designed to make money, "from a financial point", it had been Cardiff City's "most successful season ever."

Two months later, Sir Herbert was on the look-out for a new manager. When Billy McCandless accepted a lucrative offer to join Swansea Town, the board decided to split the job of secretary-manager. Trevor Morris doubled his salary to £500 a year by becoming secretary and after 'discreet inquiries' about John McNeil of Torquay had came to nothing, Sir Herbert and Cyril Spiers kissed and made up. By early December, Spiers had returned from Norwich with a much stronger hand. The minutes show that he would "take full control of the whole of the company's personnel, whether players or other employers, such as office staff, ground staff, trainers, scouts and nurseries and shall be responsible to the board for their behaviour and efficiency."

Spiers would choose all the club's teams who would play "according to his suggestions." The directors still retained their right to approve the first team but it was decided that "in the event of there being no board meeting, the Manager shall select all the teams at his sole discretion and they shall play accordingly."

In return for virtually running the club, Spiers would be paid £1,750 – more than double the salary he was offered in 1939 – and receive a bonus of £1,000 if Cardiff were promoted or reached the F.A.Cup Final.

As the crowds kept coming to Ninian Park, Trevor Morris was earning every penny of his new salary. He and Bart were simply swept off their feet because everyone wanted to see the team:

> I worked my socks off. I worked all the hours that God sent. We didn't have enough season or international tickets to go around, which created problems. The only time the police were involved was when Bart and I were trapped in the office. There were people outside wanting international tickets but we didn't have any – we had sold out. But they wouldn't believe us, they felt we were keeping the tickets from them and we scared stiff so we had to call the police. They were hammering on the windows, Bart and I were hiding in the office and the police had to come and disperse the crowd!

Bart may have been busy but he still found time to help out old friends. As the 1948-49 season reached a climax, he received a letter from Sol Shepherd, one of the original players with Riverside Football Club and a life member of Cardiff City. Could Bart supply him with a couple of F.A.Cup Final tickets for his sons?

Bart replied that, despite the 'great competition', he had obtained two 3s field tickets for the match between Wolves and Leicester City at Wembley. "This is absolutely the best I can do," he wrote. "Hope the boys will enjoy their outing. It's a wonderful spectacle. Just wait until Cardiff City get there – they are on the road but it's a long one."

In January 1950, Bart's commitment to Cardiff City was recognized when he was presented with a gold pencil to mark his eightieth birthday. Ken Hollyman had organised a whip-round among the playing staff and Trevor Morris gave Bart the surprise gift as he sat in the office.

"He didn't know anything about it when we walked in," recalls Ken, one of half a dozen players at the presentation, "and he loved it. He had done so much for Cardiff City and we felt something should be done to celebrate his birthday."

The pencil now has pride of place in the home of Bart's grand-daughter in Croydon. Alma Vosper remembers meeting him as he made his way home from Ninian Park along Llandaff Road, hat on head and crutches under his arms.

> Every Thursday, my brother John and I would go for tea at our grand-parents after school. We would stay there for a couple of hours before going home to Fairwater. I remember how Grandad used to grow geraniums, read a lot and listen to the radio. He showed me how to paint skies, but I never excelled at it, like he did. We didn't use to talk about the old days of Cardiff City because I wasn't very keen on football although I went down to Ninian Park with my mother. We used to sit in the directors' box while Grandad stood on the touchline.
>
> He was the kindest person I've ever met – he wouldn't harm a flea. It's only hearsay but there was a story that when he and my grand-mother lived in De Burgh Street, they discovered they had a mouse in the house. He had one of those humane traps, caught the mouse and then let it go into the lane. I can well believe it because that was the sort of person he was.

Six months after Bart had received his gold pencil, Herbert Merrett was also being recognized – by the King. In July 1950, he was knighted for services to public life but the chairman's honour cut no ice with the club's founder, as Trevor Morris remembers: "I had mixed feelings about Sir Herbert because he and Bart weren't friends. When the chairman was knighted, he came into the office and everyone offered him their congratulations. 'Good morning Bart,' said Sir Herbert. 'Morning, Mr Merrett,' said Bart. He was still 'Mr' rather than 'Sir' to Bart."

With radio coverage of football still in its infancy, newspapers played a crucial role in the lives of Cardiff City supporters when their team were playing away. Peter Corrigan remembers the Saturday afternoon ritual of collecting the *Football Echo* from a nearby paper seller:

> I would go down early to the old Globe cinema before the match was over and there'd be a long queue. We could see the *Echo* van coming along Albany Road and the man would throw out the bundle of papers but we wouldn't know the result until the seller cut the string and handed out copies. If they'd lost, everybody would groan. Whatever the result, I would go home and devour every word of the report.

Peter Corrigan's career as one of Britain's leading sportswriters can be traced back to those early days watching Cardiff City at Ninian Park. Although it wasn't obvious at first, Peter knew that, unlike the poet Dannie Abse, he wanted to make his living writing about football:

> Watching Cardiff City was part of the freedom process after the war. It implanted an abiding sporting passion which has never left me. When we were coming out from the enclosure just behind the goal at the Grangetown End, there was one mad rush to leave the ground so we had to wait for a bit. The press box was on stilts on the right of the Grandstand in those days and we could see the bald head of Dewi Lewis who wrote as 'Citizen' in the *Echo*. I didn't know him but people used to say 'that's 'Citizen'!' Brian and I used to stand and look at him dictating his copy after he had only made notes on a matchbox during the game. Within half an hour, we would be reading his words. We would just marvel at this man.
>
> It wasn't an ambition of mine to be him because I didn't think that was within my compass. I was twelve-years-old, going to Cathays High School and although English was the best of a bad lot of subjects for me, I can't honestly say that I was fired to become a journalist. In fact, I used to imagine myself as a commentator rather than a writer but once I stepped inside the offices of the *South Wales Echo*, that was what I wanted to be and eventually I became 'Citizen'.

When he began looking for a job after leaving school at sixteen, Peter was spoilt for choice. Apprenticeships with a local butcher and Great Western Railways were rejected in favour of an opportunity to become a tea-boy on the *Echo* at 25s a week.

The pay wasn't as much but it appealed to me. I don't know why but it stirred something inside so I applied for the job and got it. There was a crowd of us just running errands. We would go down to the courts and council meetings to pick up the copy as well as make tea.

Apart from Dewi Lewis, who was also the sports editor of the *Western Mail* as well as doubling up as 'Citizen' with the *Echo*, there was J.B.G. Thomas, the *Mail*'s rugby writer who had just come back from the war. I then progressed to running rugby copy over from the Arms Park on international days to the paper's offices in Westgate Street which meant I missed quite a few Cardiff City games. Terry O'Connor, who went on to work for the *Daily Mail*, was a young reporter on the *Sunday Graphic* then and I would phone over his copy for 3d – he was, and still is, very tight! When he started, he used to phone over copy for the legendary C.B. Fry, the former England cricketer who played for Southampton in the 1902 F.A.Cup Final and was seriously proposed as the King of Albania in 1919 – so there's a tie-up there which I'm quite proud of.

Peter Corrigan's career at the *South Wales Echo* began in 1952 – the year that the Merrett-Spiers partnership paid dividends. After four years in the Second Division – in which they finished 5th, 4th, 10th and 3rd – Cardiff City went one better and reclaimed their place in the top flight. Since replacing McCandless, Spiers had continued his policy of developing local talent as well as bringing in more seasoned professionals such as George Edwards, the Treherbert-born left winger who was signed in mid-December 1948 for £12,500 from Birmingham City. He had made two league appearances for Swansea Town and won a Welsh amateur cap before the war. Having been stationed in the Midlands, he spent two years at St. Andrews as Birmingham gained promotion to the First Division. He also attended the city's university and began writing a thesis on the Pembrokeshire coalfield for his M.A. degree. George recalls his reasons for moving back to South Wales:

I came to City because my wife Pat was a Swansea girl and although we were engaged, we were quite a long way apart. Then there was the field work for my thesis which meant travelling to Pembrokeshire and libraries in places like Aberystwyth which I could only do in the summer. I had to cry off when Wales played England at Villa Park because of a groin injury but when I met Alf Sherwood at the pre-match dinner, he asked me if I'd thought about coming to Cardiff?

Eventually, after sending a scout to watch me, Cyril Spiers came to my lodgings late at night to sign me and I made my debut in a 2-2 draw at Leicester the next day.

George scored in his first game at Ninian Park in a 6-1 thrashing of Bradford Park Avenue and became an important member of the 1952 promotion team by laying on several goals for Wilf Grant and Ken Chisholm. "George was a super player who never strayed far from the touchline," recalls Peter Corrigan. "He was an out-and-out left winger, great on the ball with a lovely touch – a very valuable signing."

After retiring in 1955, George Edwards returned to Ninian Park as a director only two years later before leaving the board in 1975. He then returned for a second spell in the boardroom before resigning in 1986.

Wilf Grant arrived at Ninian Park from Southampton in exchange for Ernie Stevenson in March 1950. He was bought as an out-and-out winger but helped Cardiff to win promotion as a free-scoring centre-forward. The switch was borne out of desperation the following November against Hull City. After six matches without a win, Spiers was away finalising the transfer of winger Mike Tiddy from Torquay. An injury to right half Bobby McLaughlin meant that, under the guidance of Sir Herbert Merrett, the side was reshuffled at half-time and eventually won 2-1. Grant finished top scorer that season and then hit 26 league goals as City returned to the First Division after twenty-three years in 1952.

"Wilf Grant was a very cultured player," says Peter Corrigan. "Not a big centre-forward by any means but he had good positional sense. He ended up as coach to Bill Jones and really helped to fashion the side that went up in 1960. Wilf was a great servant to Cardiff City." George Edwards agrees: "Wilf was the best reader of angles that I've ever known. He was a poor winger because he didn't have pace but when he was switched to the middle, he got us goals, he was so cool."

"Stan Montgomery was the archetypal stopper centre-half," recalls Peter. "He was terrific in the air. You wouldn't want to study his distribution too closely but it didn't matter so much. He was a good, strong tackler and quick enough to get in the way of people. He was fearless. Charlie Rutter was a full-back who played like his personality. He was a cheeky Londoner, very popular and adventurous and another solid man – they were built to last in those days."

Cardiff left promotion to the very last minute in 1952, having to win their last three matches, all at home, to go up ahead of Birmingham on goal average. They knew their fate was in their own hands after drawing 2-2 at Luton. "We didn't look as if we were in with a chance of promotion," recalls George Edwards, "but we were sitting in the bath at Kenilworth Road when, all of a sudden, there was a heck of a row with lots of cheering and clapping and in came Cyril Spiers. 'Birmingham lost 5-0!', he cried. 'We can go up!' We suddenly realised that he was right because that result meant we had an infinitely better goal average than Birmingham. If we won our three games in hand, we were bound to be promoted."

After beating Blackburn 3-1 and Bury 3-0, Cardiff clinched second place behind Sheffield Wednesday with a 3-1 win over Leeds in front of 52,000 at Ninian Park in their very last game in early May. With such a lot resting on the outcome, the result has been the subject of some match-fixing speculation. George Edwards remembers a very tense atmosphere in the dressing-room:

> As we were waiting in the tunnel, one of the Leeds players came up to me and told me to stop panicking.
>
> I had a feeling that here was a fellow professional saying: 'we can't gain anything out of this game, you can get promotion if you win, so OK.' But there was no suggestion that Leeds were going to throw the game – good God no! – and in fact it wasn't until Wilf scored after about half an hour that we settled down. He got another before half-time before Ken Chisholm made it safe with a third and we started to relax and Leeds scored a late consolation goal.

It had promised to be a nervous ninety minutes but, in reality, without the injured John Charles, Leeds didn't seem too bothered.

When Birmingham had gone up to the First Division in 1948, they clinched promotion with a 2-0 win over Cardiff. Now George's new club had pipped his old one on goal average. "The Birmingham side I played for was better but going up with Cardiff was the greatest moment of my club career because I was a Welshman. We had plenty of experience in that team with Doug Blair, Alf Sherwood, Ken Hollyman and Stan Montgomery. We knew what had to be done and we did it."

Five days later, Sir Herbert Merrett, by now club president, and his fellow directors officially paid tribute at a board meeting to the team's "gallant effort staged towards the close of the season when the winning of every point was so vital". The combination of Merrett and Spiers had come up trumps with the hard-headed businessman backing the judgment of a man who often seemed better equipped for one of his employers' companies rather than a football club.

"Cyril Spiers was a proper gentleman who never wore a tracksuit," says Ken Hollyman. "His work was purely done from the office. The trainers did all the running, sprinting and five-a-sides. Cyril's half-time team talks didn't need to be much because we were doing well – he just used to say 'keep it going lads'."

In 1953, Peter Corrigan was given his first taste of reporting when he was sent to cover Lovell's Athletic in Newport. The following year, after a departure to Fleet Street from the *Echo* newsroom, he was assigned to Newport County. "I was just seventeen years old and the players I'd watched at Cardiff when I was a kid were there," says Peter. "Suddenly, I was sitting in the same train compartment as my heroes, Ken Hollyman, Arthur Lever and Alf Sherwood. The players would drink a lot in those days – but only after the game and I became one of the boys. They took me under their wing."

The following year, 1954, was to prove significant both for Cardiff and its football team as well as the *Echo*'s Newport County reporter. Ninety per cent of local council delegates voted for the city to become the Welsh capital – which it formally did the following year – and two of the most important figures in the club's history, Fred Stewart and Bart Wilson died. Trevor Morris became the club's manager when Cyril Spiers resigned and eventually joined Crystal Palace.

In February, Cardiff's former secretary-manager Fred Stewart passed away at his home in Newport Road at the age of eighty-one. In May, Bart Wilson's active involvement with the club came to an end – with the full approval, gratitude and financial backing of the directors:

> In view of his age and declining health, the board agreed that Bartley Wilson's remuneration be increased to £4 per week for life and that he be retired from his duties in the office. The board wished to place on record their appreciation of his unique service to the club he had served so loyally for 44 years.

Six months later on November 19th, the man who had founded Cardiff City as Riverside A.F.C. more than fifty years earlier, died at his home in Llanfair Road from bronchopneumonia. "He had been ill," recalls his grand-daughter Alma Vosper, who was working in the accounts department of the G.P.O. in the centre of Cardiff. "Someone had asked me how he was? 'Fine', I replied, 'he's got a lot more go in him'. It was probably a silly thing to say but I was only sixteen at the time. The next minute, he was dead and it was an awful shock."

After Bart's funeral at St. John's Church in Canton, his body was taken to Western Cemetery in Ely. As the courtege made its way along Cowbridge Road, the downpour showed no signs of letting up. Trevor Morris was at the cemetery:

> It was raining so hard that the grave was flooded and the coffin wouldn't stay down. I remember someone saying: 'The old sod! He won't go!' The mourners made a joke about it. Bart was his own man and he wasn't going down – except in his own time. He had to be buried the next day.
>
> Although Bart had other interests like painting and lithography, Cardiff City was his life. It was in his blood. He was very proud of the club. I never thought about Bart being a cripple. I knew he was handicapped but you never regarded him like that – he was such an intelligent man. He wasn't the type of man you would take pity on but if you did, you'd get one across the head with a crutch! He was as good as us and he was so competent and self-assured that we treated him as an able-bodied man.

By the time of Bart's death, Trevor Morris had been promoted to manager after Cyril Spiers left Ninian Park for the second and last time. Mystery still surrounds his surprise resignation in May 1954 but it was rumoured that he and Sir

Herbert Merrett had fallen out over the signing of Trevor Ford from Sunderland for £30,000 the previous December. Six years later, just before his death in October 1959, Sir Herbert told the *South Wales Echo* that he had been opposed to the deal: "I want the public to know now that I was strongly against bringing Trevor Ford to Ninian Park. I would say it was the only Cardiff cheque I did not sign during my association with the club."

In fact, the board minutes reveal that at a meeting on December 10th 1953, the president, along with director Walter Riden, did sign the £30,000 cheque to Sunderland – a decision that virtually cut Cardiff's working profit in half. Whatever the reason for his departure to Crystal Palace, Spiers received a pay-off of a year's salary of £1,750 as part of his agreement. With Merrett's money and his belief in fostering local talent, Spiers had helped fulfill the chairman's pledge that, after being promoted to the Second Division in 1947, Cardiff City would soon be back in the top flight.

By his own admission, Trevor Morris's four years in charge were not a great success. From the outset, the team struggled and eventually he moved west to Swansea City. "We had tough times in the league," he recalls. "The 1952 promotion team had just broken up when Cyril left and the players hadn't been replaced – I should never have taken the job."

George Edwards was one of the promotion side who had stayed at Ninian Park but he realised it was time to go straight after the sixth league game of the 1954-55 season. "We were a very useful team but suddenly we all began to get old together. I remember we drew 1-1 with Sheffield United at home and as we walked across the pitch, a little kid told Billy Baker that he was 'bloody awful!' I laughed and then the boy said: 'And you George!' I went home and thought that the kid was quite right. I was thirty-four, I had a job outside football as a trainee with the Mobil Oil Company, I was doing some writing and broadcasting – I ought to retire."

As George Edwards bade farewell, Trevor Morris was trying to come to grips with his new job of manager. In his first season, Cardiff only avoided relegation by beating Wolves 3-2 in their penultimate game with Ford scoring two and Gerry Hitchens marking his debut with a goal. It was the start of a fruitful partnership with Ford which ended when Hitchens left for Aston Villa two years later. He then became an England international and moved to Italy where he played for Inter Milan, Atalanta, Torino and Cagliari. In 1955-56, Cardiff City finished seventeenth before being relegated to the Second Division at the end of the following season.

"When I stepped up from secretary to be manager," recalls Trevor Morris, "there wasn't much difference really. I wasn't in total control of the team – it was half and half because the directors would interfere." Like a number of chairmen before and since, Herbert Merrett thought he knew a lot about football. In August 1949, he informed the board that he had written to Stanley Matthews "asking if he was prepared to give tuition to Ken Hollyman on the finer arts of right wing play". Hollyman disappeared to Blackpool for some special coaching from the great man and a fortnight later, Merrett's proposal to pay Matthews ten guineas for his help was agreed by the board. Trevor Morris remembers one incident when he and his chairman didn't see eye to eye:

> In September 1955, Sir Herbert had got hold of a centre-half from Pontypridd and he insisted that I play him. I hadn't picked him because I didn't think he was good enough. But if Sir Herbert insisted it should be done, then it was done. We lost 9-1 at Wolves and it was this centre-half's last game for Cardiff. We were walking off the field at half-time, four or five-nil down, and somebody shouted out to Billy Wright, the Wolves and England captain.
> "You haven't won this yet Billy!"
> 'No', he said 'but we're favourites!'
> Sir Herbert would interfere but he wasn't a bad man. I wouldn't run him down because I got on with him. He held the purse strings and things were different in those days. He was a bit of an enigma. He would stick his oar in, but if he liked you, then you were alright and luckily he liked me, although I had a few bust-ups with him.

Although Cardiff struggled in the league under Trevor Morris, they performed better in the F.A.Cup – thanks to an incredible sequence of third round results against Leeds United. "I suppose one of the highlights of my time at Cardiff was three successive F.A.Cup wins at Elland Road from 1956-58. John Charles and Jack Charlton were in their side and I had a boy called John McSeveney who, in the first two games, stood on John Charles's toes to stop him from jumping at corner kicks. Each time we went to Leeds, we beat them by the same score − 2-1!"

In July 1958, just over a year after Sir Herbert Merrett had resigned as chairman to become club president for the second time, Trevor Morris was on his way. Like Billy McCandless a decade earlier, he was unable to resist the Swansea shilling and was replaced by Bill Jones, the former Barry Town and Worcester City manager.

Promotion back to the First Division in 1960 was the highlight of the four years Bill Jones spent in charge at Ninian Park. With the emphasis very firmly on attack, his team finished runners-up to Aston Villa and eight points clear of third-placed Rotherham United. One of City's finest and most popular defenders, Danny Malloy, along with Ron Stitfall and Alec Milne, provided the side's defensive backbone, as Derek Sullivan, Colin Baker and Alan Harrington along with wingers Brian Walsh and Johnny Watkins supplied the ammunition for Joe Bonson and Derek Tapscott to fire. A crowd of 55,000 saw them clinch promotion with a 1-0 win over Aston Villa as the teenage Welsh international Graham Moore scored the vital goal.

The club's return to the First Division could hardly have been better timed as far as Peter Corrigan was concerned. After two years covering Newport County, National Service intervened before he landed the plum job − reporting on the team he had supported as a boy:

Mervyn Thomas went off to Fleet Street and I was sent to cover a pre-season tour to Holland and Switzerland before the opening game of the 1960-61 season. Cardiff went 2-0 up at Fulham and I thought it was my birthday but they eventually drew 2-2. Phoning the copy back every Saturday was a massive job − about 2,000 words in a running commentary of the game. I'd be on the phone saying something like "Jacobs has got the ball", I'd pause and the copytaker would say "Yes?"

"Hang on," I'd say, "He hasn't done anything with it yet!"

The match report appeared as it happened in the present tense and then I would give my comments at the end inside a bold panel − you would be judged on those comments. It was the entire front page of the *Football Echo* and sometimes a turn inside. At a home game, there were 30,000 people watching as well. Thankfully, television wasn't around then.

I couldn't go out on a Saturday night because people would come up and argue with me about my comments. I was very nervous about it because, after all that ad-libbing, I was a little fearful of what I was going to read – you could say some daft things on the phone! Later, I would meet people who had watched the game and then talked about it to each other, whereas my opinion was totally fresh, completely my own without the help of interviews – I said it as I saw it and I could be in for a roasting.

The pressure on Peter was not only applied by supporters. When Cardiff were going down in 1962, the editor of the *South Wales Echo* would call him in to answer a few questions:

"What are you going to do about Cardiff City?"
"What can I do? They're playing the game."
"You've got to tell them what they're doing wrong!"
"I do my best to tell them but if they knew what they doing wrong, they'd put it right!"

Peter also had to deal with the reaction of the manager and the players to his comments. A few friendships were put under severe strain as the messenger found himself in the firing line:

The *Football Echo* was the only outlet and they used to read it as avidly as anyone else! Match reports appeared in the nationals but not as comprehensively as they did in local papers. It was worse when the City were playing away. The most dreaded sound I ever heard was when the train arrived at Newport and the newspaper seller would come on. Everyone bought the *Football Echo* and they would sit there reading my comments after they'd been beaten say, 3-0 at Manchester United, with me sitting in the corner of the compartment. That journey from Newport to Cardiff was the longest twelve miles I have ever experienced! As he was reading my report, Bill Jones would turn to me and say:
"How could you possibly write this?"
"I'm sorry but that's the way I saw it."
"Do you realise that people back home will think we played badly!"
"But you did!"
"No we didn't! We could have had a penalty in the first half, their first goal was offside... I can't believe that people will read this and not think we played badly!"
"And he'd never get over that."
I was as honest as I could be. If Alan Harrington didn't play very

well, I would have to say so. He would ask me later why I'd written what I'd written but he was very reasonable. Footballers didn't accept criticism any better then than they do now. I remember Peter Donnelly, a big inside-left, being very upset about one of my comments. He came up to me after City had lost 3-2 at Spurs in November 1960 after being two up – he'd scored both goals.

"I got those two just to prove that you were a bloody liar – for saying that I can't play!"

We actually became friends after that. I don't blame him. I'm sure I'd feel exactly the same if someone who wasn't a journalist complained about my writing! But I was speaking for the fans and not the players. The problem was that journalists were seen as the enemy by both factions – the fans didn't think I gave the players enough stick and the players felt I gave them too much. I tried to be fair because I had to live with these people.

I used to go out with some of the players and their wives – Alan Harrington was a particular friend – but we would have to go as far away from Cardiff as possible and even then people would come up to us. You couldn't have a quiet meal. My wife used to come home crying from her job at the Inland Revenue at some of the things I'd been called in the office.

Such strong feelings about the club's fortunes were, strangely, not reflected in attendances. In Cardiff's first season back in the First Division, crowds averaged only 23,000 although twice as many people saw them beat the great Spurs 'double' side in March 1961. "I remember writing a piece doubting whether the post-war days would ever return," recalls Peter. "The great bulk of support seemed to desert them and I felt they couldn't sustain a team on such low crowds."

The 46,000 who crammed into Ninian Park to see Spurs were not disappointed. Under the recently-installed floodlights, Derek Tapscott scored the winner in a memorable 3-2 victory – one of 79 goals in 194 league appearances. He had slipped through City's scouting net when he left Barry Town for Arsenal with whom he became a Welsh international. In 1958, Bill Jones paid £10,000 to bring Tapscott back to South Wales and he became City's top scorer for the next three seasons.

"Wales had beaten Ireland 9-0 at Cardiff Arms Park in the afternoon," recalls Derek, "so our match against Spurs kicked off at seven o'clock in the evening. It turned out to be one of only seven defeats for Spurs that season and we came from 1-0

and 2-1 down to beat them. It was one of those thrills of a lifetime to score the winner – especially as it was like a North
London derby for me because I knew most of the Spurs players from my Arsenal days."

"Tappy had a terrific career," says Peter Corrigan. "He never
gave less than a hundred per cent. He was a very popular
player, a genuine enthusiast who would have turned out for
nothing. He never complained when he was clattered around
the place and he had this knack of getting on the end of moves."

After the Spurs win, City lost six of their last nine league
games to finish a disappointing fifteenth. Things went from bad
to worse during the following season when the team was relegated. After beating Sheffield Wednesday 2-1 in November
thanks to a brace of Tapscott goals, Cardiff lay seventh. They
then won only once in the next 21 league games and during this
desperate run, the patience of supporters was stretched even
further when the club sold Graham Moore to Chelsea for a then
record fee of £35,000. This talismanic centre-forward had led
to club into the First Division and many fans interpreted his sale
as a sign of Cardiff's lack of ambition – a charge to be repeated
following the transfers of John Toshack to Liverpool in 1970,
Nathan Blake to Sheffield United in 1994 and Mark Delaney to
Aston Villa in 1999.

Peter Corrigan still has nightmares about the 1962 relegation
season:

> After that Sheffield Wednesday game, they just fell away and there was
> a lot of controversy when Graham Moore went to Chelsea. After a
> while, they signed Mel Charles from Arsenal for £28,000 – the first of
> my two exclusives involving the Charles brothers.
>
> I met Mel when he got off the train and was looking for a bus to
> take him to Ninian Park.
>
> 'Hello Mel,' I said, 'what are you doing here?'
>
> 'I've come to see my cousin,' he said. But he was a terrible liar.
> 'Hang on a moment' I said, 'I'll go and get a photographer'. He was
> still waiting for a bus when I came back and we got a picture of him!
>
> I'll never forget Mel's debut against Manchester City at Ninian Park
> in late March. He missed an open goal – I can still see it in my memory.
> The ball came across from the right to the far post and all he had to
> do was poke it in with his toe! It was a wet day and as he came in, he
> slid and his foot went over the top of the ball which ran up the under-

side of his leg. It was agonising! That would have been the winning goal which would jerked them out of the doldrums but it finished 0-0. After a long run of defeats, results feed on each other and I'm sure that if that goal had gone in they would have avoided relegation.

Mel was devastated but it was just a freak. Had his boot been an inch lower, I'm sure he would have just pushed the ball the necessary few feet but it ran up his leg. It would have been comical had it not been such a tragedy.

During the summer of 1962, Bill Jones paid £18,000 to bring home the first of two Welsh footballing legends. Ivor Allchurch, the 32-year-old 'Golden Boy', was signed from Newcastle United who had been relegated with City. He made his debut against the Magpies in a 4-4 draw at Ninian Park and, with his devastating body swerve and wonderful touch, went on to score nearly 40 goals in just over 100 appearances for City before returning to Swansea, his first club and first love.

After his second game for Cardiff, a 0-0 draw at Norwich, Peter Corrigan extolled the virtues of the new City skipper in his match report for the *South Wales Echo*: "Through it all strolled Allchurch, a complete footballer, a giant of a captain." Peter is unstinting in his praise for the way in which Allchurch buckled down to the new demands of his career. "Ivor Allchurch was brilliant. He just had the great disadvantage of never playing for a great side. He was in good sides at Newcastle, Swansea and Cardiff and, of course, he played for Wales but had he been in a great club side there would have been no end to what he could achieved. He was a magnificent player, a beautiful mover with a great shot."

Despite opening their league campaign with two draws and a win, City were soon in trouble and after four successive defeats, the board sacked a manager for the first time in the club's history. Bill Jones and trainer-coach Wilf Grant were sent packing in early September and replaced, in a caretaker capacity, by 1927 F.A.Cup winner Ernie Curtis, now club coach, and senior professional Ron Stitfall. By November, George Swindin had been lured away from Norwich and appointed former City centre-half Stan Montgomery, also at Carrow Road, as his trainer-coach.

At the end of another anti-climactic season, Cardiff finished tenth and Swindin put thirteen players on the transfer list as part of his policy of selling in order to buy. Promising youngsters like goalkeeper Maurice Swan, defender Frank Rankmore and inside-forward Alan Durban left Ninian Park to enable one of the all-time greats of Welsh football to return home. Against Swindin's better judgment, the club pulled off one of the most controversial deals in their history by signing John Charles from Roma for £25,000 – exactly a decade after a £40,000 bid for the 'Gentle Giant' had been rejected by Leeds.

"It was absolutely crazy of George Swindin to put virtually everybody on the list apart from Ivor," recalls Alan Durban, who was sold to Derby County for £10,000, "because we had so many good youngsters. Maurice, Frank and I were still playing ten years later but John only lasted a couple of seasons."

Peter Corrigan's second Charles Brothers exclusive was the result of his taking a holiday with Alan Harrington, the then Cardiff skipper in the summer of 1963. The pair drove to Diana Marina near Alassio on the French Riviera side of Northern Italy:

> We were staying in a tent – footballers weren't rich in those days and neither were journalists! We knew John Charles lived nearby and one day we met him on the beach. We were chatting when John asked if we knew he was coming back to Wales? 'I'm going to sign for Cardiff City next week,' he said.
>
> My ears pricked up but I assumed the paper knew about it in Cardiff so I left it until we were driving through France on our way home. When I found out that they didn't know, I had to ring the club to check it and the story made the front page lead in the *South Wales Echo*.
>
> It was marvellous when John turned up at Ninian Park and scored on his debut against Norwich. It was an indirect free-kick for offside in the centre of the pitch and he belted it from 20 yards inside his own half. The ball just kept going and going and by the time the poor keeper Kevin Keelan realised what was happening, it had come off his shoulder and was in the back of the net at the Grangetown End. If Keelan hadn't touched it, the referee would have given a goal-kick.
>
> You could argue forever about John's best position but he played at centre-half in his first season with Cardiff. John and Ivor were still class acts who could both score goals and there were some good young players coming through like Barrie Hole, Gareth Williams, Don Murray, Peter Rodrigues and Peter King.

Sadly, John Charles and Ivor Allchurch were unable to conjure up the required magic to return Cardiff to the First Division in the twilight of their careers. In two seasons under George Swindin, the club finished 10th and 15th and, on the eve of their 2-0 Welsh Cup Final win over Bangor City in June 1964, Swindin was sacked after a stormy board meeting.

"George sounded a good manager to us," recalls former director George Edwards. "I knew him as a goalkeeper with Arsenal who he later managed, but we didn't get a reference from Highbury. He was neurotic – he was always fidgeting, he lived on his nerves – and after two years of this, we decided we had to make a change. Results had been bad and we felt the job was making George ill."

Swindin was succeeded by Scot Jimmy Scoular, who had helped Portsmouth win successive First Division championships in 1949 and 1950 before captaining Newcastle to the F.A.Cup in 1955. A month after being dismissed as manager by Bradford Park Avenue, he was in charge of Cardiff City. "We went for Jimmy," recalls George Edwards, "because he was a man who knew everybody in football. He had such good contacts that he could pick the phone up and find out anything about any player."

Jimmy Scoular's arrival coincided with the start of a new era in Cardiff City's history. Victory over Bangor meant the club would be the first Welsh representatives in the European Cup Winners Cup. In 1964, they made their debut in the competition but by that time Peter Corrigan had taken his leave of the Ninian Park press box:

I left to join the *Daily Herald* because when Lord Thomson took over Kemsleys who owned the *South Wales Echo*, he made a statement that 'one good advertising man is worth ten good journalists'. I put in my notice almost the same day. The accountants were moving into the *Echo* and Thomson's attitude was that the only thing which mattered was advertising. I hadn't any real ambition to go to Fleet Street, I had only just got married and I wasn't looking to go at that time. I went to be the number three soccer writer behind Peter Lorenzo and Frank Taylor, who had survived the Munich air crash.

I didn't like leaving Cardiff City because I loved the team – they had been my life and it was a big wrench. But it was very difficult to cover them when they were doing badly, I wasn't paid very well and I took all the stick from the players and the fans. I got fed up with the paper I was working for and Lord Thomson's comments didn't bode well for the sort of journalism that I wanted to do.

It had always been a dim ambition of mine to go to Fleet Street and the takeover galvanised me. It was a relief to get away from this constant involvement with Cardiff City's fortunes. It had become so intense. I hadn't deliberately timed it like that but it was probably time to go.

After leaving Cardiff, Peter's career blossomed through a succession of newspapers before in 1978 he was appointed sports editor of *The Observer*. Ten years later, he became the paper's golf correspondent and sports columnist before taking up similar positions with the *Independent on Sunday* in 1994. Despite spells as programme editor with Fulham and Millwall Football Clubs, Cardiff City's is always the first result Peter looks for:

I take an interest in how Fulham and Millwall have got on because I still know a lot of the people involved, but Cardiff are my club, my first and most enduring love. Unfortunately, because I've been travelling the world reporting on golf and then covering other sports like the two rugby codes, it's not been easy to watch them.

For a long while, I wouldn't go to Ninian Park – there were too many ghosts. I would sit in the press box and I couldn't get my mind off the past, the mass of people on the Bob Bank. With the standard of football being not very clever, I used to come away depressed. The 1-1 draw with Lincoln City in the 1997-98 season was certainly the worst performance I've ever seen at Cardiff City, if not the worst in my whole life.

Peter Corrigan's decision to leave his home city would not be the end of his involvement with his favourite football club. From his Fleet Street base, he was to accompany them on their adventures abroad as they flew the Welsh flag almost annually in Europe. Twenty years earlier, Moscow Dynamo had whetted his appetite by providing Peter with his first taste of the game; for the next decade, the club's supporters would gorge themselves on a feast of football – in Spain, Germany, Portugal and France. Although the promised land of the First Division still proved a mirage, the continental drift was to take Cardiff City on one of the most exciting journeys in their history.

# Flying the Welsh Flag

It wasn't the goal which won Cardiff City the F.A.Cup. It didn't help them reach Wembley or clinch promotion to the First Division either in 1921, 1952 or 1960. It wasn't even the goal which kept the Bluebirds in the Second Division in the last game of the 1973-74 season.

In the end, it proved irrelevant in terms of trophies but when Brian Clark rose to head home Nigel Rees's cross against Real Madrid on March 10th 1971, it put Cardiff City on the map of Europe, if not the world. It vies with Hughie Ferguson's 1927 winner against Arsenal as the most famous goal ever scored in the club's hundred-year history.

It was classic Clark. A left-wing cross, a perfectly-timed jump and an unstoppable header into the net at the Canton End of Ninian Park. Cardiff City 1 Real Madrid 0. The Spanish team who had won the first five European Cups had been beaten by the Welsh Cup winners. Never mind that the unbelievable scoreline was followed by a 2-0 defeat in the Bernabeau a fortnight later. For one night only, Cardiff City's name was up in lights and Brian Clark, the West Country kid, has been dining out on his goal of a lifetime ever since.

> Scoring against Real Madrid was definitely the highlight of my career. The build-up, the crowd, the team we were up against – everything was fantastic. I played quite well and got the winning goal but the one disappointment was that we created a couple of chances in the second half and didn't take them. If it had been 1-1 or 2-1 then it would have been nice, but to get the only goal in front of all those people was unreal.
>
> When you're a kid, you dream of scoring in F.A.Cup Final or of doing something out of the ordinary and it all came right for me on that night. It happened in the city where I was, and still am, living which also made it a bit special.

The Real Madrid result represented the high point of Cardiff

City's adventures in Europe which began in September 1964 with a preliminary round tie against the Danish Cup Winners Esbjerg. After a solid 0-0 draw in Denmark, Peter King scored the winner in the return leg a month later in front of only 8,000. Cardiff's introduction to European football may have been low-key but it provided several emerging players with invaluable experience. As the season developed, Jimmy Scoular continued George Swindin's policy of blooding youngsters with Dilwyn John, Peter Rodrigues and Trevor Peck being given their chance to impress. A new broom was about to sweep through Ninian Park, but for the first two years in Europe, Cardiff would rely on seasoned internationals like Ivor Allchurch, Derek Tapscott and the Charles brothers.

Allchurch and Tapscott played in the return leg against Esbjerg along with King, Gareth Williams and Don Murray, all now established as first-team regulars. Murray, from Duffuss in Scotland, had signed on junior forms in 1962 and after playing half the games in the 1963-64 season, he became the first-choice centre-half under Scoular and made more than 400 league appearances in twelve years at Ninian Park. Murray recalls his European debut:

> I was on the bench for the away leg but found myself in the team for the return. It was a disappointing crowd for our first cup tie in Europe – maybe the Cardiff football public didn't know what to expect – but there was huge interest in our other games. On a personal level, it was unbelievable – a seventeen-year-old from the Scottish hills playing in the European Cup Winners Cup alongside some of the world-famous names who had been part of my cigarette card collection in school two years earlier! I had the privilege of being in the same team as John Charles, who had been the best centre-half and centre-forward in the world.

Don Murray had made his first team debut against Middlesbrough in April 1963 in the last league game of the season. In a classic baptism of fire – "I was frightened to death" – he failed to stop the then England centre-forward Alan Peacock from scoring twice in Boro's 3-2 win. Later, Don came under the influence of John Charles when the former Leeds star arrived at Ninian Park from Roma for £25,000 during the summer.

I remember him taking a Derby County corner kick on his chest around the penalty spot and knocking it back to our keeper Graham Vearncombe under the crossbar. A mere mortal like myself would have just put a head to it and knocked it out as far as I could! The first thing he pulled me up about – in the same match at the Baseball Ground – was when I headed the ball clear to the middle of the goal outside the area.

"I'll tell you once and I won't tell you again," John said as he grabbed hold of me. "You never head the ball in that direction – you always head it back in the direction it's come from." I remembered that for the rest of my life.

A few months after John Charles left for Hereford in the summer of 1966, Scoular pulled of one of his most influential signings by paying Everton £10,000 for Brian Harris. Under his tutelege, Don Murray developed into an aggressive and accomplished centre-half alongside the authoritative sweeper. "Brian had this great ability to direct and talk me through games," says Don. "When I was a little bit brash and over the top, he soon pulled me into line. I thought I was pretty good but when he arrived, he told me to aim to be as good as Everton's Brian Labone, the England centre-half – and he said I was a long way short of his standard!"

After knocking out Esbjerg, Cardiff were rewarded with a plum tie against Sporting Lisbon and shocked the holders by beating them 2-1 in Portugal. Goals from Greg Farrell and Tapscott gave City a first-leg lead which they resolutely defended at home. Their quarter-final opponents were Real Zaragoza but after drawing 2-2 in Spain, City lost 1-0 at Ninian Park. Like one or two later campaigns, Cardiff's first foray into Europe ended in anti-climax.

It was no surprise that Brian Clark became one of Ninian Park's most prolific goalscorers because the knack of putting the ball into the net ran in the family. While Cardiff City were breaking a series of records in winning the Division Three South Championship in 1947, Brian's father Don was making his own individual mark with Bristol City. His feat of scoring 36 league goals during that season – 6 more than Stan Richards' record of 30 for Cardiff – still stands today.

"I always wanted to be a professional footballer," says Brian. "I started to watch Dad play for Bristol City when I was about six – mainly at Ashton Gate but also against Bristol Rovers and at Cardiff and Newport. My grandmother took me and I would collect all the autographs afterwards. All my school reports said 'If Brian put as much effort into his schoolwork as he does his football, he'd be top of the class and go to university!' but I always wanted to play the game."

After having to retire because of knee trouble, Don Clark became secretary at Ashton Gate. As Brian's career started to develop, father and son both found that their relationship was putting pressure on the youngster:

> Dad would contact the papers and ask them not to mention it. He would say: "He is my son, I'm proud of him but let the kid do it on his own."
>
> When Dad became a scout with Birmingham, I had a tough decision to make. They wanted me, my sports master at school was a reserve team coach with Bristol Rovers, and Wolves were also interested. On my seventeenth birthday – January 13th 1960 – I signed professional forms with Bristol City and then in the last game of the season, I found myself playing against Brentford alongside my great idol John Atyeo who scored a hat-trick in a 3-0 win.

Brian ended up with more than 80 goals in nearly 200 appearances during six years at Ashton Gate before leaving for Huddersfield in an exchange deal. Fred Ford, the Bristol City manager, was determined that he shouldn't sign for a local side such as Swindon or Cardiff. Brian says that his manager wanted him out of the way:

> He felt I had to move away from my brilliant family to grow up a bit. I was spoilt like mad, I knew everybody in Bristol and I needed to form my own identity somewhere else. Going to Huddersfield for two years was a bit like National Service! It was another world up there because I lived in digs for a year, it was cold and I didn't know anybody in town. But the move worked out well for me because I did grow up, I married my wife Gillian in 1967, and became good friends with players like Trevor Cherry and Frank Worthington.

Two years later, Brian Clark returned south – not to the West Country but to Cardiff. Having badly damaged a retina in an accident with a goalkeeper on a pre-season tour to Holland, his confidence had gone and he was languishing in the reserves. Then he received a phone call from his father who told Brian that Cardiff's centre-forward Bobby Brown had been badly injured playing against Aston Villa on Boxing Day 1967"

Bobby had done his knee ligaments and through Dad's contacts in the game, he had heard that Cardiff were coming to watch me play for the reserves in the Central League at West Brom on the following Saturday. "Give it a go!" he said.

I worked hard in training on the Friday and scored two goals in a 3-1 win. The next week, I was told that the Cardiff manager Jimmy Scoular had agreed to pay £8,000 for me and, because of injuries, I was to make my debut at Derby the next day.

I met Jimmy Scoular at the Severn Bridge Services at seven o'clock that night and signed a blank contract. It had no details of my wages. 'Fill it all out on Monday,' I said, 'let's make sure I'm registered.'

The following day, I caught the train from Bristol to Derby – the Cardiff players picked it up at Cheltenham – and made a dream debut – I scored after a minute, got a second later on and we won 4-3. It was February and very wet – which suited me down to the ground – and when I knocked in Peter King's cross for the first goal, I knew my stay with Cardiff City was going to be a successful one. The gods were smiling on me. Your first league goal will always be the most important one you score but I was so pleased to have made such a good start with City.

Since my eye injury, I had been so depressed for three or four months and then, all of a sudden, I moved to Cardiff, the capital city of Wales. They had lots of good players in the side like Brian Harris and John Toshack and I was so full of adrenalin that I went running in north Bristol on the Sunday morning!

From the moment he signed, Brian Clark began a love affair with Cardiff. He and Gillian still live in Whitchurch and both his daughters were born in the Welsh capital. "I settled in Cardiff because I think you've got to live where you play. I should have bought a house straightaway but I didn't know I was going to love the city so much and stay here. Our daughters are Welsh and as far as they're concerned, Cardiff is home. I just thank goodness that I didn't say 'no' to Jimmy Scoular."

Since arriving at Ninian Park, Scoular had struggled to stabilise City's position in the Second Division. From 1965-7, they finished 13th, 20th and 20th as a number of internationals left the club. Scoular decided that fresh blood was needed so Ivor Allchurch returned to Swansea, Derek Tapscott moved east to Newport, Barrie Hole was sold to Blackburn Rovers for £42,000 while Mel and John Charles joined Porthmadog and Hereford respectively. Sixteen-year-old apprentice John Toshack scored on his debut as a substitute against Leyton Orient in November 1965 – five months before he signed professional forms.

Having just avoided relegation by beating Middlesbrough 5-3 in May 1966, City lost 9-0 at Preston North End in their penultimate league match. The margin of defeat makes the result the worst in Cardiff's history – alongside the 10-1 thrashing by Moscow Dynamo in 1945 and the 11-2 hammering by Sheffield United in 1926. The 1965-66 season proved an all-round disaster with the club losing 3-1 on aggregate to Standard Liege in the preliminary round of the European Cup Winners Cup and then failing to qualify for the following season's competition after being beaten 5-3 in a Welsh Cup replay by Swansea.

Before he signed for Cardiff, Brian Clark was aware of the club's impressive track record in Europe. In fact, it was one of the attractions of joining the Welsh Cup winners:

> I always used to be envious because Huddersfield would play Cardiff and I'd read in the programme that they'd been here, there and everywhere in Europe. It sounded great because Second Division sides don't normally get that opportunity. Little did I know that I would soon be given the chance myself!

In 1968, new players had to wait three months before they were eligible to play in Europe so, along with City's other recent signings, Fred Davies and Les Lea, Brian sat out their quarter and semi-final matches against Moscow Torpedo and SV Hamburg. Another reporter called Peter – Jackson rather than Corrigan – was now covering Cardiff for the *South Wales Echo*. The Russians arrived at Ninian Park after City had comprehensively beaten Shamrock Rovers and NAC Breda from Holland in the first two rounds. Now the chief rugby correspondent of the *Daily Mail*, Peter Jackson the two epic games against Moscow Torpedo:

A goal by Barrie Jones gave City a 1-0 win in front of just over 30,000 in the home leg before we set off on the second part of this epic quarter-final. The return leg was played in mid-March, Moscow was frozen over so the game was switched to Tashkent in Central Soviet Asia not far from the Chinese and Afghanistan borders. It was further from Moscow to Tashkent than it was from London to Moscow – about 2,000 miles – so we made a bit of an expedition of it with an eight-day trip. There were only three of us – myself, Peter Corrigan of the *Daily Mail* and Jim Hill from the *Daily Express*. Cardiff were not expected to get through.

I'd won a running battle with the paper's sports editor about whether I should go by promising that, as the game kicked off about noon our time, we would have the first report of the match in the *Echo* that evening. Communications in those days were very hit-or-miss and I heard the operator in London say to someone at the Cardiff end that the lone telephone line we had was held together like a wet piece of string – it could go at any time.

About ten minutes before half-time, Torpedo scored as I was dictating my report in an ante room. Just above the roar of the crowd, I could hear the *Echo* copytaker, a dear old chap called Gerwyn Jacob from the Rhondda, shouting down the line: "I can't hear the boy! I can't hear him!"

Every time the crowd roared, I dashed back into the stadium and looked up at the electronic scoreboard at the far end, very relieved to see that Torpedo were still only 1-0 ahead. If it hadn't been for that scoreboard, I would have been in the dark, even more than usual! Peter and Jim were in another part of the stadium and I was surrounded by thousands of Ghengis Khans, all flashing gold teeth and not a word of English.

Peter's report appeared in the *Echo*, the Cardiff City entourage finally made it home to Wales after a seventeen-hour journey and the Torpedo goal meant a third game was needed. The play-off took place in Augsberg in West Germany and Cardiff, with Richie Morgan making his debut in place of the injured Don Murray, won through a goal from Norman Dean, a £6,000 signing from Southampton who only seemed to score in the European Cup Winners Cup. S.V. Hamburg would be their semi-final opponents. Brian Clark recalls Dean's double life:

Norman was playing in the Combination League every week in front of a couple of hundred people, and then, all of a sudden, with me being ineligible, he found himself in my position playing in front of

50,000 people and he just went whoosh! The adrenalin lifted him and he scored some very important goals which won European games for Cardiff. I was the first to congratulate Norman – while wishing it had been me!

Fred, Les and I were playing in the first team on Saturday and in the Combination League in midweek. It was a nightmare because the European side would come back talking about their wonderful trip and there was a danger of us not getting a game on a Saturday if the boys had done really well abroad. But those were the rules, we had to grin and bear it. The crunch would have come if they'd beaten Hamburg in the semi-final. Les was eligible for the semi-final and played but would Jimmy Scoular have picked me and Fred? I suspect he would have put me on the bench. I wouldn't have been happy but I would have understood.

As it turned out, Scoular was spared that selectorial dilemma – but only just. Hamburg boasted three members of the West Germany team which had lost to England in the World Cup Final two years earlier – Uwe Seeler, Karl-Heinz Schnellinger and Willi Schulz – but Cardiff managed to come away with a 1-1 draw from the first leg.

"It was an extraordinary game," recalls Peter Jackson, "with Dean giving Cardiff a fourth minute lead. From then on, it was probably the most incredible game I'd ever seen – the Cardiff goal was under seige for the remaining eighty-six minutes. Brian Harris likened it to the film *Zulu* which had just been released and it was bit like that – apart from the fact there were no fatalities. The Germans equalised with twenty minutes left and with Bob Wilson inspired in goal, City hung on."

Don Murray considers Cardiff's performance in Hamburg as the best defensive display of his twelve years at Ninian Park. "We were under the cosh and it was a rearguard action second to none. I remember they had an indirect free-kick just inside the box. We were all standing on the goal-line and when the ball was hit, it stuck between Bobby Ferguson's knees. He was our full-back standing by the post and Brian Harris and I kicked lumps out of him in trying to get the ball free and behind for a corner!"

Cardiff were now just ninety minutes away from reaching the final of the European Cup Winners Cup. Forty-three thousand people turned up at Ninian Park on a warm early-May night for the second leg as Dean again hit the jackpot with a tenth-minute goal. Honig equalised, Seeler made it 2-1 to Hamburg before Brian Harris scored with his first goal in eighty-eight appearances for Cardiff twelve minutes from time. There were just two minutes left when, in a reversal of fortune of City's 1927 Wembley win, the roof fell in. Instead of Dan Lewis, it was poor Bob Wilson.

"Honig moved ran from inside his own half and fired in a 30-yard shot," recalls Peter Jackson "It was hit in hope and seemed to be going wide but Bob, until then, one of the true heroes of the campaign, dived across and the ball somehow ended up in the net. I've never heard such a deafening silence. Up in the press box, we had been talking about the play-off in Jutland and rubbing our hands at the prospect of the adventure rolling on to another place we hadn't been to before. Suddenly, it was all over and, as anti-climactic finishes go, it was pretty cruel."

"I couldn't believe it," recalls Don Murray. "It was the boob of all boobs but I would never be critical of Bob because he, more than anybody, had got us to that semi-final. He was shattered and I'm afraid Jimmy wasn't the most sensitive of managers."

"I was watching from the back of the stand," says Brian Clark, "and after the game I went down to the dressing room and poured out the tea and sympathy. There were an awful lot of tears shed that night – there was silence everywhere. Jimmy was disappointed with Bob and had a few words with him. It was a bit unfair really because Bob had performed heroics in previous European games. Once Jimmy had left the dressing room, the players were very supportive but it was sad because Bob was soon replaced by Fred Davies and later moved to Exeter."

"In many ways," says Peter Jackson, "I think that season was Cardiff's greatest European adventure because the result in Hamburg was achieved against such huge odds. They were a better team than Real Madrid were three years later."

After such an eventful campaign, City's next European trip proved a huge anti-climax. In the first leg at Ninian Park, goals by John Toshack and Ronnie Bird put them into a comfortable lead against F.C. Porto but the Portuguese Cup winners fought back to earn a 2-2 draw before beating Cardiff 2-1 in a bad-tempered match in Oporto.

"We blew the game at home," says Brian Clark. "We were 2-0 up but they scored two away goals which put us under immense pressure when we went over there. The referee was a nightmare and Jimmy Scoular fell out with him. I made sure I was near the dressing room end of the ground when the final whistle was blown to get away quickly but some of our players weren't so lucky. As they came off the pitch, the police had their truncheons out and fists were flying."

The following season saw Brian score his first European goal as City beat Mjondalen I.F. from Norway 7-1 at Ninian Park in September 1969. "I can't remember it – it was one of two I got that night – but the game was a mismatch really. They were the equivalent of a Welsh League team and we thrashed them easily in the second leg too – 5-1." There was no such easy ride in the second round as Cardiff lost 3-0 away to Goztepe Izmir in Turkey. Ronnie Bird's goal gave City a 1-0 win at Ninian Park but the European adventure was over for another year.

The following season turned out to be one of the most significant in Cardiff City's recent history. They sold their star striker, they beat Real Madrid and then narrowly missed returning to the First Division.

A generation later, the sale of John Toshack still rankles with some supporters. A few have even refused to watch Cardiff City since. They fail to understand how a team in the running for promotion could agree to transfer one of their key players with more than half the season left. After scoring 8 goals in 16 league appearances so far that season – including 5 in his last 3 games – Toshack was sold to Liverpool for the then staggering sum of £110,000. The *South Wales Echo* reporter Peter Jackson was closely involved in reporting the transfer of the first Cardiff City player to be sold for six figures:

I criticised the club at the time and I stood by every word. I think they were frightened of winning promotion to the First Division. They were quite happy to jog along in the top six of the Second Division, win the Welsh Cup every year as they invariably did and take their chance in Europe which was something that ninety per cent of First Division clubs would have given their eye-teeth for.

They certainly lacked ambition. What other club would have sold their top goalscorer when they had just won four games in a row and were top of the table? They couldn't sell Toshack fast enough – instead of, at the very least, holding onto him until a replacement had been found.

John Toshack first saw Cardiff play as a nine-year-old in 1958 and like most football-mad boys in Cardiff at the time, his ambition was to play for his home town club. In 162 league appearances, he scored 75 goals before helping Liverpool win a European competition for the first time. "When I signed as an amateur at the age of sixteen, I realised every ambition I ever had," he says. "I felt I had made it. Cardiff City were my team and I was so proud to be pulling on their shirt."

While he will always be grateful to Cardiff for setting him on the road to a glittering career as both player and manager, Toshack was surprised at the apparent ease with which he was allowed to leave Ninian Park. "Cardiff did not really do too much to persuade me to stay," he reveals in his 1982 autobiography. "Now that I am in management myself, I understand just how important it is to get money into a football club – though not at the expense of the team's progress. I must admit that I got the impression that the people at Cardiff would have been disappointed if I had stayed. They could have been right: £110,000 was a lot of money and decisions like that will always be difficult ones for people to make."

The day after Cardiff had won 1-0 at Queens Park Rangers in November 1970, Peter Jackson received a phone call at his home from John Toshack:

> "I always said I would let you know when I was leaving Cardiff City," said Tosh. "They've had an offer from Liverpool, I'm going up to see Mr Shankly in the morning and it looks as if I'll be going – it's too good a chance to miss."
>
> The next day, John went into Jimmy Scoular's office and the manager explained that there were still a few loose ends to tie up. Just then, the chairman Fred Dewey came in and expressed surprise that Tosh was still in Cardiff! The feeling was that City grabbed the money before Liverpool came to their senses and changed their mind after realising that £110,000 was an outrageous sum to pay for him.

Fred Dewey was a former Welsh international who had made his money in shipping. When his close friend, butcher Ron

Beecher, died in 1962, he succeeded him as chairman and ran the club with his son Vivian, Robert Williams, a Cardiff accountant, and George Edwards. During the 1969-70 season, Edwards had advised Toshack's father to reject a move to Fulham but once Liverpool made known their interest, he claims the club were helpless to stop the twenty-one-year-old from leaving. George Edwards says that when there was talk of a bid from Anfield earlier in the season, Cardiff had begun to make plans. He denies the allegation that the club sold their ambition the day they sold John Toshack:

> We were playing Sheffield Wednesday at Hillsborough in late August and Jimmy Scoular and I were watching from the directors box. We were 2-1 up – Brian Clark and Mel Sutton had scored the goals – but they were playing hell with us all over the place and the person causing all the trouble was their centre-forward Alan Warboys.
>
> "Are you thinking what I'm thinking?" asked Jimmy.
>
> "Are you thinking that if we've got to lose Toshack," I replied, "we could get that bugger now – he's a better player at the moment, more experienced and more aggressive – for half the money?"
>
> "That's exactly what I'm thinking," said Jimmy. We came back to Cardiff and we advised Fred Dewey that we should buy Warboys because it seemed likely that we would be losing Toshack. But Fred insisted that we sold Toshack first before committing the club to spending more money. He was worried about the size of our overdraft. It was over £75,000, we were on the limit and he wouldn't go over £100,000. He wouldn't spend £35,000 on Warboys and although Jimmy and I objected, Fred was the chairman, he controlled the club and he had his way.
>
> You could say it was bad club management but Fred had to carry the financial responsibility of the club. He decided he wasn't going to take the risk.
>
> I didn't want John to go, but you couldn't stop him. He had just got married, he was offered £5,000 in his hand – which was a lot of money then – and three times his salary. Bill Shankly had been told by his board to buy John – at that time, he didn't think that he would fit into his team but John was later to dove-tail beautifully with Kevin Keegan. John couldn't go to Liverpool quick enough. The maximum wage had gone, we knew freedom of contract was coming in and two years later we couldn't have held onto him.

Having sold Toshack, Cardiff returned to Sheffield and tried to sign Warboys only to be told that the price had risen by

£10,000. Scoular eventually got his man for a record club fee of £42,000 but the six-week delay as negotiations dragged on cost Cardiff dear. They won only two of the intervening six league matches.

"My criticism then," says Peter Jackson, "was during that period, Cardiff lost three way games on the trot against Charlton, Oxford and Millwall, all of whom were struggling near the foot of the table, and in the end, they missed promotion by a whisker – that was an indictment of the club's lack of ambition. It suited them not to go up."

To support his view, Peter can recall a conversation that a colleague Roger Malone, from the *Daily Telegraph*, had with Fred Dewey after Cardiff had beaten Bristol City 1-0 at Ninian Park in early April. It was typical of a promotion team – they had played badly but still won 1-0. "Roger turned to Fred and said: 'Well Mr Chairman, there's no doubt about it, there's going to be First Division football in South Wales next season!' Fred's reply summed up his attitude: 'Hang on a minute! If we go up, we'll have to pay more for players, higher wages etc etc.' Fred ran a very tight ship and he wasn't prepared to take any big risks – even though it was all there for Cardiff to take off."

As the directors played the transfer market in an attempt to keep their promotion train on track, Brian Clark was recalled from the substitute's bench to shoulder the goalscoring burden. He picked up two against Blackburn and another in the 2-1 defeat at Millwall as Cardiff stuttered along until Warboys arrived. Unlike some supporters, Brian bears Toshack no ill-feeling for leaving Ninian Park:

He didn't turn down Liverpool because he was travelling first-class and I don't blame him one little bit. Some people said Cardiff should never have sold him but you couldn't stop him going.

We were all disappointed because we were buzzing at the time and we were losing a celebrity – a tall, good-looking lad who said the right things. He was almost the next John Charles although I don't think he was ever as good as big John.

At the end of the day, he scored some good goals for Cardiff and having got him for nothing, they sold him for £110,000 which was a lot of money then. Tosh didn't discuss his move with us. One day he was there and the next he was gone.

Looking back, I wish Cardiff hadn't sold him because I would have loved to have known what would have happened had he stayed. I often wonder how his career – and ours – would have turned out? We'll never know. You make decisions in life and Tosh decided he wanted to have a crack at it and, let's be fair, it hasn't turned out badly for him, has it?

We had a good relationship on the field. When their best defender would pick up Tosh because of who he was, the other one would mark me. All of a sudden, I would get more room and do well. Then the shout would come from the dug-out for the big centre-half to pick me up and Tosh would have more room. The only trouble we ever had was against Norwich City when Duncan Forbes and Dave Stringer would kick us both all over the place!

Alan Warboys proved an instant hit with supporters. He didn't score on his debut – a 1-1 draw at Swindon – but was one short of a hat-trick against his former club when Sheffield Wednesday were beaten 4-1 at Ninian Park. According to Brian Clark, Toshack and Warboys were like chalk and cheese:

> Alan Warboys was a basher, a completely different player to Tosh. He was a big lad with a good left foot who used to knock people out of the way. He went on to play for Bristol Rovers where he formed a lethal partnership with Bruce Bannister – they were known as 'Smash and Grab'! Tosh was smooth, someone who wouldn't get cuts or be injured – he'd just score the goals. You could never criticise his performance.
>
> Unlike Tosh, Alan would always get covered in mud and was often on the treatment table. It was different playing alongside him – he used to upset people, they wanted to fight him all the time. He was his own man, a loner, an animal who liked to play up front by himself, down the middle with two guys wide while Tosh and I worked well together – we preferred to play in the two gaps, inside-left and inside-right. Away from home, we used to play 4-4-2 with Ronnie Bird and Peter King not working as out-and-out wingers – they tucked in a little – but at home we played 4-3-3 with Ronnie up front with us.

In early March, Cardiff's new rugged and robust striker secured a place in the record books by scoring all the goals in a 4-0 win over Carlisle at Ninian Park. After completing the fastest hat-trick in Cardiff City's history – it had taken him just ten minutes – Warboys ran to the dug-out with his arms outstretched. Jimmy Scoular had promised a fiver to any player scoring three goals and Warboys wanted to collect his reward.

"I was on the bench for that game," recalls Brian Clark, "being rested for the Real Madrid match – and I couldn't believe it! Everything he hit flew in. He wouldn't wait until the end of the game to come off – having scored four, he wanted the crowd's ovation so he was substituted by me before the end! That was Warbs, he was that sort of guy. I'm glad he came off really because I needed to have a run with an important game coming up on the Wednesday."

The 1970-71 European campaign had begun with the 8-0 hammering of P.O. Larnaca from Cyprus at Ninian Park in September as Clark and Toshack both scored twice. They then beat Cardiff's twin town Nantes 7-2 on aggregate. Clark remembers the moment he discovered City's quarter-final opponentswould be Real Madrid:

> I was driving down Queen Street when I saw this newspaper placard 'Plum European draw for Cardiff'. I quickly bought a *South Wales Echo*. I couldn't believe it – it was the one everyone wanted and the key thing was that we were at home first. The tie could well have been killed dead had we played them in Madrid before Cardiff.
>
> The build-up was brilliant. Everyone was talking about the game and we were all frightened of getting injured. Warboys had been signed too late to be eligible – which was a shame. I knew how he felt because I'd been in his position with Norman Dean when I signed in 1968.
>
> We trained on the Monday and Tuesday but it was optional on the day of the match. The ground was spruced up with industrial cleaners and everybody was allowed to do their own thing. We just had to make sure we got to Ninian Park in time because there was sure to be a big crowd. We were warned that we wouldn't get through Canton at half-past five! The official attendance was 47,500 but I reckon the actual crowd was nearer 52,000.

While Brian and his team-mates were preparing themselves for one of the most memorable nights in the club's history, kit-man Harry Parsons was busy carrying out an errand for his manager:

> Jimmy used to ask me to pull the occasional fast one. "What's the temperature in there?" he asked, pointing to the visitors' dressing room.
>
> "Oh the heating's on alright," I replied.
>
> "They come from the bloody sunshine, don't they?"

"Yes."

"It's bloody hot in Spain," Jimmy said, "let's make it bloody cold in there!"

He told me to go into their dressing room and knock off the heating. I had to get up in the corner and switch off the pipe bringing in the heating – it was like a bloody iceberg in there!

Another time, he told me to put some drawing pins in one of the opposing players' boots. I put three in the toe areas and the bugger went out and scored two goals – he never felt them! Jimmy wasn't very happy.

As the Spaniards shivered and cursed the Welsh weather, the Cardiff players were receiving their final instructions from Scoular. "Jimmy made it clear that as far as he was concerned reputations didn't mean anything," recalls Brian Clark. "He told us not to be afraid of Real Madrid because if we were, we wouldn't play. He told us just to go out and enjoy it. Maybe Real were on their way down – they certainly weren't the side they were ten years earlier when Puskas and Di Stefano played for them but they were still useful. The biggest disappointment for me was that they turned out in red rather than their usual all-white kit."

Just past the half-hour mark, Scoular's skulduggery in the dressing room appeared to have paid off when the Spaniards were caught cold. The move began down the Cardiff left and involved Gary Bell and Bobby Woodruff before the ball reached the 17-year-old left winger Nigel Rees. He knew he had been chosen ahead of Ronnie Bird the previous day when he took part in set-piece practice but it wasn't until a row between the club and the Welsh F.A. had been resolved that he was finally released from Welsh Youth team duty to play. Nigel recalls the build-up to the big match:

Jimmy gave me the chance to perform on a wonderful stage. Ronnie was obviously sick but it was Jimmy's decision, he stuck by me and said 'just go out there and play'. Everybody was there watching, my family and my mates – it was a fantastic night.

Bobby Woodruff had a wonderful touch for such a big player – he was very long-legged with a good stride. I saw the gap and went between the two defenders and then had a bit of luck. I thought I'd overrun the ball but it came back to me and once I knew I'd done them for a yard, I just went for it.

"Nigel wriggled past a couple of defenders," recalls Brian, "and got to the corner where the Grandstand meets the Canton Stand. You take a chance if you're a striker because if you go near post, there's a fair chance that the ball will go over your head! So I went in and then came out. Fair play to Nigel, he whipped the ball back to the edge of the penalty box, not far from the spot itself."

"I saw Clarky," says Nigel, "he went in and then checked back. The lie of the ball was lovely and I just clipped it in but if I'd taken one extra stride or if Brian had been a yard quicker or slower, it wouldn't have happened but that's football. I picked him out and he buried it."

"Daft as it might seem, the centre-half didn't hit me or make any sort of challenge," recalls Brian. "He was nowhere near me. Sometimes that's worse because you know you've got almost too much time – there's no excuse, it's a free header. Nigel hit the ball with his left foot and as it came in, I met it very powerfully. It was in the back of the net and I thought 'Thank God for that!' Nigel's ball was a striker's dream. I knew it was a goal the moment it left my head – I hit it perfectly. I remember running over to Nigel to thank him. The crowd were so noisy that you can't hear the commentator on the recording of the live television coverage – poor old Idwal Robling was drowned out!"

"All the players came over and jumped on me," says Nigel, "the whole place was absolutely wild. I don't remember what Brian said to me but I can tell you that he never bought me a pint – he still owes me one!"

"It was crazy in the dressing room afterwards," says Brian, "the press and the cameras were in there – everyone was ecstatic. Jimmy couldn't say a lot because there were too many people around – he wasn't too happy about that. It was bedlam really. I didn't come down that night. We stayed in the club before going into town somewhere and waited for the papers. We all wanted to read about it."

Nigel Rees opted for the quiet life. He returned to Port Talbot with his father and ended up in the late-night Chinese in Station Road. "It wasn't my best game for Cardiff but it was definitely the highlight of my professional career."

After being forced to return too early after injury, Nigel disappeared into non-league football with Bridgend in the early Seventies before moving into management and taking Afan Lido into the UEFA Cup in 1995. He now works in the poultry business and helps out at Swansea City's school of excellence.

Ronnie Bird had mixed emotions about the Real Madrid result. Having played under Scoular at Bradford Park Avenue, the left-winger had became a firm favourite with Cardiff fans who loved his whole-hearted approach to the game. Now a publican in Canton, Bird was devastated to miss one of the biggest games in Cardiff's history but delighted that the team had won. "I was as sick as a pig," says Ronnie, "because Real Madrid were my team – Gento was my favourite player. I was absolutely gutted but on the night I just had to accept it. Jimmy picked Nigel who set up Clarky's goal so Jimmy was right!"

Cardiff's dream of reaching their second European Cup Winners Cup semi-final disappeared a fortnight later in the magnificent Bernabeau Stadium. Cardiff travelled over on the Monday to train that afternoon, and everything went well for the first 45 minutes. Brian Clark remembers the reaction of the Spanish crowd:

> It was 0-0 at the break, and a few cushions started landing on the pitch as Real were booed off. They were coming down from quite a height so you had to watch out – if they hit you, they'd knock you out! Real were a different side at home and I was marked much tighter than in the first leg.
>
> The second half didn't go as well. There was a collision between Jim Eadie and Don Murray which gave them their first goal and everything changed. The whole atmosphere was different – all of their players wanted the ball and it was only a matter of time when they scored a second – quite quickly as it happened.
>
> We felt terrible. There was a horrible feeling in the dressing room. We were so disappointed because we'd come so close and then blown it.

Up in the press box, Peter Jackson too felt that Cardiff City had missed a great opportunity:

> By their standards, Real Madrid were a very poor side. That was probably their worst post-war side, they were on their way down, a team in decline and they only had one outstanding player – Pirri – who was

well-marked by Don Murray in the first leg. When we went to the Bernabeau, there weren't many in the crowd and we saw no reason why Cardiff couldn't hang onto their goal. Two bad defensive mistakes gave Real two sloppy goals and they scraped through 2-1.

It was a very flat end to the tie but it was probably the greatest European occasion at Ninian Park because Cardiff beat Real Madrid in a wonderful first leg. It captured the imagination of the entire Welsh footballing public, the *Echo* produced a special souvenir issue for the game – it was an occasion that will never come back again. At the time, Europe was taken for granted.

When City returned to their Second Division campaign, there were just ten games to go. They lost 2-0 at Birmingham before beating Bristol City and Bolton Wanderers at Ninian Park. It looked a three-horse race for the two promotion places between City, Sheffield United and Leicester City but Cardiff's challenge disintegrated in a 5-1 defeat at Bramall Lane in late April in front of nearly 43,000 spectators. "I remember Brian Harris was missing," recalls Don Murray, "so Steve Derrett again deputised and played very well. In fact, he scored our goal but I think the occasion may have got to some of us. We were outplayed by a far better side on the night with players like Tony Currie, Alan Woodward and Gil Reece outstanding for Sheffield United. It was awful conceding five and, as it didn't happen very often, it was a real sickener."

A 1-0 win over Orient and then a 3-0 defeat at Luton rounded off a thoroughly anti-climactic season. It had promised so much but City had failed to deliver – finishing third behind Leicester and Sheffield United. In retrospect, Brian Clark feels the squad should have been strengthened before the transfer deadline:

We had a bare thirteen or fourteen players and perhaps we should have gone out and bought a couple of players. We could have held our own gate-wise in the First Division but we wouldn't have been good enough to stay there. We were quite strong at the back with Brian Harris, Don Murray and Leighton Phillips coming through but we could have done with one more in midfield and attack. They would have put pressure on those in the team like Ian Gibson, a very talented player who had joined us from Coventry City at the beginning of the season. There was no strength in depth – we didn't have too many other experienced players.

While acknowledging the huge contribution by Alan Warboys of 13 goals in 17 league appearances, Peter Jackson also feels the club should have bought as the season drew to a close. "It was clear Cardiff needed a good left-sided attacking player to rectify the one noticeable weakness in the team. Leicester and Sheffield United went out and each made a significant signing, Cardiff didn't and finished third. It was perhaps the best example of the club's depressing refusal over the years to buy from a position of relative strength. So many signings have been made in times of severe struggle so few when the going has been good."

In many ways, the 1970-71 season was a watershed in Cardiff City's history. Never again would they come so close to promotion to the old First Division or create headlines in Europe. The chance of glory came and went – along with some key players. After narrowly avoiding relegation and failing at the first hurdle in Europe on penalties against Dynamo Berlin in the next season, Scoular swapped Warboys for Sheffield United's Dave Powell and Gil Reece and then sold Ian Gibson and Brian Clark to Bournemouth for £70,000. Looking back, Clark feels that Jimmy Scoular let him go because the team needed changing:

We hadn't started very well and the board were asking him to bring a few new people in. When you're twenty-nine and you haven't got much money in the bank, you look at yourself and wonder what you're going to do. I knew I only had three or four years left. I was on a basic of £35 a week with £10 for an appearance, £4 for a win and £2 for a draw on top of that. So if we won, I maybe took home £50. The man in the street was earning £40 a week. Big money was only just starting to trickle into the game.

Bournemouth's manager John Bond offered me £70 a week – double my wage – and I was also given a signing-on fee of £5,000 over my four-year contract. I really had no choice. I had a wife and two daughters and I was able to buy my first house in Ferndown, near Bournemouth.

Bond had sold Ted McDougall to Manchester United and I was meant to replace him, but nobody could. He was a legend, a bit of a freak who could score goals from anywhere. Everything was geared to Ted so the wingers would whip the ball into the box at a 100 miles an hour and Ted was so fast he would get in there.

I made some good friends at Dean Court. Harry Redknapp used to arrive for games with his wife and little boy called Jamie. I remember we once went to Jersey on a positive thinking course for four days and

Harry and Ian Gibson sat in the back of the room playing noughts and crosses and betting on horses all afternoon! Positive thinking wasn't quite their cup of tea!"

Brian then moved on to Millwall for £40,000 for two years but carried on living in Bournemouth until Jimmy Andrews approached him about returning to Ninian Park. "There were one or two other clubs interested – Swansea and Bournemouth to name two – but we discussed it as a family and Gill and our eldest daughter said they wanted to go back to Cardiff. City had a good side, with players like Clive Charles, Ron Healey, Albert Lamour, John Buchanan, but unfortunately I was thirty-three and past my sell-by date. I didn't do badly but I did struggle. I managed to buy my present house which needed doing up so I didn't rest as much as I should have done and then Tony Evans and Adrian Alston came to the club. They were in an instant success so I became their stand-in."

After helping Cardiff win promotion from the Third Division and the Welsh Cup, Brian moved on to Newport County where he linked up again with Jimmy Scoular, Don Murray, Ronnie Bird and Gary Bell. Three years later, a serious cheekbone injury led to him retiring at the age of thirty-six and taking charge of Newport's Welsh League side:

> Kids like Nigel Vaughan and Mark Aizelwood were coming through in 1980, and John Aldridge arrived on trial from Skelmersdale on Merseyside. The manager Len Ashurst asked me to play him instead of Dave Bruton against Llanelli so I put John in the team and he was hopeless.
>
> We were 2-0 down at half-time and I took him off. Bruton – who was a bit of an animal like Alan Warboys at that level – came on and we won 4-2. Afterwards, John told me he was knackered by all the training we were doing. Within a month or six weeks, he'd got back all his strength and was getting goals for me everywhere. He went into the first team and kept scoring before being transferred to Oxford and then Liverpool. He turned into another Tosh, but in his first game for Newport I took him off!

Brian later managed Maesteg, AFC Cardiff – later Inter Cabletel and now Inter Cardiff – and the Boys Clubs of Wales Under-14 side, including current Welsh internationals John Hartson and Robert Page, before finishing with football. His interest in the game has been re-ignited by Cardiff's recent revival. "In recent years, the quality of their football has been bad – sad to say but true. But I know manager Frank Burrows well, I played against him a hundred times and I know he's very keen and able – he's done very well to take Cardiff up so quickly after they finished fourth from bottom of Division Three in 1998."

While celebrating an unexpected promotion success, Brian Clark paused to reflect on the contribution made to Cardiff City by another tough-talking Scot. When he was sacked in November 1973, Jimmy Scoular had equalled Cyril Spiers's nine-year spell in charge – second only to Fred Stewart who spent more than two decades in charge at Ninian Park:

> My career was going nowhere before Jimmy bought me from Huddersfield after a lot of managers had watched me but didn't fancy taking a chance on me. If Bobby Brown hadn't done his cruciate ligaments, Jimmy wouldn't have had to buy me and Bobby would have been John Toshack's partner – it was just bad luck on Bobby.
>
> Jimmy was hard as a player and a manager. His training sessions were very demanding – especially five-a-sides if you happened to be drawn on his side! You'd never lose, he would keep them going until his team won. My five years with Cardiff under Jimmy were the hardest but the happiest of my career.
>
> It was down to Jimmy that we became a good side. He'd turned that team inside out by getting rid of John Charles and Ivor Allchurch and all the Welsh internationals who'd come home to roost. He bought Brian Harris, probably his best ever signing, Gary Bell, Mel Sutton, Les Lea and Ronnie Bird.
>
> The side did well in Europe but we didn't get back into the First Division where Jimmy had played with Portsmouth and Newcastle. He knew how hard it was but I don't think he was frightened of getting promoted. Maybe he knew that we weren't quite good enough and maybe the money wasn't there to go out and buy the players who would be needed. The support on the terraces was there – more so than Swansea – because Cardiff's a football city with a huge catchment area.

In retrospect, Scoular's fiercely competitive streak seems at odds with the board's apparent lack of ambition. How could such a pugnacious man allow his combative approach to football to be compromised by a less-than-committed chairman?

Peter Jackson believes that at the beginning of his Cardiff career, Scoular was fortunate to survive as the club narrowly avoided relegation in successive seasons:

> When he turned it around, maybe Jim felt that he owed Fred Dewey something for standing by him in those dark early days. There was a time when Scoular was much in demand. For example, First Division Ipswich wanted him before they gave the job to Bobby Robson and then just before Fred sold the club to David Goldstone in 1973, he gave Jim a five-year contract – he looked after him in that respect.

"After Jimmy left," recalls Don Murray, "I remember he told me that he'd asked the board for £100,000 to buy three new players in the 1970-71 season. But he didn't get the money."

Everyone who played under Jimmy Scoular has a story to tell about the man. All of them confirm his legendary tough style of management, which earned him the nickname of 'Iron Man', his motivational skills and his unswerving loyalty to his players which was always reciprocated. The stories reflect the esteem and affection in which Scoular was held by all with whom he came into contact.

Like most of the players, Don Murray's relationship with his manager was often fiery – as you might expect when two Scotsmen lock horns. One particular run-in followed an incident against Manchester City at Ninian Park in the mid-Sixties when the skipper's back-pass stuck in the mud and resulted in a goal. Scoular then confronted Murray at half-time with the comment: "If I didn't know you better, I'd think you'd cheated on me." Murray was appalled:

> I hit the roof, and my cup of tea hit the wall behind Jimmy's head! The old adrenalin was flowing and pieces of the cup scattered all over the place. I then took off my shirt and threw it at him: 'You can obviously do a bit better – you put the bloody thing on!'
>
> I refused to put the shirt back on until Jimmy issued this warning: 'You get that on or you'll never play for this club again! Now get your arse out there!'
>
> We eventually drew the game and afterwards in the bar, Jimmy insisted on buying me a drink. As he left, he gave my arm a squeeze which was his way of saying sorry.

"Jimmy used to criticise us but nobody else could," says

Brian Clark. "I remember Brian Clough had a go at us before a game against Derby at Ninian Park in November 1968. They'd beaten us 5-1 the previous season and after we'd drawn 1-1 and I'd scored our goal, Jimmy had Cloughie by the neck in the tunnel: 'Now say we can't play!' "

There was a kind side to his character, as Brian discovered:

> After one particularly bad home display, I went with my wife for a quiet meal in town. All of a sudden, the head waiter put a bottle of wine in a bucket on the table.
>
> 'I'm sorry,' I said, 'I didn't order that.'
>
> 'I know,' said the waiter, 'that gentlemen over there in the corner sent it over for you.'
>
> And he pointed to Jimmy who was sitting with his wife and a crowd of people. That was the sort of man he was. Two hours before, he'd been calling me all the names under the sun. We had respect for him, we would run through brick walls for Jimmy – he was hard but fair. Although we weren't the most skillful sides in the league, we were one of the fittest – thanks to Jimmy. He looked after us, we always stayed in the best hotels in this country and, of course, he gave us all those trips in Europe.

"Jim was a paradox in that he was a man with tree-trunk thighs of whom even other hard men were in awe," says Peter Jackson, "and yet the teams he produced generally played very pretty football. Don Murray was one of the original kick-them-up-the backside centre-halves who gave blood for the club but they did have people who could play – like Barrie Jones and Ian Gibson. Nobody could ever say that Cardiff muscled their way anywhere. But Jim wasn't a great manager because, despite all their European runs, they didn't win promotion. It's no good running the race if you don't get there in the end."

Like one of his predecessors Peter Corrigan, Peter Jackson's relationship with Cardiff City's manager and players was uneasy and, at times, intimidating during his nine years on the *South Wales Echo*. Unflattering headlines would be siezed upon, Peter would be harangued over his match reports and he was banned from travelling to away matches with the team for suggesting that, without new players, Cardiff were doomed to relegation. One day, he feared he was about to be attacked by an aggrieved player.

I was more friendly with Don Murray than anyone else. We both lived in the Llanedeyrn end of Cyncoed and our wives, Anne and Sue, got on well. Don always took great offence whenever I criticised him although I never meant it personally. I think I'd suggested he should be dropped and I remember Don bursting through the swing doors at the far end of the *Echo* newsroom in Thomson House – a bit like Gary Cooper in *High Noon* – and striding down the middle, jaw jutting out, not taking a sideways glance. I knew he was making a beeline for me and he stopped at my desk.

'Hello Don,' I said in a pathetic sort of way, 'what brings you in?'

'What brings me in, you bastard?!' replied Don, through gritted teeth. 'Your eyes must be in your arse. Thank God you don't pick the team or I'd be out of a job. You call yourself a friend of mine?'

With that, he did an about-turn and marched straight back out again. I was pretty relieved because I thought at one stage he was going to knock me for six!

"I think it was the result of a build-up of comments over a period of time," says Don, who now works for NCH Action for Children in Penarth near Cardiff. "Peter was quite relaxed about it which rather took the steam out of me. If he had responded differently, it could have been quite fun! I may have had a reputation as being aggressive on the field, but I certainly wasn't like that off it. Our relationship was strained for a while afterwards but I had – and still do have – a lot of respect for Peter."

"Don was very fired up, very angry," recalls Peter. "I admired him for coming in and telling me to my face what he thought of me. I can tell you that I felt about as relaxed as one of those poor centre-forwards he used to kick up in the air. We laugh about it now but we weren't on speaking terms for a while!"

As the only Second Division club to play in Europe virtually every season, Jimmy Scoular's side were unique. Cardiff was a capital city and, for a period during the late Sixties and early Seventies, they had a football team to match. The players knew they had to work hard but the rewards more than justified all the effort involved.

"Qualifying for Europe was never a stroll," says Brian Clark. "We knew that if we didn't win the Welsh Cup, we wouldn't get the trips – and we liked them. They helped us bond together. We would travel away together for four days at a stretch so we all got to know each other and we became a team. We were spoilt – we wanted new suits, we liked to travel around the world and we were treated like First Division players. Liverpool and Manchester United could not have travelled better than us at that time. It was always the best for the best side in Wales – ahead of Swansea, Wrexham and Newport."

During his first spell at Ninian Park, Brian Clark developed a particular affection for the Welsh Cup after scoring a personal record of five goals against Barmouth and Dyffryn in 1970. That 6-1 win set City on the road to another European campaign and ultimately the famous quarter-final win against Real Madrid. Clarky will always be remembered for that single goal – to be fair, one of more than two hundred he scored during his time with Cardiff – and, nearly thirty years on, he has only a single regret:

> I look back at my career and I can say that I played with great players like John Atyeo, Frank Worthington and John Toshack and I was about when John Aldridge started at Newport.
>
> I'm glad that I was lucky enough to be the right person in the right place at the right time in the first leg against Real Madrid, but if I could have scored the goal which took Cardiff City into the First Division, then I would have swapped if for the one I got on that unforgettable night at Ninian Park.

# A Man For Thirteen Seasons

Phil Dwyer can't remember the first time he went to watch
Cardiff City – but he knows it cost him nothing.

The archetypal local boy made good who would eventually
play a record 471 league games for his home town club was
one of a gang who used to sneak into Ninian Park for free.
Admission prices were a mystery, an irrelevance, something for
other people to complain about and then pay. During the early
Sixties, Ninian Park was open house to Phil and his friends.
From the age of about eleven, he would leave his home in
nearby Penarth Road on alternate Saturday afternoons and
make tracks for the railway line behind the Bob Bank:

> I very rarely paid to watch City play. We would get into the ground
> by putting a railway sleeper up against the wall around the back and
> then climbing over. We would then mingle with the crowd before slip-
> ping to the back of the Grange End. It was easier for night games
> because we could go there early, climb into the ground and then hide
> before the crowd came in and then, when they arrived, we'd jump out.

Had his parents found out, Phil would have been in their bad
books as well as, eventually, in the club's record books. Luckily
for him, Ted and Connie Dwyer were unaware of his antics:

> I told them I was going down to watch the City, but I don't think they
> would have been very pleased had they known I wasn't paying to get
> in! We were a good Catholic family but, to be honest, there were so
> many people doing it in those days. You'd see railway sleepers up
> against the wall of the Bob Bank until the club got wise to it and started
> putting barbed wire and red tar up there. But we still managed to get
> in – most of the time. I remember getting caught and being thrown out
> or being forced to drop down the wall – but only occasionally.
>
> I can't see it happening nowadays but I was nicking in until I was
> about fifteen because I remember seeing players like Don Murray,
> Peter King and Bobby Brown.

This highly irregular but apparently quite common way of watching his heroes continued until Phil Dwyer joined them as a member of the Cardiff City groundstaff. The youngest of a family of five, Phil had always been football-mad and attended two Catholic schools, St. Patrick's in Grangetown and then Bishop Mostyn in Ely.

"I always thought I wasn't a bad player," Phil says, "and every spare minute I had I'd be out with a ball. My mother would always know where to find me – either in the back streets or over the park. I didn't get in the Cardiff Boys team until the Under 15 stage – the same year as I was picked for the Welsh schoolboy team at centre-half. It was Cardiff City's kitman Harry Parsons who asked me to go training at Ninian Park and I attended a few sessions."

Phil Dwyer was not a typical footballer. With his splayed feet and lack of pace, he was blessed not so much with natural ability but the biggest of hearts. Pretty effective but certainly not pretty, Phil was the unsung hero always in tune with the public. Willie Anderson, Andy McCulloch, John Buchanan, Dave Bennett and, briefly, Robin Friday may have excited the crowds with mazy runs or explosive finishing but Phil won their lasting respect. They appreciated his reliable and unfussy approach to the game and he was the solid rock on which the Cardiff City defence was built for thirteen long though largely unsuccessful years. By the time he reluctantly left Ninian Park in 1985, he had become the club's record appearance holder.

"He was solid and hard when I first saw him play," recalls Harry Parsons, "although he didn't look much like a footballer with his shovel feet. He was doing a good job at schoolboy level so I took him on. Jimmy Scoular wasn't going to sign him as a professional but Phil then developed a knee problem. He had a cartilage operation but when he came back, he never looked back. If he hadn't have been injured, he might have been sacked!"

Phil was about to start work as a carpenter with the Docks Board when, just after his sixteenth birthday, the call came from Cardiff City. His contemporaries included Jimmy Hobby, Jimmy McInch and Nigel Rees who, unlike Phil, were sadly not to last the pace. Along with youngsters like John Impey and Billy Kellock, who developed their careers with other league clubs, Phil was part of the City side which lost to Arsenal in the 1971 F.A. Youth Cup Final.

"I was playing in the Combination League side against full backs like Eddie McCreadie and Ron Harris of Chelsea and Joe Kinnear of Spurs," recalls Nigel Rees. "They were all great defenders in their own right but when I was marked by Phil in practice games, I always found him as difficult as anyone I came up against! He was a hard bugger to get past and I always felt he was going to become a great defender. When he later moved to centre-half and captained the side, he did just that. He was a players' player who gave a 120 per cent in every game and became a legend at Cardiff."

Life was pretty simple for young professional footballers in the early Seventies. They would train with the first team in the morning and then carry out their jobs in the afternoon. Phil has fond memories of his apprenticeship at Ninian Park:

After a home game on the Saturday, we would clean up the ground on the Monday. We had to sweep the stand which was a bit like working down a mine. We would lie on our stomachs and then crawl right to the front to pick up all the paper which was obviously a fire hazard. When we came out, everything was black. About twenty of us would then have to sweep the terraces as well as help the groundsman with the pitch, replacing divots.

All of us had individual jobs as well – like cleaning the passage, scrubbing the tiles, cleaning the dressing room and the bath and the medical room. At the end of the day when the lads had finished training, Jimmy Scoular would inspect each job and we wouldn't be allowed home if he found one mark on anything.

I was lucky enough to be involved with the first team kit – it seemed to be the easiest job. It helped that I could walk to work every morning – it would take me exactly fifteen minutes and I'd be there by nine o'clock. I had to put the kit out for the players when they arrived at 10. They all had a number and I used to sort out their shirts, socks, shorts and tracksuit tops in the warmth of the dressing room while the other lads were outside in all sorts of weather!

During the close season, we had to whitewash every wall at Ninian Park – inside and out – and paint the gates blue. That was all down to us. We accepted it because we were part of a football club and, as far as we were concerned, every youngster at every club did the same.

Another footballing tradition is the allocation of nicknames by players for their team-mates. When Phil Dwyer arrived at the club, his resemblance to the Everton centre-forward and current Manchester City manager Joe Royle was quickly spotted by the City keeper Fred Davies. "Fred called me Joe in training one day and it just stuck," recalls Phil. "It spread through the club like wildfire and players who later came to Ninian Park didn't even know my name was Phil! Everybody but Jimmy Scoular called me Joe – he wasn't keen on first names!"

Scoular was keen on maintaining hands-on involvement with his forty or so players. He would take training himself either at Jubilee Park, opposite the ground, Coronation Park, where Grange Albion now play or Corinthian Park off Llandaff Road which has since been turned into a housing estate. Phil has nothing but respect for his first manager:

> We were all part of his team, and he would treat everybody exactly the same on the training pitch. I progressed from the youth team on a Saturday morning to the first team via Welsh League and the reserves.
>
> Jimmy was hard but fair. If he thought you'd done something wrong, he told you to your face. After he had criticised me, I didn't bear any grudges and neither did he. Once we were back in the dressing room, everything was forgotten.

His pre-training kit ritual ended when he became a full-time professional on his eighteenth birthday in October 1971. It would be another year before he made his league debut. In fact, as the first-team door opened for him, it was closing for Brian Clark whose first spell at the club came to a rather abrupt end.

After beating Luton Town 2-1 at Ninian Park in their opening 1972-73 league fixture, City's form nose-dived dangerously. They lost eight of their next ten matches and, despite the arrival of Albert Lamour for £10,000 from Linfield, the defence conceded an average of two goals a game. Having already sold Alan Warboys to Sheffield United, Scoular decided to let Brian Clark and Ian Gibson move to Bournemouth after a 3-0 defeat at Queens Park Rangers in late September. As they left the senior squad, Phil Dwyer was about to join it:

> I was sad to see Clarky and Gibo go. Obviously I'd watched them both play – Gibo had so much skill for a little lad that he made a lot of difference to the side and Clarky was one of the fittest players I've ever

seen. Another one was Gil Reece who was also a Grangetown lad.

I knew my name had been in the frame for the game at Loftus Road. After training on a Friday, Jimmy would pin the squad on the board. If you were in the squad but not the team you would get half the bonus. I didn't travel with the party up to West London but I knew I was knocking on the door.

When I heard they'd been beaten 3-0, I felt that I might have a chance and I was told by Jimmy that I would be making my debut at Orient after training on the following Friday. He pinned up the team sheet on the dressing room notice board and it was just tremendous to see my name there against the number 2.

Most of the players came up to congratulate me – even Dave Carver, whose place I took, wished me all the best. I knew I had to grab my chance with both hands. I was in the first team and that's where I wanted to stay. Dave was a good footballer and a good bloke but it was our living and I just had to get on with my job.

It was the realisation of a dream for me – a local lad playing for his home town side at the age of 18! It all went so quickly, everyone told me to play my normal game – it was a bit scary. But once you go out and start playing, you try to forget about everything.

Most of the 6,284 crowd did just that after having to endure a grim 0-0 draw. The game was memorable only for the sending-off of Alan Foggon in his last match for Cardiff. The former England youth international had arrived from Newcastle for £25,000 in 1971 but never made an impression during his 17-match stay. "He was overweight when he arrived and Jimmy put him through hell to try to lose some pounds," says Phil. "During my debut, I can remember keeping an eye on players like Ian Bowyer, Gerry Queen and Barrie Fairbrother but the game went so quickly. The main thing was that we had kept a clean sheet and got a point – I had done my job."

With the help of senior players like Don Murray, Gary Bell and Bobby Woodruff, Phil quickly established himself at right-back and made 31 league appearances in the 1972-73 season. "Don was a legend at Ninian Park, a real Jimmy Scoular player who would run through a brick wall for him and a good man to have in your side. He took me under his wing, as did Gary who I knew pretty well because my fiancée and I used to babysit for him. All the experienced players helped me as I played right through to the end of the season."

As Phil settled down to life as a first-team regular, there was frantic activity – both in the manager's office and in the board-room. Soon after selling Foggon to Middlesbrough for £10,000, Scoular recruited midfield player Johnny Vincent from Ayresome Park for £35,000 and then paid another £45,000 to Queens Park Rangers for striker Andy McCulloch. When a road accident laid low chairman Fred Dewey, the Swansea-born London businessman David Goldstone, who had been chair-man at the Vetch Field, was invited to join the board.

"I resigned my position at Swansea City because I didn't agree with the decision to part company with the manager Roy Bentley," recalls Goldstone. "The Deweys were contemplating disposing of their shares and it seemed a good opportunity for me to renew my interest in Welsh soccer. I think I paid about £100,000 for the club."

Almost immediately, Goldstone sanctioned a then Cardiff record fee of £60,000 to buy the former Manchester United winger Willie Anderson from Aston Villa and City avoided rele-gation by drawing 1-1 with the surprise F.A.Cup holders in their last game. Two days after beating the favourites Leeds United at Wembley, Sunderland pitched up at Ninian Park with the famous trophy and just over 22,000 spectators saw City secure a point and, with it, their Second Division status.

During the summer of 1973, the new extensions to the Grandstand along the Sloper Road side of the ground was completed at a cost of nearly a quarter-of-a-million pounds. Another £45,000 was spent on bringing George Smith to Ninian Park from Birmingham City and the 1973-74 season began well.

Three consecutive draws represented a solid start, McCulloch scored a hat-trick against Oxford but after drawing 2-2 with Crystal Palace in late September, City slid down the table. They lost five of their next seven league games, and then their manager. Jimmy Scoular was sacked on November 9th and replaced by trainer Lew Clayton for one match only – the 2-0 defeat at Millwall. Goldstone was saddened by the need to change managers:

I had a very good relationship with Jimmy, who I remembered from my schooldays when he was a wing-half with Newcastle. But we'd had a run of bad results and we had to see how we could best improve matters. It's the manager who chooses the players in his squad, he selects the eleven who go out each week and if the results aren't there, unfortunately it's the manager who takes the stick.

Jimmy was a very sensible bloke who knew there was pressure. He was the executive, the rest of us were non-executives and we reluctantly had to part company with him. I had a great affection for Jimmy, we worked closely together and I was very uncomfortable about it, but we didn't perceive there was a realistic alternative.

Scoular's sacking came as no big surprise to the players. Having returned from training on November 9th, they were told that their manager was leaving after nine years at Ninian Park. Phil Dwyer was amongst them:

I remember all the first-team players going into Jimmy's office to wish him all the best. There was a lump in my throat because I wouldn't have got my chance without him.

It was one of the saddest moments of my career to see such a hard man in everyone else's eyes just sitting there – having been told that he was no longer needed. He looked shocked – as if he couldn't believe it was happening to him. I was too upset to say a lot and obviously, in the back of my mind, I was wondering who the directors were going to bring in next.

Unbeknown to the players, Scoular's replacement had been casting a furtive eye over his new charges at Millwall. Frank O'Farrell was standing on the terraces at the Den and obviously wasn't deterred by their performance. In appointing the former Leicester City manager, Cardiff City undoubtedly landed a very big fish – albeit one out of water. After a brief spell in charge of Manchester United, he had left Old Trafford after failing to solve the George Best disciplinary problem. The backwater of Wales gave O'Farrell a different type of headache. "Frank had been with a big club," says David Goldstone, "we had aspirations and we thought he could wave a magic wand. It's very difficult for any manager to do that – such wands are in short supply."

"It was strange because Frank would sometimes take training with a tracksuit over his suit," recalls Phil Dwyer. "He was a softly-spoken Irishman and I don't think people knew what to expect – Jimmy had been there for so long. Frank didn't really fit in. It was a different set-up to Old Trafford and I don't know whether he could adapt to his new surroundings."

After recruiting his former West Ham team-mate Jimmy Andrews from Spurs as coach, O'Farrell began making use of David Goldstone's money. A new club record fee of £62,000 was paid to Leicester City for winger John Farrington while the experienced Willie Carlin came for nothing to shore up the side's midfield.

"Willie was one of the smallest players I'd ever seen but also the most tenacious," says Phil. "Frank thought the club needed someone to grab the players by the scruff of the neck and sort them out. Willie was only 5 feet 4 inches but he was a born leader – he wasn't afraid to square up to anybody. He was a good talker – in fact, he wouldn't shut up on and off the pitch!"

As the relegation battle intensified, Phil Dwyer scored his first goal for Cardiff in a 2-0 home win over Preston North End, and goalkeeper Ron Healey and defender Clive Charles were drafted in as reinforcements. After beating runaway champions Middlesbrough 3-2 at Ninian Park in April, the club suddenly announced that Frank O'Farrell was leaving – four games from the end of a season in which Cardiff looked likely to go down! After a mere 158 days in charge, O'Farrell had decided that he couldn't refuse an offer to coach Iran and promptly disappeared into the Middle Eastern sunset. David Goldstone remembers the moment:

> We were at a reserve game one day and Frank said he'd had a call from Iran – would it be OK if he talked to them? I replied that although I wasn't happy about it, I wouldn't stand in his way. If a bloke doesn't want to work for me, I'm not wildly enthusiastic about him staying.
>
> It was disappointing but I didn't blame him for leaving. I can't remember how long his contract was but the fact is he wanted away. Would anything have been achieved by holding him precisely to the terms of that contract? Where would have been the motivation? I didn't feel let down – I'm a businessman who lives in the real world.

"Frank didn't think there was a great future for the club," says Jimmy Andrews. "He couldn't see them getting in quality players so he put two and two together and accepted the very good offer from Iran."

Don Murray was nearing the end of his Cardiff City career

The Yo-yo years. Derek Tapscott's goal in a 5-1 win over Leyton Orient in October 1959 helps City back to the top flight after two seasons in Division Two. Derrick 'Ginger' Sullivan looks on in admiration.

Two Welsh legends tread the green green grass of home. Ivor Allchurch, on his debut against his former club Newcastle United in August 1962, and John Charles in a practice match after his arrival from Roma a year later.

Who said Tosh was no good on the ground? One of the goals in his first hat-trick, as City beat Queens Park Rangers 4-2 in September 1969 – in front of City's first 30,000 crowd for eight years.

The Iron Man is honoured. Even receiving his Manager of the Month whisky in December 1969, Jimmy Scoular finds it difficult to smile. Six consecutive league wins up to the turn of the year prove to be in vain as City finish seventh.

The 1970-71 squad are all smiles but, after John Toshack's £110,000 transfer to Liverpool in November, they miss out on promotion for the third successive season.

Brian Clark scores the *second* most famous goal in Cardiff City's history to beat Real Madrid on that unforgettable March night in 1971.

Phil 'Joe' Dwyer in typical action against Brighton in January 1976 as Ci
bounce straight back into Division Two.

The 'double' celebrations after City beat Hereford 3-2 in the 1976 Welsh Cu
Final replay. David Giles, with trophy, stands in front of Phil Dwyer, with bottl
and Brian Clark.

Veteran striker Bob Hatton goes close in City's 2-0 win over Orient in May 1983. His mid-season signing proves crucial as Len Ashurst's side returned to Division Two at the first attempt.

The Gaffer and Mr Chairman. Frank Burrows and Tony Clemo after their 1988 promotion and Welsh Cup 'double' end in a 2-0 win over Wrexham at the Vetch Field. Five years later, Eddie May and Rick Wright celebrate winning the Third Division Championship at Wrexham.

A Welsh Cup Final win over Rhyl at Cardiff Arms Park completes a 1993 'double'. Kitman Harry Parsons (right) celebrates promotion for the fourth time.

Player of the year Kevin Nugent pops in league goal number fourteen in a 2- win over Carlisle in March 1999.

Goal of the season? If, not, then certainly a contender: Jason Fowler chips in to help City beat the eventual champions Brentford 4-1 in January 1999.

Saturday May 1st 1999. Manager Frank Burrows acknowledges the applause of an ecstatic Ninian Park crowd as promotion is secured. Now, where's that champagne?

All's well that ends well. The 'Grand Old Man' of Cardiff City pictured ju
before his death in November 1954. Heavy rain on the day of Bart Wilson
funeral forces the burial in Western Cemetery to be postponed. When th
headstone is not returned, Bart lies in an unmarked grave for almost forty-fi
years until the stone is rediscovered by chance and then refurbished to reco
Bart's details. In June 1999 close family members and club representatives gath
for a short rededication service and the contribution of the founder of Card
City is finally and officially recognized.

when O'Farrell jumped ship. After nine years of playing under the abrasive Jimmy Scoular, his replacement took some getting used to. "I think Frank saw Cardiff City as a launching pad because in no time he was off to the Middle East," says Don. "He was a very distant manager. We had been used to Jimmy Scoular for so long, to his team talks when sometimes the air would turn blue while Frank had a very laid-back approach."

The board had little alternative but to promote O'Farrell's trusty lieutenant to caretaker–manager. The odds may have been stacked against Jimmy Andrews but he applied himself to the job in hand with real relish during a remarkable climax to the season.

After a defeat and two draws, City needed a point from their final home match against Crystal Palace to stay up. To add to the tension, Palace needed to win to avoid being relegated from the First to the Third Division in successive seasons.

The contrast could hardly have been greater. The shy, almost retiring Scot versus the flamboyant and outspoken, fedora-wearing Englishman. Jimmy Andrews against Malcolm Allison, former team-mates at West Ham, now locked in a relegation dog-fight. The Crystal Palace manager was sure his team would rise to the occasion and they took the lead on the half-hour through Stewart Jump. But, in front of an ecstatic crowd of nearly 27,000, Tony Villars scored the equaliser at the Grange End just before half-time to keep City in Division Two.

"I felt that if we worked hard enough, we had enough quality to beat Palace," recalls Jimmy Andrews. "Tony was a brilliant player on his day – he could win any match, a little bit like Ryan Giggs. He had marvellous ability but he was inconsistent – good one day and not very good the next. When he scored at the end of a brilliant run, it was fantastic! The right man did the right thing on the day – I didn't expect it to happen but it made it even better."

City finished 17th – one point away from relegation – and Jimmy Andrews became the new permanent manager. "It was another challenge because everyone has called Cardiff City a sleeping giant and I found that the ground was bigger than the club. We didn't have the blend or quality to win anything. We wanted to win but didn't have the drive or the money to do so. The prospects were pretty grim"

"I got on well with Jimmy," says Phil. "He was probably the first real coach to be involved with Cardiff City. He made a difference by making players better. Jimmy Andrews had been a skillful winger, the total opposite to Jimmy Scoular, a hard man who gave 100 per cent. Jimmy Andrews liked to work with the ball to improve our skills."

City's stay of execution proved only temporary because twelve months later, they were relegated. The message was spelt out by David Goldstone at the start of the season: there would be no money for strengthening the squad. To make matters worse, key players were sold as Cardiff made a £28,000 profit when Andy McCulloch moved to Oxford United for £73,000 and then banked £80,000 from Aston Villa when a transfer request by Leighton Phillips was finally granted in September 1974.

"I told the chairman that if Leighton went, we would go down," recalls Jimmy Andrews. "David said it couldn't be helped – that was the way it was going to be and sadly I was proved right."

Andrews had little chance of averting the inevitable. Swop deals and loan transfers were his only option so John Farrington was exchanged for Northampton's John Buchanan, and Steve Finnieston arrived from Chelsea.

By the end of September, Don Murray had played his last game for Cardiff – a 2-1 home defeat by Hull. A month's loan to Swansea was followed by a permanent move back to Scotland to Hearts where he spent two enjoyable years before moving to Newport County and then helping out with Cardiff City's youngsters.

"Jimmy Andrews said I could go," Don recalls. "I wasn't that surprised as I was one of the Scoular School who had to move on. I was quite prepared for it really. I was sad to leave Cardiff and my biggest disappointment was not playing in the First Division with them. I've no regrets apart from wishing sometimes that I had moved to a bigger club. I had the chance to join Everton and Birmingham but I always felt we were good enough to get into the First Division. I'm very fortunate to be happily settled here in Cardiff. My wife Sue was born and brought up here and I like Cardiff and its people."

During the 1974-75 season, Jimmy Andrews was forced to

blood a succession of youngsters and although a run of just one defeat in twelve games from late October augured well, a 5-1 thrashing by Millwall in January sent City spiraling towards Division Three. Finnieston had returned to Chelsea and the tension in the Cardiff camp surfaced during a scoreless draw with fellow strugglers Sheffield Wednesday at Ninian Park at the end of March. Johnny Vincent had missed a penalty and then Andrews decided to substitute George Smith. As he walked to the tunnel, the stocky, ginger-haired midfielder threw his shirt at the bench in disgust as the 6,637 crowd heckled him off. He wasn't the only disgruntled person at Ninian Park that day.

From his season ticket seat in the grandstand, lifelong City fan Dannie Abse was so annoyed by Smith's substitution that he wrote an open letter to Jimmy Andrews which was published by the *South Wales Echo*. 'Why I was booing...' ran the headline as the doctor-poet launched a fierce attack on the manager's tactics and general handing of the club.

"I wasn't booing Smith who I thought was playing quite well compared with most of them," recalls Dannie. "I felt that Clive Charles or John Buchanan should have been taken off instead and I felt very strongly about the way Andrews was using players like Gil Reece, Phil Dwyer and Willie Anderson."

After detailing his complaints, Dannie's letter concluded with a question: "Who, finally, has to take responsibility for City's poor showing this season but you, the man in charge? I should be most interested to hear your comments on these remarks and I should be glad if you could give me reasons why I should support Cardiff City next season."

Dannie didn't receive a reply from the manager although at one stage he did think that his letter had hit home. As he was preparing to leave for a reading tour of America on the day it was published, the phone rang. A man with a Scottish accent was on the line.

"Is that Dannie Abse?"

"Yes, it is."

"This is Jimmy Andrews. I've just read your letter in the paper. I'm going to sue you."

I'd taken the call on the extension in our bedroom as my wife Joan and I were packing and when I put my hand over the receiver, she exploded with rage – "you stupid idiot! You shouldn't have written that letter!" After a while, we heard the caller laughing on the other end of the phone. It was my close friend, the late John Ormond, the poet and television director, playing a prank. It worked well – he had me going for what seemed like a couple of minutes!

The real Jimmy Andrews remembers both the George Smith incident and the letter very well. "I thought about replying but it was purely Dannie's opinion and he was entitled to that opinion. One of the fascinations of football is that everyone has a view and they can argue and disagree about points of the game."

"Relegation in 1974 was a real blow," recalls Phil Dwyer. "Peter Sayer broke his leg in our last-but-one game at Southampton and then we lost 2-1 to Bolton at home."

The 2-0 defeat at Southampton sent Cardiff City down and the chairman on his way. David Goldstone decided to cut his losses and during the summer sold out to a consortium of businessmen. Local politician and hotelier Stefan Terlezki became chairman with travel operator Tony Clemo, North-Eastern businessmen Bob Grogan and Jack Leonard, from the engineering company Kenton Utilities, among the other members of the board. Goldstone explains why he decided to sell the club:

> I had made a major investment in Cardiff City and I was very disappointed when we were relegated. Whatever the fans may think or say, you are in the hands of the players and the manager. He can do everything during the week in training but ultimately, it's down to those 90 minutes when those guys either do the business or they don't. I remember it was a very, very long drive back from Southampton.
>
> Not unnaturally, the fans were upset but who do you blame? Not the players because they're your heroes, so it's the faceless directors. There were rumours of people wanting to buy me out and although nowadays people try to make a profit out of football as a business, I was very happy to accept what I had put in – with no inflationary increase whatsoever. If they felt they could do better, I said OK – the club was more important.

"I got on well with David apart from when it came to money," recalls Jimmy Andrews, "and he had decided not to come up with anymore. He wanted out because he saw the club as a business."

"I don't know any football club chairman who gives his

manager an open cheque book," says Goldstone. "Any business requires a modicum of restraint – it's called living within one's limits."

"It was very difficult because the new board had never been in football before," recalls Andrews. "They knew very, very little, they're were in another world. Football is not like ordinary work – it's a different environment altogether. In fact, the players are in charge of you very often and the new directors couldn't understand that. They thought that if you paid the players, you were entitled to get so much from them. That's fine in theory but it doesn't work like that in practice. They're up and down and in and out, sometimes they're up against better players and sometimes worse players but it's not a permanent, steady rock-like thing."

The manager's extensive knowledge of football enabled him to attract a number of experienced players to Ninian Park as City aimed for an immediate return to the Second Division. The former Wales and Spurs international defender Mike England arrived from America, having been persuaded by Andrews to postpone his retirement, and £18,000 was somehow found to enable Norwich City's Doug Livermore to anchor the midfield. Brian Clark returned from Millwall and fellow striker Tony Evans joined on a free transfer from Blackpool.

"Jimmy had seen that we were struggling in certain positions and he brought in the right players to do the job," says Phil Dwyer. "I was lucky because in the earlier part of my career, I played alongside Don Murray and then Mike arrived – he was tremendous and I learnt a lot from him too."

The return of Willie Anderson from a summer in America after a brief dispute with the club proved a turning point. "He was a wonderful player," recalls Phil. "In that season, he was on one wing with Peter Sayer on the other. Willie scored 6 league goals but set up loads more with his fantastic runs and crosses."

Anderson inspired Cardiff to a 3-0 win over Wrexham in early October as Phil Dwyer narrowly missed out on a hat-trick when City were awarded a last-minute penalty. "The keeper saved it and I remember getting a right rollicking from Jimmy Andrews who said that if we missed promotion by a goal, I'd be hung, drawn and quartered."

In fact, Phil experienced a fate close to death just over a month later when he swallowed his tongue in the club's 2-2 draw at Gillingham:

> I think I was playing in midfield and our keeper Ron Healey kicked the ball out. It bounced about chest height and as I went to head it, I was caught by one of their players – probably with his knee – on the back of the head. The next thing I realised was that I'd been taken off on a stretcher and placed in an ambulance at the side of the pitch. The bump caused me to swallow my tongue and our physiotherapist Ron Durham came on and managed to get it out. I had apparently stopped breathing and he gave me the kiss of life.

Back home in Wenvoe, just outside Cardiff, Phil's wife Ann had just returned from a shopping trip with her mother:

> Mum went into the lounge and put on the television. I was in the kitchen and I heard the name Dwyer followed by a gasp from my mother. I presumed Phil had been sent off again! When I went into the room, my mother was absolutely white and they then repeated that Phil had died on the pitch after swallowing his tongue. It was then just a mad panic ringing around until we eventually found out, through friends, that he was alive.

"I'll always be grateful to Ron for what he did," says Phil, "his quick action saved my life. Luckily, I recovered quickly and was back in action within a week."

There were to be more heart-stopping moments – especially during heavy defeats at Swindon and Hereford – but City eventually secured runners-up spot behind Hereford after conceding just one goal in their last nine games. Adrian Alston's finishing – 14 in 33 league matches following his £20,000 transfer from Luton – and Alan Campbell's industry in midfield were crucial to the final promotion push. Campbell scored the second goal in a memorable 2-0 win over Hereford at Ninian Park in front of more than 35,000 in April. Three matches later, Bury were beaten 1-0 and City had clinched promotion.

During the summer of 1976, Mike England led the exodus of City players to America when he left Ninian Park under a cloud. It has been suggested that Jimmy Andrews had offered but then withdrawn a coaching post. Apparently, he had felt under threat. Immediately after the Bury win, the future Wales manager left to join the New England Teamen but, nearly a quarter of a century later, he receives little sympathy from Jimmy Andrews:

> I never worried about being replaced by anybody because if it came down to the wire, they would have no chance. In fact, I asked Mike if he wanted to join in with the coaching. I would have been delighted and it would have been good for the club and the players who all thought a lot of him. He refused – he said he had too much to do at home. That would give you an idea of whether I was afraid of Mike or not!

According to Phil Dwyer, some of Cardiff City's players were more than a little wary of Robin Friday, one of the most controversial signings in the club's history. After a disappointing start to the new season, Adrian Alston left for the Tampa Bay Rowdies for £20,000 and the money was used to buy Reading's star striker. Friday was a one-off, a wild and wonderfully-gifted player who made his debut in a 3-0 win over Fulham on January 1st 1977. It was a New Year and a new start for the wayward striker. Fulham's problem player, George Best, was missing but City's version more than made up for his absence with two goals in a sparkling display.

"I signed Robin after seeing him star in an F.A.Cup game against Burnley," recalls Jimmy Andrews. "He was brilliant, there was no two ways about it – the boy could play, he had eyes in the back of his head. At that time, I didn't know what his major problem was so I bought him for £25,000. I felt he would be worth it and that I could sort him out."

For the record, Robin Friday scored six goals in 21 league games in just under a year with Cardiff. He was sent off twice and went missing countless times.

Phil Dwyer, the exact opposite of Friday says the signing came as a big surprise to the players::

> He had a reputation for being a bit of a wild man and we didn't think Jimmy would be able to handle him. On the day he arrived, the club received a phone call from British Rail explaining that Robin was at Cardiff Central with nothing more than a platform ticket. Harry Parsons had to go down to pay his fare and bring him back to the club to sign on.

He had a touch of the gypsy about him with his long hair – he was a real loner. He would come down on the train from Reading most days in a pair of jeans, a T-shirt and a carrier bag. And he'd go every-where like that, although for away games he'd find a tie from somewhere. On the return journey, he'd ask to be let off at the next roundabout – and the next we'd see of him would be the next day in training!

He was very volatile. I remember playing five-a-side in the gym at R.A.F. St. Athan once when I was keeping goal for the opposite team to Robin's. I threw the ball out and as he turned away, the ball hit him on the side of the head. Steve Grapes, who was on Robin's side, laughed and Robin turned round and hit him! Steve was in a collar for a couple of weeks – that was the sort of chap Robin was.

He was a tremendously skillful player but so unpredictable on and off the pitch. The one goal he scored which sticks in my mind is the famous one against Luton when he stuck two fingers up to the goal-keeper. We beat them 4-2 and I scored as well but I can't remember it!

We felt Robin was a very good player who could win us a few games so we indulged him. Nobody would say anything against him. He went out onto the pitch and did his own thing. You could always give the ball to him and know that defenders wouldn't be able to get it off him. He held it up so well and just the sight of him would terrorise the opposition. He would tackle anyone, anywhere. If some-one did take the ball of him, he'd be upset and try, whichever way he could, to get it back. In a good side, he would have been an asset, but because we struggled, he was a bit of a luxury.

I never saw him take any drugs but it was common knowledge that he was on something – he was so high! He was never calm, he was always bouncing around – it wasn't normal. Some of his team-mates were frightened to talk to him, even to look at him!

After doing his best to sort out his wayward signing, Jimmy Andrews eventually had to admit defeat. "For a period, I handled it but I'm afraid Robin was a hopeless case. He was lost, he was never professional in his outlook towards the game. There were some great players who had similar problems but when it came to the day, they would perform. They could turn it on, they were fit to do the job but I'm afraid Robin wasn't in several games. By the end, he was uncontrollable. You could never depend on him. He would vanish and I would get Harry Parsons looking for him. If Harry couldn't find him, then nobody could!"

In recent years, Robin Friday has assumed almost cult status

among Reading and Cardiff supporters. After playing in the 6-
3 defeat at Bolton in December 1977, he left Cardiff for good
and his career petered out. He died alone in a flat in Ealing in
West London in 1990 at the age of 38. His controversial life is
the subject of a recent book, *The Greatest Footballer You Never
Saw.* "When I heard of Robin's death," says Jimmy Andrews,
"I felt sick for him and his family but I'm afraid I wasn't
surprised. It was almost as if something drastic had to happen
to him."

With or without Friday, City were a poor side. A week after
his debut, the new signing was cup-tied and Peter Sayer came
in to secure a famous F.A.Cup victory over Spurs. During
Friday's self-imposed absences, defenders Paul Went and occasionally Phil Dwyer were pressed into service as strikers with
Went scoring the winner against Notts County in early May to
keep City up. In their last game against Orient, Cardiff were so
lacklustre that they were heckled by their own supporters as the
London side secured the win they needed to avoid relegation.

Cardiff's shortage of goals could probably have been solved
if John Toshack had returned to the club where his career had
begun nearly fifteen years earlier. Before becoming player-
manager at Swansea in March 1978, the former Liverpool
striker had offered his services to Cardiff City. Tony Clemo,
who was then vice-chairman, claims that he fought a losing
battle to make use of Toshack. "I thought it would be brilliant
to get John on board," he says, "particularly as we were struggling at the time. It would have been a tremendous boost as
John was a huge name with Liverpool and Wales."

But Clemo was outvoted by the other directors including Bob
Grogan who was an admirer of Jimmy Andrews. In his 1982
autobiography *Tosh*, John Toshack revealed details of a meeting
he had with the manager during which they apparently
discussed the striker's coaching qualifications. "I explained to
him that I had taken my preliminary badge and passed it at the
age of sixteen but some of the things I had seen had turned me
off the coaching manual. I told Jimmy he could look in my
trophy cabinet any time to see for himself what qualifications I
had."

When Toshack's offer wasn't accepted, he moved on to

Cardiff's arch-rivals and the rest is history. Between 1978 and 1981, he took Swansea City from the Fourth to the top of the First Division before successfully managing a string of foreign clubs including Real Madrid twice. More than twenty years later, Jimmy Andrews recalls his meeting with the embryonic player-manager in a rather different way:

I'm not a bad judge of people, and I think he just called in on his way to Swansea. I would have liked Tosh, he was a good player and a brilliant header of the ball – one of the best I've ever seen – and I was disappointed that we couldn't use him. He would have been a great asset.

During the meeting, I was trying to size him up all the time and I thought he was maybe using us a little bit as a bargaining tool because I'd been told by a very source that Swansea were interested in him. Like anybody would do, I think he was trying to get an offer from us to take to Swansea. If you get two clubs interested, you can guarantee you're going to get more from one of them. I was very disappointed but I felt rightly or wrongly – I think rightly – that Tosh was on his way to his next club.

It's absolute nonsense to suggest that we discussed his coaching qualifications. He did not say that I should look in his trophy cabinet. I certainly wouldn't haven't have offered him a job as a coach unless I needed one – which I didn't. It was a very cagey meeting altogether and I formed the opinion very early on that he had no intention of joining us. I have never felt threatened by John or any player or anything – apart from, that is, when the end is coming. Everybody senses that when things are bad and there's a possibility that you're going.

Nearly three months into the new season, that possibility became a certainty when Jimmy Andrews was sacked. Despite spending £75,000 on Newcastle's Micky Burns as player-coach and £70,000 to bring Hull City's Welsh international defender Dave Roberts to Ninian Park, City continued to struggle. They won just four of their first 13 league games and after a 4-1 home defeat by Charlton, Andrews lost his job – halfway through a five-year contract – to be replaced by long-serving defender Richie Morgan as caretaker-manager.

"I had a legal fight for two years before I got my money which was very unfair," says Andrews. "I can't forgive the directors for that. They knew I was a professional but unfortunately the club was being run by amateurs. It doesn't bother me now. I'm not bitter because bitterness just turns in on yourself."

After spending over a decade scouting for Southampton, Jimmy Andrews severed his links with football. He now lives very happily in retirement in Cowbridge in the Vale of Glamorgan with his wife Dorothy.

Within a month of his appointment, Richie Morgan's enthusiasm had persuaded the board to make his position permanent and he surrounded himself with experience. Brian Harris, Doug Livermore and former Newport County manager Dave Elliott became his assistants.

"We were near the bottom of the table," recalls Phil Dwyer, "so it came as no surprise when Jimmy was sacked. Richie hadn't played that many first team games despite being at the club for a long time. He held a clear-the-air meeting with the players and got us on his side. He said he'd look after us and he did. He might not have had our respect at the beginning but we finished ninth in the league so we obviously responded."

From then on under Morgan, City started to slip – from 15th in the following season to 19th the next. Only goal difference prevented them from going down instead of Preston. Midway through that 1980-81 season, John Buchanan was responsible for one of the most fondly-remembered goals ever scored at Ninian Park.

Two days after Christmas 1980, Cardiff met Swansea in a Division Two match as John Toshack's charge up the divisions was about to reach its climax. Injury time was being played when Buchanan grabbed a point for City in a 3-3 draw with an unstoppable drive from a tapped free-kick from at least 35 yards. "It was the best goal I ever scored," recalls Buchanan. "When the referee told me it was indirect, I told Wayne Hughes just to touch it to me and I just hit it right. I caught it perfectly."

"It was one of the best goals from distance that I've ever seen," agrees Phil Dwyer who, having contributed to Swansea's first goal, was replaced through injury at half-time by Paul Giles. "Form went out of the window in those derbies, both sets of supporters were fanatical and it was great to salvage a point against Swansea."

The result tasted all the more sweet when Toshack revealed in a post-match interview that he had hoped Buchanan would shoot because "he'll never score from that distance!" But the Swansea manager had the last laugh when his club secured the third promotion place on goal difference from Blackburn Rovers with a 3-1 win at Preston in their final game.

City were ninth in Division Two in November 1981 when the directors decided it was time for another managerial change. Three years after taking over from Jimmy Andrews, Richie Morgan was moved into an administrative position and former Welsh international Graham Williams swapped running a health club in Weymouth for the coach's job at Cardiff City. Four months later, after 9 defeats in 11 league matches, both men were sacked. Len Ashurst arrived from Newport County to become the club's sixth manager in nine years but, despite three successive wins in late March and early April, he failed to keep them up.

Throughout the various personnel changes since Jimmy Scoular's sacking in 1973, one person had remained a permanent fixture at Cardiff City. Phil Dwyer was now as much a part of the furniture at Ninian Park as the Bob Bank. He had Fred Keenor's 369 league appearances in his sights and was even looking as far ahead as the record of 445 games held by Tom Farquharson. But in the summer of 1982, his Cardiff career nearly ended when Ashurst decided to clear the decks. Phil recalls how he heard the bad news:

> I was in hospital recovering from a knee operation when I read in the *South Wales Echo* that I was one of several players being released or given free transfers. I had missed half of the season through injury so it was a bit of a shock – Len had hardly seen me play.
>
> He later said that if I could prove to him that I could recover from my injury, there was still a place for me there.
>
> During that summer, I worked on my own in the house building my leg up – I had something to prove. One day, Frank O'Farrell, who was back at Torquay as general manager, rang me. Would I like to go down to Plainmoor and play for them? I turned out in a couple of pre-season friendlies and then had talks with Brian Godfrey at Exeter. If we could have agreed terms, I would have gone there because I didn't want to stay where I wasn't wanted.

"I left Phil out initially," recalls Len Ashurst, "because I didn't think he was up to it – his attitude was poor but he showed me that he wanted it. Phil was a difficult nut to crack – and there's more than one way of skinning a cat so I put him on the transfer list to gee him up. I took the opposite posture by fighting him and showing him that I didn't care about him – I wanted to see if he would come round that way."

"I didn't know it at the time but Len had had me watched during the friendlies," says Phil. "Keith Pontin played centre-half in City's first four games of the season but, after beating Wigan 3-2, Len decided to replace Keith with me and I was virtually ever present as we won promotion."

"Keith was a smashing chap, a good club man and very honest," says Ashurst, "but although he'd won a Welsh cap, I didn't fancy him. I made decisions on the professional ability of players not on how nice they were. Keith quickly disappeared to be replaced by Phil who duly proved to be as good as everybody had said he was. Despite being crippled with back and knee problems, he fought on to become just about our best player by the end. He was the rock – with Jimmy Mullen – around which I built the side."

Ashurst's working of the free transfer market produced the perfect mix of youth and experience. From eighteen-year-old Andrew Dibble in goal to thirty-six-year-old striker Bob Hatton, who arrived in early December from Sheffield United, the side blended together superbly. As they had under Andrews, City returned to the Second Division at the first attempt, with Phil Dwyer rehabilitated at his home-town club:

That was a great team. There were the Bennett brothers, Dave our right winger and Gary, the tall defender – both tremendous players in different ways, Gary was so elegant on the ball while Dave was quick and skillful. Whenever we were in trouble, he was our main outlet. David Tong in midfield had clear instructions from Len: 'whenever you get the ball, give it to Benno' – which he did. Roger Gibbins was a workhorse in midfield, someone who would sit in the middle, win the ball and pass it. In defence, there was Jimmy Mullen, who Len brought down from Rotherham, and Paul Bodin in what was a good, hard-working side. Bob Hatton used all his experience to get us goals and worked well with Jeff Hemmerman up front. John Lewis was another local lad, skillful and quick.

Like Jimmy Andrews had done, Len brought in experienced players in crucial positions – Jimmy Mullen at the back and Bob Hatton in attack. Bob's job was to get us promotion and when he'd done it, he retired. Sadly, Jeff Hemmerman was badly injured in our last game of the season at Bristol Rovers after we'd already been promoted. He collided with Phil Kite, the Rovers goalkeeper, and the injury effectively ended his career.

Although the crowds were still disappointing – they averaged just over 7,500 – Cardiff City had stopped the rot and a rejuvenated Phil Dwyer had played a key role. He missed just two games in the promotion season and was an ever present as City finished 15th in Division Two. By that time, the managerial merry-go-round had begun turning again. In March 1984, when Ashurst was unable to resist the call to return to Sunderland where had spent fourteen years as a player, his assistant Jimmy Goodfellow and Jimmy Mullen assumed joint control.

"People were talking about me taking over," recalls Phil, "but I didn't actually apply for the job. Had they offered it to me, I don't think I would have turned it down but I hadn't thought about becoming a manager because I was still playing and only thirty-one – I thought I had a few more years left in me. It was a popular arrangement because the two Jimmys had worked with Len. They were in charge for the last two months of the season and Jimmy was then appointed manager by himself."

At the end of the 1983-84 season, Cardiff City showed a working profit of nearly £250,000 but the club's overall debt stood at £1.4 million, most of which was owed to the club's parent company Kenton Utilities. As City equalled their worst-ever start to a season – six defeats in seven games in 1921-2 – Phil Dwyer deservedly took his place in the record books on Saturday 18th September when he played his 446th league match for the club at Ewood Park in Blackburn. The game ended in a 1-0 defeat and Phil received a memento from the supporters club to mark his achievement in breaking Tom Farquharson's record.

Just over a week later, Jimmy Goodfellow, now in sole charge, was sacked in the wake of a 3-0 home defeat by Manchester City and his subsequent criticism of the board's transfer policy. "Being manager was something I wanted to do," recalls Jimmy, "because if I hadn't, I would never have known if I could have done the job. Having kept the club up, we then lost Andrew

Dibble, Gary Bennett and Gordon Owen in the summer. They were difficult to replace, I gave it my best shot and it didn't work – in other words I wasn't good at it – but I don't regret taking the job."

According to Ron Jones, Cardiff's managing director, Goodfellow's inexperience counted against him, so the former Welsh international Alan Durban was appointed. "I suspect that Alan will be more dynamic and determined as a manager," said Ron Jones at the time, "and hopefully will push the club up the table."

In fact, Durban's arrival achieved precisely the opposite effect as he presided over one of the most wretched periods in Cardiff City's history. Port Talbot–born Durban had started out on a glittering playing career at Ninian Park and had won promotion with both Shrewsbury and Stoke before being sacked by Sunderland after keeping them in the old First Division for three years. He will be forever remembered as the man who took Cardiff City down from the Second to the Fourth Division in successive seasons. Phil Dwyer, now serving under his eighth manager, initially welcomed the new appointment:

> Everybody thought it was a good decision because he had done it before as a player with Wales, Cardiff and Derby and as a manager. I remember he called me into his office early on and told me he was building his side around a few of the more experienced players. But then he brought in a few youngsters like Mike Ford, Paul McLoughlin, Graham Withey, Vaughan Jones and Jake King, and it all seemed to go downhill. The former England captain Gerry Francis was signed by Jimmy Goodfellow but he only played a couple of games under Durban – and then the Welsh international Brian Flynn joined us for a season.

Alan Durban was happy to return to his native South Wales but admits that his two years at Ninian Park were among the most frustrating of his whole football career:

> It was a disastrous eighteen months for me. After ten very good years as a manager, I lost all credibility. Cardiff had sold their top three players and Jeff Hemmerman had to retire. The best two players were me, aged forty-four, and Hemmerman the physiotherapist!
> I made a big mistake in thinking I could do it on my own – I should have brought in my own people to work with me. And I was always

fighting Ron Jones at the same time. He wasn't a football man although he'd spent four years with Jim Gregory at QPR. It was a problem from Day One. I realised I had made a mistake when, on my first day at the club, they put me up in the worst hotel in Cardiff!

There were too many things wrong which I didn't change because they were always pleading poverty. When we bought Phil Brignull from Bournemouth for £9,000, we had to have a whip-round to raise half the money! A club that size ought to have had their own training facilities – we used to go over to Jubilee Park and we'd sometimes get thrown off there.

I couldn't get anything done, the board were up in Newcastle and I was travelling back and forth for the first year – it was highly unsatisfactory. I tried to do it with kids, many of them local, because we had no money but it didn't work. I was in a trap of having to borrow and use players in a temporary situation – I could never plan for the future because there was no long-term policy. All the power was in the North East but I have to take a certain responsibility for what happened. It was just one big mess which unfortunately I couldn't clear up.

"We were looking for another Len Ashurst," recalls Ron Jones, "someone who could use his contacts to bring players to the club for virtually nothing – like the Bennett brothers and Jeff Hemmerman. If Durban thought he was going to come and spend a million quid which nobody had, than he was naïve in the extreme. He thought Cardiff were a team with a lot of money like Sunderland but he was completely wrong."

"Jack Leonard had his own ideas," recalls director Tony Clemo, "and because of his position as chairman, everyone went along with him to a certain extent. Alan Durban was a name. Jack felt he was the right guy, he saw him as the saviour but he was a disaster from day one. I didn't get on with Durban and I had a personal go at him a few times in board meetings. He would come up with the most ridiculous comments, including the one at a board meeting near the end of the 1985-86 season when we were heading towards our second successive relgation. His answer was to blame the switchboard telephonist's treatment of the public. He felt the first point of contact with supporters had to be improved because otherwise it would spread through the whole club."

"Jack had appointed Alan," recalls Ron Jones, "and it was Tony's decision to get rid of him as part of his takeover deal. Durban may have thought I manoeuvred him out, but I didn't.

I have to say that his record as a manager didn't lead me to believe he was going to take Cardiff City anywhere so I concurred with Jack."

The whole experience left Alan Durban deeply scarred. He later become manager of the National Tennis Centre in Telford for nine years before returning to football with Derby and then Sunderland. By the time he had left Ninian Park in May 1986, Phil Dwyer had already made history – as well as his exit.

Phil's record 471st and last league appearance for Cardiff City was in a 4-1 defeat by Notts County at Ninian Park on Saturday February 17th 1985. In all, he played 573 games in league and various cup competitions and won 10 Welsh caps. Nearly fifteen years later, he is still saddened by the way he was forced to leave Cardiff City.

"Along with a lot of the team," recalls Phil, "I didn't have a very good game against Notts County and afterwards, I admitted it. I then said there were players who wouldn't accept they'd played badly. I was prepared to speak up and accept the blame because I knew I'd had a bad game but others weren't – that was my last appearance. It seemed to me that Durban didn't actually want the experienced players around him so Dave Grant and I signed for Rochdale on the following Monday."

"I had tried to buy Phil when I was manager at Stoke," recalls Alan Durban, "and I appreciated him as a player because I'd seen him in a couple of internationals. But he and Jimmy Mullen were supposedly the biggest influences at Cardiff and yet we had leaked goals all season and gone down. My opinion was that he had lost his pace, things had to be changed and I thought I might as well do it then as leave it for another couple of years."

"It was clear I was no longer required," says Phil, "and I wasn't the sort of person to stay. The sooner I got away from Cardiff the better. I had seen quite a few managers leave Ninian Park and I was grateful that I'd had such a long run – I had loved every minute of it. Ann and I agreed to meet up at weekends because she didn't want to move to Lancashire!"

"Phil had been a good servant to Cardiff," says Durban, "but I can't remember receiving a letter from anybody saying I shouldn't have let him go or any articles in the papers saying what a bad mistake I'd made. I had a great respect for Phil but I didn't think he could give anything more to Cardiff City in the long term – I might have been wrong but we'll never know that."

"If I hadn't signed for Rochdale on that first day," recalls Phil, "I'm sure I would have come back to South Wales and joined either Swansea or Newport who I later found out were interested in me. I don't think Durban wanted me to sign for a local club – he wanted me out of the way so he kept their interest quiet."

Cardiff and either Swansea or Newport's loss was Rochdale's gain as Phil helped them stay up. He trained at Ninian Park from Monday to Thursday before heading north for the game on Saturday and although Rochdale wanted him to sign on for another season, Phil decided to retire and join the South Wales Police. "It was great being paid for something I loved doing and I could have stayed in local football. But I had my wife and our two children to consider and I wanted security for them. I had thought of joining the police before and although I'd recovered from my knee injury, Ann and I decided that I should look for something new."

As well as working as a detective constable in the CID at Penarth, Phil still maintains his involvement with football. As assistant manager of Cardiff Civil Service in First Division of the Welsh League, he steps into the breach when the team are short. "Last season, I was on the bench a few times and I actually played in goal twice when our keeper didn't turn up – I kept a clean sheet but we lost 2-0 in the other game. Up until last season, I had been playing regularly and I really missed not being involved all the time rather than just helping out in an emergency."

In football's current climate, it seems unlikely that Phil Dwyer's appearance record will ever be beaten. Apart from that one season at Rochdale, Joe spent all his playing career – man and boy – with the club just around the corner. For thirteen years, the consistent and totally committed defender sweated blood for Cardiff City. In becoming the talisman for a team which majored in mediocrity, he endeared himself to a generation of supporters and served under eight different managers.

"I'm very proud to hold the record," admits Phil, "and although the way it all ended was a bit sad, I don't have any regrets. I suppose I could have played more games for Cardiff had it not been for Alan Durban but these things happen in football. After all the dreadful years, it was great to see the crowds coming back."

The record books show that Phil Dwyer made 174 of his 471 league appearances while Jimmy Andrews was in charge at Ninian Park. In true footballing fashion, his name was always the first on the team sheet from 1974-78 as City, apart from one season, struggled to stay afloat.

"Phil's main strength was his strength," recalls Andrews. "He was brave and he had a good professional mentality. He wasn't a great player but a good scrapper who would always give you everything he had. He was over-physical at times, a bit like a rugby player, but you could always depend on him. If there was any stick needed, Phil would provide it and the crowd loved his whole-hearted approach."

"Phil was one of the old school," according to Roger Gibbins, a team-mate from the 1983 promotion side. "He was a captain-cum-leader, a man mountain sort of player. He was a very intimidating colossus who you always admired for what he put into it. He was to Cardiff what Tony Adams has been to Arsenal, an out-and-out centre-half who was good in the air, competed very well and who put his head in where it hurt. I played most of my games in midfield then and it was reassuring to look back and see Phil working hard at the heart of the defence."

"When we had problems up front," recalls Jimmy Andrews, "I played him as a striker and he scored one or two very important goals. That was the thing I liked about Phil: he was always happy to have a go – wherever I wanted him to play. He was a true pro and that's what you need in your side. Every time Phil went out to play, he wanted to win. In a way, he represented the team – he was 'Mr. Cardiff City'."

# A Woman's Place

Football has always had more than its fair share of superstars. They appear in a blaze of glory, burn brightly for a few years and then fade away – often as quickly as they've arrived – before being replaced by another generation of very special players. Some – like Birmingham City's Trevor 'Superboy' Francis and Newcastle United's Malcolm 'Supermac' MacDonald – are good enough to earn an individual superlative sobriquet.

Then there are the supersubs, the less exalted fringe players whose introduction can turn a game with a late match-winning goal, cross or pass. David Fairclough had the uncanny knack of coming up trumps for Liverpool shortly after leaving the substitute's bench in the Seventies, and Gareth Sheldon shattered Swansea City's dreams of reaching a Wembley play-off final with two extra-time goals for Scunthorpe in May 1999.

And who will ever forget the Super Spurs, the Tottenham team which in 1961 became the first twentieth century side to win the coveted Double? In the Nineties, the creation of a Super League in the form of the English Premiership has produced the rise and rise of the Super Reds as Manchester United have outstripped the previously unparalleled success of Liverpool during the previous two decades.

Then there are the spectators. Despite the growing influence of television, football is nothing without the paying public. From the drawing up of the first rules in *The Simplest Game* published back in 1862 to the 1998-99 season's tense title climax, there have always been superfans, the supporters for whom football isn't just a game but a way of life.

Sue Goodfriend is a superfan. For most of her forty-four years, she has followed Cardiff City – come hell or high water, rain or shine, in good times but mainly bad. The freelance management training consultant has collected programmes and autographs, travelled to faraway places like Hartlepool,

Darlington and Carlisle and served behind the Grandstand Bar at Ninian Park. For four years in the early Eighties, she was secretary of the Cardiff City Supporters Club and later helped to run the Junior Bluebirds. Sue Goodfriend is Cardiff City through and through – and proud of it.

Sue was born in Tremorfa and brought up in Riverside where the club was formed a hundred years ago. She lived just around the corner from Bart Wilson's home in De Burgh Street which served as Cardiff City's first headquarters before they became a professional team. Her father, Maurice, would watch City with his father and from an early age, Sue followed suit, nailing her colours firmly to Cardiff City's mast and setting sail on a life-long voyage in support of her home-town club:

> I was probably about seven or eight when I went to my first game, but I didn't go frequently then – my father wouldn't have been able to take me because of the cost. I remember more about the atmosphere than the football itself – as I think most kids do.
>
> We had to walk under the Grange End to reach the Bob Bank, dodging the cigarette ends as we went and smelling the smoke up above. We always used to stand in the same place just in front of the television gantry to the left of the halfway line. My sister Sandra, who's four years younger than me, wasn't allowed to go at that stage – she was too young.
>
> By my teens, I was going quite often but there was a problem because Saturday was the day I was supposed to visit my grandmother in Tremorfa with the rest of the family. We'd stay there for tea and then come home in the evening. Occasionally, after a lot of negotiation, I would go to the game with a group of school friends – I've always gone to football predominantly with women. My father doesn't go now – he thinks I'm completely mad! To be honest, I don't think I can tell you why I love the game so much.

Sue thinks her fixation with football – Cardiff City in particular and the game in general – can be traced back to the 1962 Tottenham v Burnley F.A.Cup Final. From then on, whenever she and her father kicked a ball around the back garden, he would be Spurs and she was Burnley. "I remember hearing that their average crowd meant that one fifth of Burnley's population used to watch the team play. Because I knew that London was big, I was going to be the underdog and it's stayed with me ever since. I've always had a soft spot for Burnley. I remember listening to the football results on a Saturday afternoon with my father and being fascinated by the intonation of the reader. I'm sure the results get a lot of kids interested because you try to predict the scores."

After the 1966 World Cup, Cardiff City's European Cup Winners Cup semi-final against Hamburg and Manchester United's European Cup win in 1968 both played a crucial part in developing Sue's interest in the game. "I remember Manchester United beating Benfica 4-1 at Wembley very clearly," she recalls. "It was the first football game on television which sticks in my mind. By then, I was old enough to stay up and watch *Match of the Day!*"

Like all football supporters, Sue Goodfriend has heroes. Ruud Gullitt, the player rather than the manager, is her all-time favourite but John Toshack, a predecessor of Sue's at Canton High School, was her first:

> He was in the team at sicteen scoring all the time. He was a striker which appeals to young people because midfield subtlety isn't so obvious when you're twelve. He had sex appeal and I suppose I might have fancied him – I was certainly at the right age to do that.
>
> There was a section of the crowd who really got on Toshack's back and I liked him all the more because of that – it was so unfair. I had other heroes as well, like Brian Clark and Don Murray who was a bit of a contrast to Toshack. Barrie Jones was a fantastic, tricky little winger who was wonderful to watch.
>
> Toshack seemed very good at building partnerships with people – Bobby Brown, Brian Clark and then Kevin Keegan at Liverpool. He was a figurehead who was attracting attention, a famous player in a side which nearly got promotion in three successive seasons.

By the third near-miss, Toshack had departed to the bigger stage of Anfield. His transfer in November 1970 proved to be a defining moment in Sue Goodfriend's life:

> I was walking along Neville Street to catch a bus to school when I saw the *Western Mail* billboard. It read 'Toshack leaves for £110,000': I couldn't believe my eyes. That was probably the first time I bought a paper! I knew he was attracting the interest of scouts but I thought he'd stay with Cardiff because this time we were going to get promotion. I felt let down and to a certain extent, I thought that he'd let Cardiff down too. Why couldn't he stay for just another season?

Then again, it was £110,000 and he was only the sixth player in the game to go for that sort of money. I bought a paper but I can't remember what I read. I just remember thinking 'God! It really is true!' I began to fill up with tears, through frustration more than anything – it just wasn't fair for Liverpool to come along and take him away just like that. Why did he want to go anyway?

Memories of that particular day in school are as vivid now as they were nearly thirty years ago. Sue was trying to comes to terms with a trauma – and it showed:

It was one those fuzzy days when everything happens with a sense of unreality. I was probably in mild shock and I would sporadically burst into tears throughout the day. I remember sitting in double chemistry and the teacher, Mr Ackryll, a nice man, was very worried about me. He didn't quite know what to do because I was a girl but he came over to investigate.

"What's the matter?" he asked.

"Oh! You wouldn't understand!" I cried, brushing away his concern. I think he just left it at that and made good his escape – which is exactly what I would have done in those circumstances! I was better when I got home to talk it over with my family. It was particularly upsetting because Toshack had just scored a hat-trick against Hull.

If they had a choice, I don't think the club were right to sell him. I have no idea what the board machinations were at the time but, as a supporter, I felt, along with many others, that by selling him Cardiff City sold any ambition they might have had too. I can see the reasoning behind it now, but I didn't then.

I remember people saying that if Cardiff knew they were going to sell Toshack, why didn't they get a replacement in straightaway? That six weeks until Alan Warboys arrived might have made a difference to their promotion campaign.

Sue may have been disgruntled but, unlike some Bob Bankers, she was not disillusioned. Cardiff City could still count on her support although her view of football was changed forever. "The club was bigger than any one player so I still wanted to go but I guess it was all part of my growing-up process. I now realised that football wasn't a fairy tale – it was the start for me of thinking of it as a business. I can articulate it that way now, but I don't suppose I did then. John Toshack's transfer shattered a few illusions."

Sue remained a regular until 1971 when she found a Saturday

job – in a bridal shop in St. Mary's Street for 25s a week – but it wasn't her style and only lasted a month. She left to work in a boutique before spending three years at the University College of North Wales in Bangor from 1972-75. "I followed the team through the papers when I worked on Saturdays. I still felt as affectionate towards them but I didn't see as many games and being eight hours away at college was always going to make it difficult to keep up my support."

But by the end of the 1975-76 promotion season, Sue was back in Cardiff and back on board. For the next four years, she could indulge her passion while working at Les Croupiers, a city centre casino. "The shifts were broadly eight in the evening to four in the morning plus one afternoon, so you were unlucky if you had to work a Saturday afternoon, but it meant I couldn't go to many away games."

Another Canton High School old boy hit the headlines in January 1977 as, for once, Cardiff City made it past the third round of the F.A.Cup. Peter Sayer's goal in an unlikely 1-0 win over Spurs made him a household name by propelling him onto the opening titles of *Match of the Day*. It also helped him to win the first of seven Welsh caps.

"Peter was a good cross-country runner at school," recalls Sue, "and I knew him quite well. That goal was really a one-off because although he later joined Brighton for £100,000, he never rediscovered his Cardiff City form. I hear he's now running a pub in Preston."

Wanderlust meant Sue missed the end of the 1979-80 season as City finished mid-table under Richie Morgan. She decided to go to America for three months with a couple of friends. "I must have been pretty confident that Cardiff weren't going to do anything special because I would never have missed a home game! One of the stupid superstitions which real die-hard fans follow is that, if you don't go and the team lose, it's your fault! It was your duty as well as your pleasure to go to a home game. Sometimes recently it's been more of a duty than a pleasure."

While Sue was in the United States, Wales played Iceland in Reykjavik in early May. Despite the growth of the North American League, football received little coverage so Sue knew she would struggle to find out the result. "I couldn't see anything in a couple of newspapers I bought so I decided to stop people walking down the street with newspapers to see if they had a football section. Amazingly, the second person I asked actually knew the result – it was 4-0. Not only that, he said he used to know Mike England quite well when he played in United States soccer before and after his spell at Cardiff City!"

On her return from America, Sue decided to take a year out rather than look for a proper career job. While working in tele-sales and the Wales Tourist Board before joining British Telecom, she began her association with the Cardiff City Supporters Club. Until then, the role of secretary had been strictly a male preserve. Sue Goodfriend, with some sterling support from her sister Sandra, broke the mould.

"One of the things about being female in football at that time was that there weren't many of us," Sue recalls. "There had always been some women involved but when you got two like me and Sandra, both 5 feet 9 inches, standing together on the Bob Bank, everybody knew us – we were distinctive."

The Goodfriend girls became actively involved with the supporters club in the 1980-81 season – the same time that Ron Jones joined the club as chief executive. One afternoon, they weren't able to register their vote in the man-of-the-match competition run on the Bob Bank and Sue complained to the officials:

They then asked us to do it, so we went around marking off the various choices of the crowd. At the end of the year, the player who'd won the most awards would be given a trophy. We got a normal reaction – the odd person would try to chat us up and we occasionally might have a conversation about their choice. It turned out to be a stepping stone.

The supporters club wasn't doing very well – it was meant to make a profit so it could give some money to the club. It was clear to the committee that I was going to be able to write a decent letter and get a few things organised so they asked me to become secretary.

As a secretary you do everything; as a chair you're a figurehead. So there was a man as the figurehead and I, as a woman, did everything else. We used to design membership cards, print them, sort out the constitution and then collect the fees as well as taking bookings for coaches for all away games.

Although three or four of us would go to negotiate with the coach companies, I was the one who made sure the contracts got signed and therefore my name was on everything. We had to arrange pick-up points and renegotiate our coach contracts every year which got more difficult because there'd be the more than occasional problem with coaches.

One of my first away trips before I became directly involved with the supporters club was to West Ham in November 1979. Sandra and I were a bit worried during the game because we were only separated from their supporters by a thin blue line of police. We were concerned that the line was going to break at any minute. We were just a bit too close and it wasn't segregation as I knew it. It was a fantastic but scary atmosphere.

We came back to our coach to find every window smashed in – although it was in a car park. One of the Cardiff supporters was asleep amongst the debris on the back seat!

The 'English disease' of hooliganism was to plague football in general and Cardiff City in particular throughout the Eighties until the Hillsborough disaster brought everyone to their senses and helped to restore the game's respectability. Cardiff were also having to implement the 1977 Safety of Sports Ground Act which meant money was even tighter. Ron Jones, a former Olympic runner and British team captain, had spent nine years as sprinting coach at Queen Park Rangers and another four as chief executive before arriving at Ninian Park.

I took over the commercial and administrative part of the club. I did everything but run and select the team. There was an expectation at the time that Cardiff City should be a First Division club and people were always telling me that it was a sleeping giant. Our chairman Bob Grogan has assumed that, as a capital city, Cardiff could become another Newcastle United from where he came from but he failed to appreciate that he'd invested in a rugby stronghold. An advertising board would bring in about £5,000 at the Arms Park whereas we'd be lucky to get £500.

My job was to try to keep Cardiff City on an even financial keel – it didn't please some of the supporters who felt we should be putting millions into the club. We tried to get businessmen interested but nobody wanted to know – who wants to invest in a club where you've got nutters smashing the place up every two minutes?

I still don't understand why we had the football violence problem but it obviously discouraged people, especially families, from coming to our matches. It got to the stage where I actually met a bunch of these hooligans – many of them were professional people. I remember one was a solicitor, another a butcher – they weren't unemployed yobos. They went to football for the aggravation – they were killing the game.

They told me they came to Ninian Park just for a punch-up not to watch the football. It was almost as if they relished the prospect of getting their name in the papers and on television.

Sue was happy to be the supporters club's Girl Friday for the first couple of years. As well as secretary, she also undertook some of the treasurer's work and a slight loss was turned into a £900 profit in the first year. Gradually though, she became disillusioned with the job:

> I began to notice that if things went well, everybody took it for granted – anything that went badly somehow reflected on me. Some of that was my own sensitivity because I like things to go well but I also felt that I was an easy target as a woman.
>
> What they were actually expecting was for a coach to always turn up on time and to be allowed to do whatever they liked when they were on it. It had to get them to the match in time to have a drink in the pub, pick them up immediately afterwards with no problems and ferry them home. That would happen thirty-nine times out of forty but nobody ever got any thanks for that.
>
> As I started to make more suggestions, say about overnight stays on away trips, they didn't go down too well. Nobody articulated this, but my impression was that you were alright as a woman as long as you were seen to be efficient and nice but knew your place. Indeed, everyone used to say that Sandra and I were nice girls. It became a bit of a problem as soon as we were thought to want to do things above our station.

The Safety of Sports Ground Act was causing the supporters club a few problems too – especially on the coach trips to away games. As secretary, it was Sue's job to make sure that the alcohol ban was enforced.

> Drink was banned from many grounds and we certainly weren't supposed to carry alcohol on the coaches. There was a constant battle between a coachful of blokes in their twenties and me – and because I was responsible for anything that happened, I used to enforce the ban strictly. They resented it – they would have resented a bloke doing it as well but I don't think a bloke would have done it.
>
> From time to time, I would stand on the coach steps and take a can of drink out of people's hands as they were boarding at nine o'clock in the morning. 'Either you get rid of this or you don't come on the coach!'

I would say. There'd be some swearing but they'd then get rid of the drink and board the coach. You'd then get this rumble all the way along.

The silent majority were fine, we had a few allies, there was a whole bunch of people who wanted a quiet life, to watch the game and come back and then there was the vocal minority who could make your life a misery. They could turn what was meant to be a pleasant experience into a wearying one. It became worse and worse, more and more wearying.

We always said we didn't carry hooligans, only genuine supporters, but we always knew in our heart of hearts, that one or two of the 400 blokes would go a bit too far. We always said that if any of our members were convicted of any crime, then we would ban them. To my knowledge we didn't have to go that far but I'm quite sure that some of them got involved in things they didn't get arrested for.

Cardiff then had a reputation for trouble which I don't think was deserved, but we had it. I can put my hand on my heart and say that in my time it had nothing to do with the supporters club. I'm not saying there was never an isolated person who might have been involved or an incident but we never had any organised problems at all.

However, our reputation meant that we were often harshly treated by police who would march us along the pavement to the ground. If we arrived an hour before kick-off, they wouldn't let us stop or get something to eat. We would be herded straight into the ground and we all know what football facilities were like in those days.

We always had good support away from home although the numbers travelling would depend to an extent on who we were playing. There was also another supporters' club, 'Adar Glas' from Pontypridd, with whom we had a kind of uneasy co-existence. They ran coaches along different routes with some alternative pick-up points. It didn't really make a lot of sense to have separate groups but historically there had been some rivalry between the two which I never fully understood as it stemmed from events before my time. That made thoughts of amalgamation difficult. I wasn't against us having close links but somehow I knew it wouldn't happen.

By the time Sue resigned as secretary, the club had over 400 members – three times as many as when she had begun. As well as her stressful role as coach steward, Sue found herself having to fight her corner on another front – rampant male chauvinism. Some of the club's members refused to accept that she and Sandra knew anything about football:

They would then start casting aspersions on our motives. I always had to prove myself. They didn't give me twenty questions about the game, they just wouldn't take any notice unless I made them take notice. I would have to trot out all the finer points of football – which they would take for granted from another bloke who might be totally ignorant about the game. He was a bloke so it didn't matter. It was just a difference of opinion with him but with a woman, it was a case of 'well you would think that, you're a woman!'

There was also the stuff about just being around to see the players' legs – which one did we fancy most? Most of it was lighthearted but there was that element in it. Nowadays, if you're a twenty-year-old standing on the terraces, you can freely admit to liking somebody's legs best – and nobody thinks anything of it. It's quite normal – it doesn't mean to say you ignore the football.

Before returning to his native Cardiff four years ago, Ken Gorman spent twenty-five years as journalist in Newcastle and London. He covered the Welsh national team for most of that time and he now freelances on boxing and football for a number of national newspapers. He also came across the Goodfriend sisters:

I can remember Sue and Sandra as two of the keenest supporters Wales had. It was very unusual then because football wasn't the game it is today. I suppose they were a bit of a novelty. Most people initially thought they were football groupies but, in fairness to them, they weren't. They did actually understand football – they knew what they were talking about.

It surprised me because I suppose I'm a bit old fashioned, from the old school if you like, and I've always found it difficult to accept the whole idea of women being involved in football. We'd talk on planes and in hotel bars and they'd mix quite easily with the press lads. It still strikes me as odd when you come across women who follow the game – they're actually talking about tactics not just who they fancy.

When Sue and Sandra worked behind the Grandstand Bar at Ninian Park – now the John Charles Suite – on match days, they became the victims of rumour and innuendo – particularly from other supporters.

We would serve at the bar until a quarter to three and then after the game. There was quite a bit of what some people might call harmless banter because we had a lot of contact with the players when we were behind the bar. They would come in for a drink after the game and we got to know the Cardiff lads quite well – players like John Lewis, Roger Gibbins, David Giles and Jeff Hemmerman.

Our friendship with them probably didn't help our relationship with other club members. They made make all sorts of inferences that they had no right to make – as men tend to do – about the nature of our relationship with some of the players. They had no evidence to support this and, even if they had, it was none of their business. I wish I'd had such an exciting sex life as they imagined! I remember asking one of them if they were jealous?

"Yes," he said, "in a way, we are. We'd screw them if we could!"

They didn't mean it literally but they saw it as our way of getting closer to the players. They could see us occasionally having a laugh with a couple of the lads and you could almost hear them say 'those girls, they get everywhere!' They would also see us waiting outside the dressing room for the players to get our free tickets for away games – our reward for working behind the bar. Although they hadn't done anything to deserve them, some supporters would wait around for spare tickets so there was a bit of resentment about that. I suppose it might have been more tactful if we'd collected the tickets differently, but really it was none of their business.

"We realised that the two sisters organised quite a few things which a lot of people didn't know about," recalls Roger Gibbins. "If they approached us about making presentations, we were only too willing to go along – those type of people are invaluable to a football club."

But according to Sue Goodfriend, there was little or no help for the supporters club from Cardiff City. "The club didn't dislike us," claims Sue, "but we didn't have any real backing from them. Ron Jones used to talk about charging us to have space in the club shop to do our bookings. He used to say that football would be better if there were no spectators – he could run it much more smoothly then. Part of it was to wind us up and part of it was serious."

Ron Jones denies ever talking about charging Sue to use the club shop in this way. He claims he gave all the supporters' clubs as much help as he could:

Sue and Sandra were extremely vocal as was Mair Daniel who ran the 'Adar Glas' supporters club. Rightly so. I understand that their heart and soul were in the club – but they didn't really want to know about the economics of football.

From the players point of view, there's no doubt that support at away games is important and Sue did a good job. But that's only half the story. It was a major thing for her because she was only concerned with the team – I looked at the club. Without the club, you wouldn't have a team. They didn't want to know about how the players got onto the pitch, who bought the kit or who paid the wages for the police and the stewards.

It provided enjoyment, even euphoria, for them, but I had the responsibility of keeping the club from going bust. Bob Grogan wanted me to represent him as chairman because he was up in Newcastle. We did achieve quite a bit – I remember, when Tony Clemo was chairman, a deal worth £40,000 from Buckleys Brewery for shirt sponsorship over three years which I thought it was a major coup.

In all, there were three bona fide Cardiff City supporters organisations – 'Adar Glas' in Pontypridd, the official one in Cardiff and another group in Barry.

"At one point," recalls Ron Jones, "I had the temerity to suggest that they should get together! They were all in the same business but they said independence was critical. It made me question if they were there for the club or their own gratification? Surely, if they were interested in the club, then they'd pool their resources? If I wanted to hold a meeting, I had to write three separate letters to each organisation and then when they came in, they'd have three different views on policy."

"I was concerned for the club's long-term well-being," says Sue. I thought Ron's policies would be counter-productive." Ron Jones insists that he had no alternative but to take a wider view if Cardiff City were to survive:

I tried desperately to get all the supporters' organisations on my side. We met at the old Bluebirds Club and I tried to explain our economic problems. I gave them what information I had so they could understand that it was more than just about coming down and yelling support. The financial situation was so precarious that, towards the end of my eight years, we used to regularly have the bailiffs down at Ninian Park – I used to hide underneath the table! It was crazy! Maybe I shouldn't always have related it to money but that had to be my main priority. If you don't attend to that area in any soccer club, you go bust – like Newport County did and like Swansea City nearly did. My remit wasn't to stand on the terraces but to keep the club alive. If Bob Grogan had pulled out, we would have had no club for Sue to support.

After four years at the helm, Sue Goodfriend decided it was time to sever her links with the supporters club. There was no particular reason, just a gradual build-up of disillusionment.

Repeated racist attacks on Cardiff's black players, sexist treatment and football violence didn't help.

The worst case of racism was at Millwall in 1982-83. We were sitting on the side where Dave Bennett was running down the wing and there were literally five-and-six-year-olds chanting racist abuse at him and his brother Gary. They were being totally offensive. I had been in grounds where bananas had been thrown before but that was in the Seventies. This was the Eighties and it was horrendous. Dave's answer was fantastic – he scored two goals in a 4-0 win.

As we returned to our coach after the game, stones were being thrown at us and then we found that all the windows had been smashed in. I had to go and negotiate with the coach company – I think in that case we paid half and half – but it was one of the things that made me question whether I wanted to be involved in running the trips anymore.

I was beginning to get more and more wound up by all the problems involved in organising the supporters club so I dropped out. I would make the occasional trip by coach but basically I didn't enjoy travelling on a smoky coach with forty blokes and three other women and then being herded around by the police.

The final break came when Sue and her friend Liz Rogers were asked to steward a coach travelling to Wrexham for a Wales match. They had just passed the half-way point of the journey to the Racecourse when someone put on a porn video.

Liz and I were nominally in charge and there was one other woman on the coach. There was no way I was going to sit and watch that video with all these blokes around – I knew that some of them would make an issue of it.

I don't know how soft or hard the porn was because I didn't wait to find out. I just told them to switch it off! That caused a bit of a row so I went up to the driver and told him to pull in. I gave them an ultimatum: "get that off – or we turn back!"

The driver removed the video, the coach continued on its way and Sue Goodfriend vowed never to become involved with organised football travel again. "Ironically, several of the men on that trip came up to me afterwards and offered their support for my actions. Frankly, it would have been much better if they'd stood up to be counted at the time."

When Liz Rogers returned to Cardiff from university in

Liverpool in the mid-Eighties and set up the Junior Bluebirds at Ninian Park, Sue lent a hand as treasurer. On one Sunday a month, children were invited to Ninian Park for a training session with some of the players. Paul Wheeler and Cohen Griffith were among the most supportive of the first-team squad.

> Every season, we would try to go and see a First Division game, we'd have a Christmas party – things just to get the kids involved. They would to pay a nominal membership fee of about a fiver but Ron Jones said we should be charging them because they were getting the services of the players. The idea was that these were the supporters and potential sponsors of the future – bonds built in childhood are longer lasting. We were trying to build ties between the club and the community. I saw myself as an ambassador and could have been much better used by the club.
>
> It was all very well lending a hand answering phones, selling match tickets and being bar hands but we had much more to offer. But once again, here were two women not being treated at all seriously by the club. It was supported in principle but was seen as totally insignificant. They felt because it was only women running it, they weren't proper coaches but Liz, in fact, is a qualified coach.
>
> By the end, we had over a hundred members – sometimes there would be twenty, at other times sixty. They didn't have to be good, just keen. It was for anybody, there were no standards to meet. I wanted to do more rather than just watch the team – I wanted to get involved, to do something for the club.

Sue's spell with the Junior Bluebirds ended after Rick Wright bought Cardiff City in the early Nineties. The scheme was replaced by one drawn up by the club in conjunction with the *South Wales Echo*. Nowadays, Sue Goodfriend is just like any other Cardiff City fan. She has a season ticket but no official connection with the club.

> It's very strange not being more involved. When I was twenty or thirty, I was quite happy to do all the things I did in running the supporters club – it was fun but I wouldn't want to do that now. If I were to become involved again, I'd want to have more clout.
>
> My hands-on involvement with Cardiff City in various guises lasted nearly fifteen years so I stopped with mixed feelings. I felt quite sad but there was a little bit of relief as well – it's fun to be just an ordinary fan. My voice through the supporters club was not fantastically influential but at least I had the chance to say something and I miss not having that now.

As she sits watching City from Seat 10 in Row E of Block C of the Ninian Park grandstand, Sue Goodfriend can reflect on a significant improvement in the lot of women in football. The game has a growing female audience and their influence is being felt in boardrooms throughout the country. Karen Brady is managing director at Birmingham City and Britain's most famous chef Delia Smith has bought herself a large slice of Norwich City.

"The role of women has changed in some ways because we've now got female referee's assistants and even referees in the lower divisions," says Sue. "We've got chief executives and masseurs who are female so women have started to infiltrate and, on the surface, I think attitudes have changed tremendously – especially over the last five or six years, though there are still very obvious prejudices like the Professional Footballers Association's awards and 'gentlemen's' dinners."

According to journalist Ken Gorman, there is room for women in the box housing the directors but not the press. He still feels uncomfortable when such a traditional male bastion is invaded. But he pays tribute to Joan Hill, Cardiff City's former chief executive, who left in the wake of chairman Samesh Kumar's unexpected resignation in May 1999.

"Karen Brady and Delia Smith are fine as long as they don't get involved in the football side of it," says Ken. "Clubs need thriving commercial offices and women can do that kind of job well. Joan Hill was a very good hostess, very friendly and outgoing, and, all in all, she was a good influence on the club. I wasn't that close to it but I did feel that she projected a good public image for Cardiff City."

Former managing director Ron Jones, now director of the Welsh Sports Aid, the organisation which helps promising young sportsmen and women, is full of praise for the way in which Cardiff City is marketed. "The matchday programme is very impressive. I see a far wider range of sponsors than in my day. We found it very hard work to find even one – now there are far more companies involved. The commercial staff have done a good job. Joan Hill was fantastic – clever, with-it, very accommodating, she made you feel welcome all the time – I can't speak too highly of her."

Former player and manager Alan Durban, who returned to Ninian Park in August 1998 to run the rule over Cardiff's Mark Delaney for a First Division club, also noticed a dramatic change. He saw City lose 2-1 to Kevin Keegan's Fulham in the Littlewoods Cup and was impressed with both the promising full-back and, in particular, the warmth of the welcome.

"The hospitality was absolutely magnificent in the board-room," he recalls. "They had let in scouts and friends of the club and Joan was top-class. The Doc, Leslie Hamilton, and Harry Parsons were there, I hadn't seen them since I left Ninian Park and the mood at the start of the season was great. She had lifted up Cardiff's profile so much that you felt that they deserved success."

"The whole role of women in society has changed in the last thirty years," concedes Ken Gorman. "I've got three daughters so I've noticed women's lib at first hand! But in many ways, I still think that football is a man's game. Women in the board-room are OK but when they start to think they understand football, then that worries me. And if they had any kind of influence in who a manager signs or who he plays or what tactics he employs, then that would really worry me."

On the terraces, Sue Goodfriend has detected a significant change of attitude by men although verbal abuse – of the players and in particularly the referee – is still an accepted part of the game.

I haven't come across any obvious incidents of sexism or racism personally for quite some time. I'm sure black players will tell you they are still abused but I think it's improved. Football has become more of a family game, less male-oriented although it's still obviously dominated by men. On the whole, I don't feel I have to prove myself half as much as I used to – there's more respect for women and their knowledge of football.

I do get annoyed by the general level of abuse from spectators towards players and officials though.

Everybody knows everybody where Liz and I sit and the only bad language comes from infiltrators, not the regulars. I do swear when something goes wrong – the odd expletive comes out – but I object to systematic thoughtless swearing when every second word is effing this or that. Usually a look will stop someone swearing but sometimes it doesn't. When we played at Rushden and Diamonds in the F.A.Cup a couple of years ago, a local man, who was with his wife and child, would just not stop swearing – even when I asked him politely to.

His reaction was to pour scorn on me while his wife wondered what I was doing at the game if I didn't like swearing. I felt sorry for their poor child who was standing with them.

I used to love being in the with the boys at Ninian Park when they were chanting and there was a lot of atmosphere, some banter and humour, but I prefer where we sit now because you can actually see what's going on.

First and foremost, Sue Goodfriend is a football fan. She loves the game and has travelled around Wales and the world to watch it. Her commitment has involved her once seeing a hundred matches in a year and travelling to and from a New Year's Day game in Plymouth by taxi, train and the players' coach. She watched two games at Italia 90 – including the final – either side of seeing the artist formally known as Prince perform at Wembley. She went to Euro 96 and also saw Manchester United's historic European Cup win in Barcelona and the 4-0 humiliation of Wales by Italy in Bologna in the summer of 1999.

"My job as a management consultant means I'm totally flexible now," she explains. "I can do what I like as long as I can afford it. I teach subjects like communications skills, assertiveness, working in teams and leadership to organisations which, like football, are going through lots of changes. As well as going abroad, I go to every Cardiff home game, but over the last couple of seasons I haven't seen them play away much. It's been so awful so I've watched Chelsea at home instead, but Cardiff improved so much last season that my enthusiasm returned and I saw quite a few away matches."

Like most football fanatics, Sue is a creature of habit and superstition. As well as taking chocolate money to Christmas games, there is the ritual of wearing the same jumper to matches throughout a successful season: "Cardiff won once when we had the money so I had to sit and eat it during the Shrewsbury game on Boxing Day 1998 – even though I didn't much feel like it! To be honest, I deliberately forgot what I was wearing last season so I wouldn't get caught up in worrying about it!"

Despite all the talk of superstars, supersubs and Super

Leagues, there will always be a place in football for the super-fan. Indeed without them, there would be no game. Every club has them; they are football's lifeblood and its future.

"Love and despair I think sums up my relationship with the club," says Sue. "Wherever I go and whatever I do, I will always be a Cardiff City supporter – even if I can't go to all their games. Obviously, the relationship has had a huge influence on me – it's never been the only thing in my life but it dominates, maybe a little less as I grow older. In a sense, football came before boys and men – not because I didn't like them, but because if you were travelling back from Doncaster on a Saturday night and working hard during the week, it was diffi-cult to form a meaningful relationship.

"It has been an obsession at times but I think I've always had the balance right. I like other things – I go to the theatre, I love ballet, I play tennis. I have a life outside football but the rela-tionship with Cardiff City has been a dominant force in my life – even when I haven't been able to stand what's going on at Ninian Park. I feel I've put more into it than Cardiff have. I've lost count of the number of times I've said that if they'd have put as much energy into playing as I've put into supporting, we would have done a lot better. I think all supporters, male and female, would say that."

# Pleasure Before Business

Why do they do it? Who, in their right mind, would want to become a director, let alone the chairman, of a lower league football club? What makes apparently sensible self-made men get involved in a largely loss-making operation which brings them nothing but trouble and strife? Who are these hard-nosed businessmen with a soft spot for football?

Answers on a postcard please to the boardroom, Cardiff City A.F.C., Ninian Park, Sloper Road, Cardiff. After the club's promotion to the Second Division in May 1999, the directors began looking for financial help to take the club forward. So what's new? Cardiff City have been down this road many times before. A brief burst of success is almost inevitably followed by a long period of stagnation. Boom and bust, start and stop, one step forward, two steps back. The club's history is littered with similar appeals for investment which have mostly fallen on deaf ears. But every now and then, some philanthropic soul steps into breach to make some progress – and occasionally some money.

Sir Herbert Merrett saved Cardiff City when the desperate days of the Thirties threatened to strangle the club. Without his intervention, it is unlikely they would have survived. In the Forties and Fifties, Merrett financed a return to the old First Division but since then a variety of local, and not so local, businessmen have owned the majority of shares but failed to build on Cardiff City's occasional success.

In the continuing absence of the Penarth-born David Sullivan, the soft-porn publisher with a major stake in Birmingham City, the word went out. Anyone with any money to invest in the most somnolent of sleeping giants was asked to contact the Ninian Park board as they sought to cash in on the club's ninth promotion.

With Cardiff City celebrating their centenary at the dawn of the new Millennium, it was time for the fastest-growing capital in Europe to show that it deserved, if not a Premiership club, then at least one in the First Division. The board had delivered their first promise – promotion to the Second Division – and surely it was time for a major company – or companies – to rally round and support their local football team?

At least, that's how the argument went. Just how many people will be persuaded to part with their money is another question. Tony Clemo will not be answering the call. He feels he has done his bit and it's somebody else's turn. To be fair to him, he has a point. As chairman and director, he spent seventeen years on the Cardiff City board. The champagne flowed during three promotion parties but Tony Clemo was left with a huge financial hangover – he estimates he lost nearly three-quarters-of-a million pounds and his travel business to boot.

"I would never invest in a football club again," he says, "I just feel I'm past my sell-by date. You don't get any thanks from the public for it – none at all. If I personally had gone bankrupt, they wouldn't have cared less. Although I enjoyed my time there, if I'd known what I know now, I would never have become involved in the first place."

Tony Clemo was born in Pwllheli and moved to South Wales when his parents started up a restaurant business in Cardiff in 1958. After leaving school, he worked as a confectionary salesman before qualifying as a teacher at Cardiff Training College – now UWIC – in 1961. Among his contemporaries was the future Olympic gold medalist, long jumper Lyn Davies. Athletics, rather than football, was his main passion during the Sixties and he ran for Wales in the half-mile. Tony spent two years teaching and then bought Red Dragon Travel from the Dewey family who also owned Cardiff City. The company used to organise the club's domestic and European away trips.

"I was approached by Clive Griffiths, an accountant and a Cardiff City nut who was putting together a consortium to buy out David Goldstone in 1975. He thought I would be interested but initially I didn't want to get involved – I had so many other things on the go at the time."

Although retired from athletics, Tony was still coaching with, among others, the late Ron Pickering. He also commentated on

231

the sport and owned a Cardiff nightclub. Against his better judgement, Tony allowed himself to be cajoled by Clive Griffiths into joining the board.

> I also spoke to former manager Jimmy Scoular who said I would really enjoy it and his recommendation convinced me to step in – I think we all put in £20,000 each. My decision might also have had something to do with being a frustrated sportsman. With my physical education background, I like sport which is played at a high level. I was too old to run anymore, I'd had my time and I thought now I could achieve success through another vehicle, football.
>
> But the difference is you've got to rely on eleven guys on the field doing it for you – and they don't do it for you a lot of the time. If I say I'm going to do something in my business, it's going to happen. But football, and indeed all sport, is different. It's not an exact science and you're dealing with human beings. You can do everything right off the park, but if the players don't do it on the field, then you're a loser. The problem is its unpredictability which, of course, is what makes it so fascinating.

Initially though, Tony Clemo's investment in Cardiff City paid dividends. A year after the 1975 takeover, the club were back in Division Two and the board were starting to settle into their new role. "At the beginning, directors don't know what day of the week it is," claims Tony, 'they don't even know where the toilet is! They are taken to the cleaners totally by the manager because they agree to all of his demands. They don't want to upset anyone so they go along with everything he proposes. The problem is that the heart rules the head – instead of the other way round – and smart businessmen start making silly mistakes."

Two years after joining the board, Clemo and his fellow directors were struggling to come to terms with a far more serious problem. The Safety of Sports Ground Bill became law in 1977 and Cardiff City were refused a safety certificate by the local council until Ninian Park had been made safe for spectators. Clemo was unhappy with the way the club were treated:

> There was no common sense, the Act was being interpreted to the letter. The Grangetown Stand had to be demolished in 1978 when the council's safety officers said that if there was two feet of snow and an 80 mile an hour wind blowing, it would be unsafe.

We maintained that if there was two feet of snow and an 80 mile an hour wind, we wouldn't be playing football anyway! They insisted and down it came! It was a total waste of time and money. These guys didn't know where they were going, they were petrified of their own positions in case something went wrong and they were left out on a limb.

Luckily for Cardiff City, chairman Bob Grogan was able to carry out most of the safety work at a reduced rate through his engineering firm Kenton Utilities. His involvement with the club had stemmed from his friendship with Clive Griffiths and lasted until just before his death from cancer in 1983. By that time, his plan to establish rugby league in Cardiff with the Blue Dragons had failed. Grogan was criticised for launching the venture and for living in the North East of England rather than in South Wales but it emerged later that he had been largely instrumental in keeping the club afloat.

Tony Clemo maintain there had been very little investment in Ninian Park before Grogan assumed control and, without his backing, the improvements would not have been carried out:

We were trying to use the ground more and Bob thought rugby league might be worth a try in a rugby area. David Watkins became involved and we had a good couple of seasons. I would go down there every other Sunday because it was a great game to watch but, after an encouraging start, the numbers tailed off to an average 600 gate.

It wasn't costing as much to run as people think. Two or three months of Cardiff City expenses would keep the rugby league team going for a season! It didn't take more than £50,000 to put the whole Blue Dragons together – and, in those days, you couldn't get a single footballer for that kind of money. It was bringing revenue into the club every other Sunday and the social side – especially through the bar – was making a fortune.

We weren't getting many through the gates but rugby league helped to keep Cardiff City going – it certainly wasn't taking money away from the football club as was alleged at the time. The Blue Dragons income was paying the rents and rates and there was always a small profit at the end of the day. But Bob had problems when the team didn't make the top grade of rugby league so the project withered and died after a couple of years.

During his involvement with Cardiff City, Grogan presided over a regular turnover of managers – from Jimmy Andrews to

Len Ashurst – as the club struggled in the late Seventies and early Eighties. As the local man on the spot, Tony Clemo found himself having to do the chairman's bidding:

> It is a very common misconception that I sacked the managers. As a director, my views were sought and considered but I wasn't a dictatorial type. In the end, the decision was Bob's.
>
> Jimmy Andrews went because the results just weren't good enough and we were under pressure from the public. He and Bob were quite friendly so Bob fired him but then, as vice chairman, I became the bearer of bad news. Bob couldn't get down from the North East so he told me to sack Richie Morgan. He was giving the instructions and I was doing all the dirty work.
>
> We were doing OK but we weren't making progress toward the First Division. Richie and coach Brian Harris had done very well in my opinion but the pressure was on in the boardroom for a change – they wanted a big name manager and, for some reason, they went for the ex-Wales full-back Graham Williams, then a health farm manager in Dorset.
>
> Len Ashurst was good appointment – he couldn't save us from relegation but he took us up in 1983 before going off to Sunderland. Then there was the double act of Jimmy Goodfellow and Jimmy Mullen before Goodfellow took over by himself. After we lost six of our first seven league games, panic set in and Jimmy was sacked.

With Grogan's death, his partner in Kenton Utilities, Jack Leonard, had become the majority shareholder in Cardiff City. Again, the search was on for a high-profile manager and it resulted in Alan Durban's appointment in September 1984 and two years of misery for the club's supporters as City dropped into the Fourth Division for the first time.

A month after Durban's departure in May 1986, Tony Clemo took full control of the club and appointed the Sunderland coach Frank Burrows as manager.

> I was left holding the baby to a certain extent. Jack wanted out and there was talk of a consortium putting something together but nothing seemed to be happening. I was worried because I thought that if Jack closed the club down, I'd still be living here. I paid him about £250,000 which gave me 80-odd per cent of the club's shares.

The new chairman's game plan was simple: he would stay for a maximum of three years and hope to gather support from other directors along the way. After a season of consolidation under Burrows, Cardiff City did the 'double' – winning promotion from Division Three and the Welsh Cup in 1988:

> At that moment in time, I said "Right, I've done my bit." I didn't have the money to take us on. "Here it is," I said, "We're up and flying, come in and help." We needed two or three other people to come in with some money and say "C'mon Frank! Let's go again!" – but nobody wanted to know. I was stuck holding the baby again and from then on, it was all downhill.

As well as hooliganism and the need for ground improvements, Tony Clemo was faced with a problem even closer to home. From about 1986, the holiday business went into decline and his company, Red Dragon Travel, started to feel the pinch:

> In the early Eighties we were flying – in every sense of the word. We were turning over £5 million, we had the airline Airways Cymru going but we were hit by a general downward trend in the UK travel business, so much so that big companies like InterSun collapsed taking with them airlines such as Air Europe.
>
> The football club were paying out £50,000 a month in wages – money which wasn't coming in through the gates. We needed somewhere about 6,000 instead of the 3,000 we were getting. We were losing about £2,000 a week. We didn't lack ambition but we did lack money.
>
> During the dark days of 1990-91, it was hard but, contrary to what some people say, cheques were not bouncing. Players' cheques were re-presented and then they were cleared. It was tight, we were living from hand to mouth because we'd been relegated and the crowds understandably weren't coming in. You cannot survive on crowds of 3,000.

According to Tony Clemo, Cardiff City owed Red Dragon more than £350,000. The money had been used to pay football club wages over the years and, following the slump in the holiday industry, the company, under pressure from the bank, wanted it repaid. The whole operation was tottering:

> It was like a pack of cards and, in the end, I had to choose between my business or the club going under. My feeling at the time was if Red Dragon goes, who'll remember? If Cardiff City goes, I'll go down in history as the chairman of the club when it collapsed. That was one of the reasons I tried to keep it going – I felt I had a duty to look after

the club for the people of Cardiff. I had no option but I would dearly have liked to have kept my travel business. Looking back, I think the bank could have supported me better – that's why I'm taking legal action against them now.

Tony Clemo's knight in shining armour appeared to ride into town when Rick Wright took an interest in Cardiff City in 1991. A former Army frogman and commercial diver, Wright was a self-made businessman who had transformed Barry Island's Majestic Holiday Camp. As Tony Clemo struggled to deal with a growing financial crisis, there were consortium and takeover rumours before Wright made his move. Initially, Clemo was grateful for the helping hand:

I didn't know him from a bar of soap but he seemed a nice, plausible guy. I was under enormous pressure and he said he would help me out of a bit of a difficulty. I had the council trying to repossess the ground, the bank were on my back about my travel business and I was sitting there on my own wondering if we're going to get next month's wages. Rick Wright put in £30,000 to help deal with that problem and then he got more and more involved. He said he'd sort things out and he put in more money to cover us as we went along.

He paid the wages of a couple of Second Division players who we bought to try to reach the play-offs but we just missed out. I thought I'd found the person I'd been looking for at last but the more he got his feet under the table, the more I felt duty bound to go along with it. There was a lot of acrimony and, in the end, I'd had enough and I walked away. I sold my shares to him but I didn't get the money – that went to the bank who turned us over six months later when Red Dragon Travel went into receivership. I'd saved the club but we couldn't save my business.

The £350,000 which the club owed us had to be written off and the bank foreclosed on Red Dragon in October 1991. The company is back in existence because of my legal action against the bank but it's not trading.

Tony Clemo stayed on as chairman until the end of the 1991-92 season and then severed his links with Cardiff City after seventeen years on the board. "I was relieved in one way to get away from Wright because we eventually didn't get on very well at all, yet I was sorry because of my long association with the club. But once I'd made the break, it was amazing how quickly I found other things to do on a Saturday afternoon."

By the time Tony Clemo had raised the white flag, Frank Burrows had moved on, via Portsmouth, to Swansea City where he would spend four years. With Eddie May having replaced Len Ashurst as manager, Cardiff City completed another 'double' by winning the Third Division Championship and the Welsh Cup in Rick Wright's second season in charge.

Under Wright, Ninian Park underwent a facelift similar to the one carried out on his holiday camp. Seats were installed on part of the Bob Bank, the Grandstand roofing was extended to cover the family enclosure as the idiosyncratic millionaire began to reawaken the sleeping giant. Admission prices went up if the team did well and down if they didn't, the Junior Bluebirds Club took off and the feelgood factor returned to Ninian Park with a vengeance. Cardiff City bade an impressive farewell to Division Three with a 3-0 win at Scunthorpe United and then beat Rhyl 5-0 to win the Welsh Cup.

The canny Wright had taken out an insurance policy on Cardiff City doing the 'double' which resulted in a £1.4 million payout. The supporters flocked to Ninian Park in their thousands as 'Ayatollah fever' took hold. The roots of this peculiar craze lay in the scenes of despair witnessed at the Ayatollah Khomeni's funeral when thousands of Iranians beat themselves around the head – many using rocks – as part of the mourning process. For the next couple of years, pockets of Cardiff City supporters sporting tea towels on their heads, could be spotted on the terraces 'doing the Ayatollah' – minus the rocks.

Utility player Roger Gibbins says that when the craze started he didn't know what was happening:

> The fans started putting their hands on their heads and singing and when it caught on, they started asking the players to do it. We were doing it and I didn't know why! The last game of the season at Scunthorpe was incredible with about four of the five thousand supporters there dressed up as the Ayatollah. It was strange but fantastic, everyone was doing it – including Eddie May and the chairman!

But then, with Cardiff City in Europe and the party in full swing, the music suddenly stopped. Rick Wright, self-publicist supreme, attracted more headlines when, almost Ayatollah-like, he showed everyone who possessed the real power. He had promised to stay at Ninian Park for two years and he was as good as his word.

The former Football League and F.I.F.A. referee, Jim Finney, worked under Rick Wright as Cardiff City's secretary. He says the problem stemmed from the owner's lack of interest in the game:

> He was going and that was the end of it. Had he issued season tickets out straight after the Welsh Cup win, we would have made a killing but he wanted out. Unfortunately, the business community of Cardiff didn't back him. It was fantastic working under Rick – I couldn't fault him in a lot of ways. He was a man who made a decision to do something and then did it, but I was very disappointed when he just walked out. Had he stayed, I think we could have made more progress – he was that sort of charismatic man.

Now managing Merthyr Tydfil in the Dr Martens Premier Division, Roger Gibbins has few fond memories of Rick Wright.

> He was not my favourite person because he decided that Cardiff City could do without an assistant coach and I was sacked. I had spent nine years at Ninian Park in two spells and it was obvious that if a club of Cardiff's size wanted to do well, the coach or manager must have some help.
>
> Wright had his good points and he did a lot to improve Ninian Park and bring the place to life again, but if you had a poll of the fans and asked them about his contribution and the way he left Cardiff, he probably wouldn't be everybody's flavour-of-the-month.

Eddie May was another frustrated member of the Ninian Park staff when Rick Wright pulled the plug. Having narrowly missed the play-offs in his first season as coach, it all had come together with the 'double'. Eddie recalls that the celebrations were short-lived:

> From the day Rick came in, there had been a buzz about the place. He mentioned that he would be leaving towards the end of the 1993 season and raised the subject again when we were in Geneva for the European Cup Winners Cup draw in July.
>
> "You won't leave here," I said, "not with the way things are!"
>
> "Watch this space!" Rick typically replied.
>
> I think he had made up his mind to go to live in Australia. We got on very well but I think his decision had a lot to do with his family who

wanted to go there. Unfortunately, afterwards the team fell apart – we lost six of the championship side and we didn't replace them so we struggled during the 1993-94 season. Rick seemed to communicate more and more from Down Under and then a consortium put together by Cardiff City's vice chairman Michael Boyce, which involved Terry Yorath being coach, tried to take the club over on a sort of trial basis before the whole thing went pear-shaped in April 1995.

From August 1993, Wright had held discussions with the world and his wife as he tried to dispose of Cardiff City. Boxing promoters Frank Warren and Frank Maloney were among those interested in the £500,000 asking price in March 1994 but it was Michael Boyce's consortium which nearly pulled it off. Working under the slogan 'Premier Football for a Premier City', the consortium made three attempts to do a deal. They even commissioned a feasibility study of Ninian Park from the Tarmac Construction Group. Their 'master plan' for the redevelopment of Ninian Park was priced at £4.6 million with the club paying nearly £2 million towards the cost.

By January 1995, the takeover price had risen to £800,000 but Wright objected to the involvement of marketing executive Jim Cadman so the consortium's first bid failed. Lack of consultation between Cardiff City and South Glamorgan County Councils scuppered the second attempt a month later. The third and final bid fell through at the eleventh hour in June 1995. The consortium had decided that about £1 million would be needed to take over the club – £850,000 to buy Wright's shares and pay off every creditor and £150,000 as working capital. When South Glamorgan County Council refused to guarantee the Co-operative Bank's loan of the money over the following two seasons, the consortium had to admit defeat and an outsider Samesh Kumar stepped in with a bid said to be worth £850,000.

With business interests in clothing and real estate, Kumar had spent three-and-a-half years as chairman of Birmingham City until the collapse of the Bank of Credit and Commerce of India forced him to resign. Birmingham had won the Leyland Daf Trophy in 1991 under Lou Macari in their first visit to Wembley before the manager left for Stoke City. His replacements Ian Atkins and Terry Cooper then won Birmingham promotion to Division Two. Kumar recalls how he became involved with Cardiff City:

I had been out of football for a couple of years and I was beginning to miss it. I only really wanted to get involved with a club which had potential and Cardiff was up there with the best of them. When I arrived at Birmingham, most people said to me: 'the situation's too far gone – you'll never rescue it' but I managed to take that club out of intensive care and within three years, we were in a comfortable situation with the bank who had wanted to get out. We refurbished the stadium's facilities, we stabilised things and built some solid foundations for the club to progress.

With Cardiff, I was told the situation was worse and when I arrived, I discovered an old ground with no facilities and a team which had just been relegated to the old Fourth Division. There were two people working in the office, the club had no bank, the playing squad was weak and all the best assets had already left.

Cardiff was a club which nobody wanted – it was considered too big a job. When I look at what's happened to clubs like Oxford, Luton and Portsmouth, who are all facing very difficult financial problems, and the way we virtually eradicated hooliganism at Cardiff – from about six arrests or ejections per match to fewer than three a season – then I feel a degree of achievement. It had always been a priority of mine to make Ninian Park a safe ground to visit – so that women and children could return to football as a whole and to Cardiff in particular.

After being appointed by him in the summer of 1994, Samesh Kumar's former fiancée, Joan Hill, played a key role in transforming Cardiff City's image She had been commercial manager at Peterborough and Birmingham before joining Lincoln City as head of marketing and then becoming chief executive at Ninian Park. Kumar assesses her contribution until her departure in May 1999:

Under Joan, the club had made good commercial progress. She wore her heart on her sleeve and added an awful lot of fire, as well as heart and soul to the place. She used all her experience to build up commercial and administrative departments from a very small staff and made the whole thing look more professional. All of sudden, we were acquiring a reputation for having the best hospitality in football. Visiting directors, sponsors and football people all felt welcome – in fact, the greatest accolade that I've received in the last couple of years was from Richard Scudamore, the Football League's chief executive, who, as part of his job, has probably visited every club.

He went on record saying that he enjoyed coming to Cardiff the most – he couldn't believe the hospitality he received. That was one of the reasons I was able to convince Frank Burrows to join us. He told me he had heard that we were going places, that we had really taken off and Joan deserves all the credit for that.

Supporters rightly only associate success with the team's performance – whether they got promotion or won a cup. By those yardsticks, I think we were successful.

In Kumar's first season in charge, Cardiff, under chief coach, Kenny Hibbitt, finished third from bottom but reached the play-offs in 1996-97. When the former Liverpool and England full-back Phil Neal was appointed manager and then abruptly left to join Manchester City, Hibbitt returned from his director of football post and, alongside newly-appointed Russell Osman, managed to steer the club to a play-off semi-final defeat by Northampton Town who eventually beat Swansea City at Wembley. Hibbitt was in charge for most of the 1997-98 season before Frank Burrows returned and won the club promotion in May 1999. His only serious rival for the job was Colin Addison, the present Scarborough manager then at Merthyr. After making a few enquiries, Kumar decided that Frank Burrows fitted the bill.

When Burrows returned to Ninian Park in February 1998, Cardiff were heading towards one of their worst-ever seasons. They finished fifth from bottom and drew half their 46 league games. A 2-1 home defeat by Macclesfield in late April proved a turning point. As usual, a number of the club's vice-presidents had travelled to the match – including Philip Jardine, a Cardiff solicitor and Steve Borley, a director and later to become club chairman, who runs an engineering company in the city.

"We were third from bottom of the Third Division, it was possibly the lowest point in the club's history and we had to endure Macclesfield celebrating their promotion," recalls Jardine. "A few of the regulars in the boardroom, who weren't yet directors, looked at each other and said: 'we can't allow this to happen again.' Almost immediately, we held a meeting of like-minded individuals in my office at Morgan Cole and invited along Frank Burrows and Paul Guy. Paul is the club's vice chairman and a well-respected Cardiff-based property developer who had already, with fellow directors Bob Phillips and David Temme, injected a huge amount of their own money to help the club keep going. We wanted to know if we could make a difference and become involved in the football club. Frank said the financing of his plans for the future was within our reach for the following season."

The 1995 Bosman Ruling barred transfer fees for players out of contract and removed limits on the number of foreign players a club could sign. It was to prove crucial to Cardiff City's revival.

"Frank was looking to use Bosman to bring in new players and he wanted about £300,000 to re-build the team," recalls Steve Borley. "We had released quite a few of the first-team squad and he needed money to pay the signing-on fees and re-location expenses for about half a dozen players."

"We were a collection of twelve largely self-employed businessmen in a variety of different fields ranging from computers to engineering," says Jardine, a City supporter from Pontymister for the last thirty years. "None of us had amassed huge amounts of wealth but we all had a passion for the football club. It became obvious that our relatively small sums when put together could actually achieve the amount Frank needed. Two people put in six-figure sums and the rest was made up of smaller donations of between five and ten thousand pounds."

The supporter-investors received shares in the football club in and were represented by two new directors on the board – Jardine and Rhondda-born computer systems programmer Mike Price. Kim Walker, a Newbridge builder, later joined on a similar basis. The new investment meant Samesh Kumar lost his controlling interest in the club.

In the last three years up to 1999, Cardiff City had lost about one-and-a-half-million pounds; they don't own their own ground – Ninian Park is leased to the club by the City Council – and, at the end of the 1997-98 season, they were one of the worst teams in the Football League. So why did a group of self-made businessmen want to invest a not inconsiderable amount of their money in what appeared to be, at best, a loss leader?

Steve Borley was born and brought up in Cardiff and worked his way up from apprentice to general manager with a national engineering company before setting up his own business CMB six years ago. His childhood home was in St. Donat's Close, behind Ninian Park's Bob Bank.

> I became involved with Cardiff City because I believe I could change things. It's not a case of making money – I have a genuine feeling for the football club. My grandmother lived in Sloper Road, three doors away from the ground and I remember seeing people climbing over her walls to get in without paying.
>
> I watched my first game against Hull City in 1970 from the Grange End. City won 5-1, John Toshack scored a hat-trick in his last home game before joining Liverpool, and I picked up Bobby Woodruff's sock tie-ups!
>
> I could see that the club were shipping big losses and I felt that I could attract some investment and help turn things around. We may have lost money over the last year or so but I believe that, with the way football is changing these days, the value of a club is in the badge on the shirt and the league status. If nothing else, we've increased the value of the club by pushing that badge into the Second Division. The days are gone when the players and the ground are a club's assets – in my view, the only asset these days is the badge.

Philip Jardine's commitment to the club is no less keen but, by his own admission, he lacks the financial clout of the other directors. Nevertheless, he belives that a wide range of people and skills has produced an effective Ninian Park board:

> Paul Guy is an astute businessman with an excellent understanding of financial and accounting matters, Bob Phillips has tremendous experience in the leisure industry and a well-known commitment to fostering Welsh sport. He has also been instrumental in introducing a state-of-the-art computerised ticketing system into Ninian Park for which he has received very little credit.
>
> David Temme's property and construction background is proving most valuable to the club while Mike Price has brought his IT expertise to bear and has already been responsible for promoting a number of excellent commercial initiatives like the Bank One Bluebird credit card and the Cardiff City Internet web site. Kim Walker another long-standing City fan, who has created a very successful building company and his and Steve Borley's knowledge will help with any future developments of the ground. It's hugely prestigious to be a director of a football club and I'm very proud to be one. But I'm on the board to see if can make a difference, to help Cardiff City achieve what I believe it should achieve – ultimately a place in the Premiership.

As the 1998-99 season wended its way to its nerve-racking conclusion, chairman Samesh Kumar and his growing band of fledgling directors were faced with a dilemma. The rave reviews being garlanded by full-back Mark Delaney had attracted the attention of a host of scouts and there were strong rumours that Cardiff were going to sell their hottest property: they were about to do another Toshack and transfer one of their best players as promotion beckoned.

After playing a mere 28 league games since joining from League of Wales side Carmarthen Town for nothing, Delaney had made huge strides under Frank Burrows. The Portsmouth connection – Burrows had worked under John Gregory in the late Eighties – was instrumental in the Aston Villa manager making an offer at the beginning of March. Delaney could join the nearest Premiership club to Cardiff for the staggering sum of half a million pounds! With City having just been replaced by Cambridge at the top of the Third Division, some support-ers began to wonder whether Cardiff would win promotion – some even questioned the club's ambition.

"There were a number of offers on the table,' recalls Steve Borley, "and this one was just too good to turn down. We received half of the money the day Mark signed and because we were operating the club on a Second rather than a Third Division budget, we needed the money. We were losing a lot but not as much as the previous season."

"When Frank returned," says Samesh Kumar, "I wanted him not to have to worry about achieving overnight success. He needed the time to bring in youngsters and to improve them. I told him the name of the game was obviously a winning team which I was sure we would have. But I also wanted to build up this club and if that meant we had to sell a player or two every season, then that was the name of the game too. I wanted to make sure that we didn't lose so much money that we couldn't reinvest any sales in players. I regretted having to sell Mark Delaney but we were on course to lose a million pounds. I would have liked to have kept him but it was half a million pounds for a full-back playing in what was the old Fourth Division!"

"I deny the claim that we sold our ambition along with one

of our best players," says Steve Borley. "It's a fact of life that 82 of the 92 Football League clubs have to sell to survive. If we hadn't gone up, it would have been the result of results – too many draws – rather than the sale of Mark Delaney."

"We did lose the attacking option he offered," concedes Philip Jardine, "but one player doesn't make a team. There is an argument that if you transfer a 30-goal striker, then you are selling the club down the river but not in the case of a full back. A fee of that size for a Third Division full-back is unheard of."

When promotion was finally secured with an understandably tense 0-0 draw against Scunthorpe United at Ninian Park on May 1st, the board's decision to sell Delaney was vindicated. A huge wave of relief swept around the ground – from the Canton Stand, across to the Bob Bank and the Grange End and on into the Grandstand and the directors box – depositing the new chairman onto the floor. "It was an amazing feeling really," Steve recalls "because the tension throughout the last month of the season had been incredible as we inched towards the finishing line. I didn't travel to Southend but I couldn't bear to listen to the game on the radio – we won 1-0. When the final whistle went against Scunthorpe, it felt as if a huge weight had been lifted from my shoulders. My legs went and I fell onto my knees!

"There was a tremendous release of emotion," says Philip Jardine, "and I think we all felt pleased for each other because we'd achieved our objective. It had been very much a team effort from day one. For every other promotion, I had been on the pitch so it was nice to be up in the Grandstand this time!"

The celebrations were barely over when Samesh Kumar dropped his bombshell. Less than a week after the Scunthorpe game, he unexpectedly announced his resignation. At the end of a normal lengthy board meeting, the chairman gave the directors a letter which contained his surprise decision.

"It seemed strange," says Steve Borley, "but thinking back, he seemed to be on edge throughout the meeting. He gave no reason for his resignation in his letter but told us that he had considered going nine months earlier but decided to stay on to support Frank Burrows."

Kumar then withdrew to allow his colleagues to discuss the letter and returned to hear that they had accepted his resignation. As the owner of just over a million shares – about 35 per cent of the club – the former chairman would leave Cardiff City but remain on the board. The question remained too: with the club in such a healthy position both on and off the field, why did he resign?

It seems that Samesh Kumar felt that certain members of the board were undermining his position at the club through their relationship with some office staff and the manager. Despite setting Cardiff City on their way with promotion, in these circumstances he felt it was better to leave Ninian Park:

> I had made my decision at the beginning of last season but I stayed because I felt obliged to – I had just appointed Frank as manager. It didn't seem right to go so soon afterwards, I knew he needed my full support because we had long-term plans for Cardiff City.
>
> Certain things were happening behind the scenes which I felt were undermining my position at the club and making it untenable, to the lasting detriment of Cardiff City. I'm not prepared to go into them – it's not my style. They were making me very unhappy but I tried to keep them from everybody at the club, especially the manager.
>
> I had established a marvellous relationship with Frank and I'd wanted him to be totally focused on promotion – I had no doubt that we would go up last season. My biggest regret in football, if not life, is that I felt I had to resign from Cardiff. It was heartbreaking.

It appears that the move to relieve Joan Hill of her duties as chief executive played a significant part in Kumar's decision to leave. A week after his announcement, she returned from helping to organise the Football Legends exhibition in London and then left for a 'well-earned holiday'. The former chairman is unhappy about the way in which backroom staff are treated:

> There's a unique type of person who works in the football industry. When the team's winning, these people don't get any attention or accolades – fair enough, that's for the players and the manager – but when the team loses, they take the brunt. The board take the flack to a degree, but by and large, it's the people who are the hub of the club who have to accept a great deal of unfair criticism. They have to go in every day, phone the sponsors and they sometimes work very unsocial hours.
>
> When we start to lose sight of them and how they make a football club special – and they don't always have to be the best at their job – then something's wrong.

Joan is someone who I consider to be a very important individual but the problem went deeper than that. It also involved Frank. Some members of the board were talking to him without consulting me beforehand. When it got to that point, I had to draw the line. I couldn't give him my one hundred per cent attention because I was being undermined when I was trying to make various decisions.

Samesh Kumar's allegations of boardroom skulduggery have been vehemently denied by the remaining Cardiff City directors. Philip Jardine resents any suggestion that they interfered in any way with the relationship between Frank Burrows and the chairman. "In fact, as far as Frank was concerned," says Jardine, "having given him the finances to rebuild the team throughout the whole season, we deliberately took a hands-off approach when it came to footballing matters. They were entirely his preserve."

For legal reasons, no Cardiff City director is able to comment on Joan Hill's departure from Ninian Park. A month after resigning, Samesh Kumar put his shares up for sale through an advert in the *Financial Times*:

I'll just see what people are prepared to offer. I might get involved with another club which would mean having to sell my interest in Cardiff City but I don't need the money. The most important thing is that Frank Burrows and his assistant Billy Ayre are staying at Ninian Park.

Whatever he chooses to do, there is no doubt that Cardiff City owe Samesh Kumar a huge debt. He bought the club when Rick Wright had tired of football and his successor pays tribute to the work carried out by the former chairman over the last four years as Cardiff City reached Division Two. "Sam came in when nobody else would", says Steve Borley, 'and for some time, he ran the club with little or no help. It's in a far healthier state thanks to him than it was back in 1994."

During his spell at Ninian Park, Samesh Kumar received his fair share of personal abuse from supporters – usually over the team's poor performances, the financial state of the club and especially over the sale of Mark Delaney. But like any football club chairman, he knew that criticism comes with the territory. For instance, Tony Clemo was a regular target of supporter unrest during the late Eighties and early Nineties:

The insults didn't get to me personally because they were part and parcel of the position. You're chairman of the club and you're there to be shot at – you take it on the chin or you get out. It wasn't very pleasant sitting in the directors box and having people standing up and shouting abuse at me but I was doing the best I could in the circumstances. If they were so bloody keen why didn't they come forward to help?

But there was no need for the amount of flack my wife Linda took. She was often stopped in the street and harangued by supporters. She's quite a tough cooky and she gave as good as she got, but it wasn't nice. It's the old story: when the club's doing well, it's all down to the manager. When it's doing badly, it's all down to the bloody chairman and his board. It's all about bottomless pits of money in football. It's a hard fact of life that you don't make any unless you're Man United or Arsenal.

It certainly helped having Frank Burrows around. He's the only manager I've come across who was thinking as the managing director as well as the manager. He would always have the financial position of the club at the back of his mind. He could see the problem and he did his best to help out. Of course, it was in his interest too because his wages were dependent on a successful club.

There are always three barren months at the end of every season and Frank was fantastic about the problem.

"How're we looking Mr Chairman?" he'd ask.

"Not too bad," I'd say, "although we're struggling a bit."

"Don't worry," replied Frank. "I've just sold so and so for x thousand pounds _ that should get us through the summer!"

We had to sell Mike Ford for a record £150,000 to Oxford to pay the bills at the end of the season in 1988 – some went to the tax man and the rest took care of the summer wages.

Since resigning as Cardiff City chairman in 1975, David Goldstone has spent nearly twenty-five years building Regalian Properties into one of the biggest development companies in Britain. He once owned Land's End and his company built the new London HQ of the spy agency MI6 in Vauxhall Cross and the *Financial Times* Building in Southwark Bridge. Regalian Properties are currently refurbishing the Marble Arch Tower. He says rugby, rather than football, is his main sporting interest now:

I think I made a contribution to Cardiff City but unfortunately we did not achieve our ambitions – life is often like that. I've been invited on many occasions to go back into soccer but I didn't think it was appropriate. I miss the camaraderie but I don't miss the stress. At the moment, I'm fairly heavily involved in London Welsh rugby club as a director and deputy chairman and that's enough for my limited appetite. Cardiff City did very well last season and although I know nothing about their financial circumstances, I assume they are regulating their affairs appropriately. I regret that it was necessary for me to leave because I am a football enthusiast – I still keep an eye on the Welsh clubs' results.

Hard on the heels of Samesh Kumar's resignation in May 1999, the club announced that promotion to the Second Division would hit supporters in the pocket. Prices were being dramatically increased with the cheapest season ticket rising from £96 to £170.

"It's a big hike but we've had a very favourable response from supporters," says Steve Borley. "Sales have taken off despite the increase and by the middle of June 1999, we'd sold £320,000 worth of season tickets compared with £80,000 at the same point the previous year. Just to put the price rise in perspective, Forest Green Rovers in the Conference charged £150 for their 1998-99 season tickets."

"It's a question of value for money," says Philip Jardine. "We're playing a better quality of football in a higher division and, as with any industry, people will pay if the product is good enough."

New admission charges, a new chairman and a new season but what price the beginnings of a new era? Is the growing feeling that Cardiff City are about to wake up after six years of slumber justified or will the old habit of failing to capitalise on a promising position return to haunt them again? Are the optimists being carried away on a tide of euphoria or are the foundations for a successful start to the Millennium being laid down at Ninian Park?

The answers to these and a whole series of questions may be known at the end of Cardiff City's centenary season but it's impossible to avoid a feeling of *déjà vu*. After the 1988 promotion, a combination of a shortage of money and occupational hazards forced Tony Clemo to sell out to Rick Wright who, in turn, lost interest in the beautiful game and, true to his word, disappeared Down Under. Now the sleeping giant of South

Wales has another chance to wake up but not everyone is sure that the opportunity will be taken.

Steve Borley is a Cardiff City fanatic who played for Llanrumney Mad Dogs, a city parks team he helped to form. Indeed, some people might say that the 41-year-old chairman has indeed taken leave of his senses in taking over at Ninian Park. Others maintain that the former goalkeeper possesses a very safe pair of hands.

"I think the club will make progress under Steve," says Cardiff's former secretary Jim Finney, who works closely as a consultant with club secretary Ceri Whitehead. "He's got a good board of directors behind him and he strikes me as a man who makes a promise and carries it out. There's a wonderful feeling about the club now – it's better than it was in 1993 – and I'm predicting great things. The sponsorship potential here is astronomical. There are one or two companies already nibbling and I just hope they get behind Steve Borley. I've been around, I've seen clubs come and go and this is one place where I sincerely hope the awakening giant is going to roar."

The new chairman wasted no time in trying to raise the money which everybody agrees is needed for Cardiff City to move forward. Plans are being made to raise over £1 million through the issue of new shares. "It is a brave decision to take," says Steve "but it tells people that we have an open door policy and they can help make the club a success. We've opened people's eyes and shown them what's possible, the supporters are hungry for success and I believe we will reach our target. A substantial part of the money will be made available to Frank to strengthen the team and we're hoping to finally complete the executive boxes in the Canton Stand."

More than £100,000 has been spent during the summer on increasing Ninian Park's capacity to 16,500 – especially at the Grane End. "Obviously we have to work within our budget," says director Philip Jardine. "It's a case of doing what we can, when we can. The structure for the fifteen executive boxes is there – it's now a case of fitting them out during the next twelve months."

From his detached position as an occasional spectator, former chairman Tony Clemo agrees with the board's priorities:

The bulk of the money has to go towards strengthening the team. It's no good saying you're going to improve the ground – if you haven't got a team, forget the stadium. Some of the money will need to be spent on modernising Ninian Park but it's going to be difficult to get out of Division Two this season. The top six or seven teams will be spending money and unless someone comes along with a substantial investment then Cardiff City won't get past the First Division and into the Premiership.

I've lived in Cardiff for more than forty years and businessmen I speak to, like Stan and Peter Thomas, are into rugby, which is their choice. They don't like football – if they did, I'm sure they'd be there.

So, in the absence of a philanthropic millionaire, will there be enough companies in Cardiff and South Wales willing to lend their support to the city's football team? In the past, there has been little sign that the business community cares enough about the future of Cardiff City. Steve Borley believes the problem is not confined to his football club alone:

Both the Welsh football and rugby teams and the League of Wales can't attract sponsorship worthy of the name. Wales is full of very large plcs who, for various reasons, want to remain anonymous or whose headquarters are outside of Wales. Cardiff is being billed as Europe's fastest-growing capital city but it's difficult to attract sponsorship because most of the new companies setting up here are outsiders. They don't appear to be interested in any of the country's sporting activities.

It looks nigh-on impossible to attract one large company so we're looking at a few. As individual directors, we may be financially weak but collectively we can be strong and the same applies to our search for commercial backers. Back in the Fifties under Sir Herbert Merrett, Cardiff City were so successful in terms of playing in the First Division, they didn't need to worry about the off-the-field activities – the gate receipts were more than adequate fund the operation of a football club. But when you're not so strong, you need the commercial side to help sustain the business and we've not exploited the ground enough.

Two of the handful of journalists who have covered Cardiff City for the *Football Echo* over the last forty years, Peter Corrigan and Peter Jackson, are reasonably optimistic about the club's future.

Peter Corrigan, now at the *Independent on Sunday,* says that Cardiff have never suffered from an excess of philanthropy

Directors get involved because they want to help – and they stick their money in because they're enthusiasts. But when you're talking about people like Jack Walker at Blackburn who pour money into a team, they're just not about in Wales.

Everything Cardiff City have done, they've had to do more or less as a club and the only way you're going to do it is if you get big crowds through the turnstiles. I wonder whether they will?

Cardiff City have given us a focal point for civic pride – we have a lovely civic centre but you can only show that to visitors. "How did the City get on?" is the question on a Saturday evening. Not "How did Cardiff Rugby Club do?" Even when you go down to the Arms Park, it's the same question. It's part of us.

I remember receiving a letter from a vicar who said that football is like religion. Everybody has got their church, they don't go to it but it's there – "that's my church" they say. It's the same with football – people say "that's my football club". And I don't think it ever leaves you. When you get a little bit of flurry, you suddenly find that 20,000 people will turn out to watch a cup-tie! Most of the time they couldn't care less but they're there for the big occasion. I'm beginning to think it's there still with Cardiff. With what's happening in the city, especially with the Millennium Stadium, I'm more optimistic than I've been since the Sixties.

Peter Jackson, of the *Daily Mail*, also believes that the Millennium Stadium could have a role to play – but not until well into the twenty-first century:

> The advent of Premiership football means the gap between the twenty top teams and First Division football has widened to a depressing extent. Historically, Cardiff City have never been very good at investing from a positive position – in other words, supplementing a team that's winning as opposed to shoring up one that's losing. The new Millennium Stadium would give them the perfect facility. It's far better than anything in the Premiership but, at best, we're five or ten years from ever having a team which could play in it.

Former managing director Ron Jones has returned to Ninian Park having completed the circle. His football career began as sprint coach to Queens Park Rangers and he now fills a similar role with Cardiff City as well as working with Welsh Sports Aid:

> I remember our chairman Bob Grogan being interviewed during the euphoria of the 1983 promotion. He said everything was right at the club but now it really depended on people outside.
>
> The same thing applies now: Cardiff City could be a good invest-

ment for a company or companies in the city. If they're going to make the Premiership, they need corporate support which they haven't had in the past – apart from the small entrepreneurs. The fans have got to support the team, even if they lose a few matches, and if the supporters come along in their thousands, then they'll get a Premier League club in due course.

We've got to get back into the habit of supporting soccer as we did in the post-war years but inevitably it's money that will make or break a club down here. Shouting for the team is very important but you have to have the team there to shout at first. If you don't have the money, you don't have the team.

A clarion call from the current boardroom sounds a slightly different note. Philip Jardine, a director for just over a year, believes that although finance obviously has an important role to play in Cardiff City's revival, it won't be enough on its own to move the club forward.

Our promotion has given me a heightened belief that Cardiff City can actually do something about the 'sleeping giant' tag. We all feel that we can now go forward and give Wales the Premier League football club it deserves. The people of Wales have been cheated in my lifetime because they haven't had a top-flight club. Wales needs Cardiff City to be successful.

If we begin winning honours, our success will have a far greater impact on the Welsh economy than rugby can ever achieve. Football is the world's number one game and rugby is a minority sport by comparison. It's going to be a long, hard road but we've got the fans, the passion and the vision and we will get there. Money is a vital ingredient but clubs like Wimbledon, Charlton and Leicester didn't get to the Premiership on the back of money alone.

Tony Clemo was one of the longest-serving board members in Cardiff City's history. Sid Nicholls, Walter Parker and Sir Herbert Merrett were three of his predecessors who, like him, put their hands in their own pockets to keep the club going.

A passionate love of the sport seems to draw in successful businessmen but a poor return on their investment usually drives them away; Sir Herbert Merrett and Rick Wright proving the rare exceptions. When the football bug bites, so intoxicating are the potential rewards that its victim is often helpless to resist.

Tony Clemo may have sacrificed his company on the altar of

professional football but he still takes a keen interest in the game through Sky TV and he's back in the travel business organising Welsh international trips abroad.

"My involvement with Wales is enough for me now," he says, "I really enjoy it. I might go down to Ninian Park once in a blue moon but I'm not interested in following them week in, week out. I do keep an eye on their results though. I've still got a couple of hundred shares in the club and I go along to the AGM. I'm interested in how they get on because I'll always have a soft spot for Cardiff City – especially with Frank being there."

# Never Go Back?

Cyril Spiers did it. So did Len Ashurst. Eddie May had a go too. And so, after a fashion, did Kenny Hibbitt as well. In all, five men have twice managed Cardiff City in the last hundred years. Three of them won promotion in the Football League but only one has taken a team up during both his spells at Ninian Park.

Frank by name and by nature, the latest manager to challenge the maxim 'never go back', created history when Cardiff City were promoted on May 1st 1999. Having taken the club up in 1988, Frank Burrows then repeated the feat eleven years later. Different decades, different teams but the same single-minded determination.

To be fair to Spiers, the side he created won the Division Three South Championship in 1947 immediately after he left after a disagreement over money. He then took Cardiff back to the First Division five years later. But the history books show that Frank Burrows is unique. He alone has returned to the scene of his greatest triumph and succeeded for the second time.

Frankie didn't go to Hollywood but he's a star – as far as the players, the directors and the supporters of Cardiff City are concerned. The feeling is mutual: The Gaffer's pretty keen on Cardiff City – love, in football if not in life, can indeed be sweeter second time around. But there's one marriage vow which must not be broken.

"I've worked in South Wales with two great clubs at Cardiff and Swansea," says Frank, "and I sold a lot of players during my time at both. If Cardiff City don't match my ambition, then it's not for me – I'll step aside and let a younger man take over. At the moment, I haven't a clue how long this romance will last. If we can keep going forward, then I would love to stay here."

Frank Burrows arrived at Ninian Park in the aftermath of the

Alan Durban débacle in the summer of 1986. For the first time in their history, Cardiff City found themselves in Division Four and their new owner Tony Clemo, having bought out Jack Leonard and Kenton Utilities, decided that the Sunderland coach was the man to turn the club around.

"Frank's name had come up when a lot of contenders were being bandied around," recalls Clemo. "I spoke to Len Ashurst and he gave me a very good recommendation. We instantly clicked – I just had this feeling about Frank. He didn't want a contract – he said he'd do the job for two years and see how we got on and that's what happened."

Like Len Ashurst, Frank Burrows was steeped in football. He had begun his career as a no-nonsense centre-half with Raith Rovers for whom he played part-time while completing a six-year engineering apprenticeship at a local whisky distillery. In 1965, he moved south to Scunthorpe Utd and then on to Swindon Town where he helped the Wiltshire club beat Arsenal 3-1 in the 1969 League Cup Final at Wembley. The future – and now former – Welsh manager Bobby Gould was one of many centre-forwards to find themselves shackled by the tough-tackling Scotsman as Swindon produced one of the greatest cup upsets of the last thirty years.

After coaching at Swindon, his first managerial job took him to Fourth Division Portsmouth who gained promotion in 1980 and Burrows then went on to coach at Southampton and Sunderland before moving to Cardiff.

The new manager shared Len Ashurst's ability to play the free transfer market well. New signings included Welsh international Alan Curtis from Southampton, Southend's Alan Rogers and Graham Moseley, a former F.A.Cup Final goalkeeper with Brighton, while Jimmy Goodfellow returned to the club as assistant manager and physiotherapist.

Inconsistency plagued City as they finished a mediocre 13th in the Fourth Division but reached the fourth round of both the F.A. and Littlewoods Cups. Average home gates dropped to below 3,000 for the first time with a 4-0 home win over Hartlepool attracting a crowd of 1,510 – the lowest ever home league attendance. Desperate rather than happy days were here again.

The close season saw Burrows making good use of the £100,000 Cardiff received from Watford for goalkeeper Mel Rees. With some money to play with, the shrewd Scot started to establish his reputation as one of the most successful operators in the lower divisions. Shrewsbury's Mark Kelly, Nigel Stevenson from Swansea, Oxford's Brian McDermott and Phil Bater from Brentford all arrived on free transfers while a cheque for £17,500 secured the services of striker Jimmy Gilligan and softened the blow of Lincoln City losing their league status. Top scorer Gilligan was to play a key role in Cardiff's 'double' as the club finished runners-up to Wolves in Division Three and beat Wrexham 2-0 in the Welsh Cup Final at the Vetch Field in Swansea.

But it all turned sour during the following season when lack of money undermined Cardiff's attempt to capitalise on promotion. Little of the £150,000 raised from Mike Ford's sale was reinvested in players as City struggled against relegation before finally finishing 16th. Managing director Ron Jones left for Portsmouth and was soon be followed by Cardiff's manager and top scorer. A month into the 1989-90 season, having lost four of their first five league games, Frank Burrows left to go to Fratton Park as assistant to the present Aston Villa manager John Gregory. He may have left a sinking ship but he threw his old club a lifeline by taking Gilligan to Portsmouth in late September for £215,000.

"I left Cardiff the first time because I thought the club were lacking ambition," recalls Frank. "I thought I wasn't going to be able to give the supporters what they wanted. I had a good relationship with a good chairman Tony Clemo who never pretended that we had buckets of money. Fans want a winning team playing good football but, despite all the hard work, I didn't think I could sustain it."

Frank Burrows was promoted to Portsmouth manager in 1990 and after stabilising the club, fell out with the chairman before moving back to Wales, this time with Swansea City. Again, there was little money available to bring in new players and it was at the Vetch Field that he honed the art of prospecting to perfection. Supposedly run-of-the-mill players were moulded into money-making assets as £2 million flowed into the club's coffers. Des Lyttle (£375,000 to Nottingham Forest), Jason Bowen (£350,000 to Birmingham City) and John Williams (£250,000 to Coventry City) were among those who benefited from working with frugal Frank.

In 1994, Frank Burrows became only the fifth Football League manager to both play and win at Wembley when Swansea City lifted the AutoWindscreens Trophy by beating Huddersfield on penalties. Kenny Dalglish, Graeme Souness, Terry Venables and Gianluca Vialli make up the illustrious quintet.

But the constant need to sell players began to take its toll and, for the second time, Frank decided to walk away from a South Wales club. Hard though chairman Doug Sharpe tried, he couldn't persuade Frank to stay and his manager left for London and a three-year coaching spell with West Ham United:

> Through a lot of negative publicity, I felt Doug had lost some of his interest in the football club and, over the last couple of years, we had made a lot of money but I had spent very little.
>
> I felt I had taken Swansea as far as I could under the circumstances and rather than wait to fall out or get the sack, I decided to leave. Any club I'm with becomes my professional life and I work very hard. For four-and-a-half years, I ate, slept and ate the Swans, and in view of all the hours I was putting in and all the money I raised, I felt it was time for me to move on and let somebody else have a go.
>
> For three years West Ham was my whole life. The only thing I couldn't do at Upton Park was talk with the Cockney accent – to Harry Redknapp and Frank Lampard!
>
> I had just turned fifty-four when I was asked to come back to Cardiff. You don't get too many offers after that sort of age and I wanted to manage a football club at least one more time. I had a house in South Wales, Cardiff were in a poor position, they were going nowhere fast and I thought I would give myself two years with a limited budget to turn it round.

Armed with the money raised at the end of the previous season, Frank began to assemble a new squad. Experienced players were brought on free transfers with defenders Graham Mitchell from Raith Rovers and Oxford United's Mike Ford proving his most astute signings while Mark Delaney re-entered the Football League after being rejected by Manchester United and resurrecting his career with Carmarthen Town.

I used the Bosman ruling to bring Mark Bonner from Blackpool and Richard Carpenter from Fulham, but my directors played an important part because good players weren't going to come here for nothing. The board financed signing-on fees and re-location expenses – it's all hidden money but, when you don't have a pot to pee in, it becomes a lot of money.

Thanks to them, I was able to bring half a dozen new faces in and let eleven players go, as well as change the backroom staff. My assistant Billy Ayre has possibly been the best signing I've made. I'd had three years with West Ham where I was looking at world-class Premier League players and I'd lost touch with the lower divisions which Billy knew very well.

The board allowed me to increase the staff so I got George Wood in as goalkeeping coach and expanded the medical side by bringing in physiotherapist Mike Davenport from Swansea. I don't want to kiss their arses but the directors did put their hands in their pockets – it was their money, not from the fans.

Despite all the close season activity, Cardiff lost three of their first five league games, but an encouraging performance in a 2-1 defeat by Fulham, the eventual Second Division champions, in the Littlewoods Cup in August hinted at the team's potential. An own goal winner against Plymouth at Ninian Park in early September proved the turning point. It set City on their way up the table and a 1-0 win at Carlisle on December 1st lifted them into top spot. Only six goals in their last eight league games saw their promotion bid falter but until the 3-0 defeat at Mansfield on the last day of the season, Cardiff had not been out of the top two since the beginning of December. They conceded the least number of goals in Division Three (39 in 46 matches), which augers well for next season when goal difference rather than goals scored with be taken into account.

Frank Burrows displays typical honesty in summing up the 1998-99 season:

We had a very poor start, but we played well against Fulham and then we had a steady run of success and a very good middle part of the season before dying off a little bit at the end. We had a good season all the way through in terms of playing football but not in terms of results. We drew too many games which we should have comprehensively won. When you run into a bad patch, you've got to look at your team, see what's happening, keep a cool head and keep faith with your players. It was simply that John Williams and Kevin Nugent stopped scoring goals and we didn't get enough from midfield. But the big prize was always there and we got promotion.

The big prize was won in front of 12,500 at Ninian Park on the penultimate Saturday of the season against the club with whom Frank Burrows began his career in English football. Scunthorpe United needed to win to keep alive their hopes of automatic promotion; City needed a point to wave goodbye to the Third Division.

When referee Andy D'Urso blew his whistle to end a perhaps predictable scrappy goal-less draw, Frank quickly shook hands with the Scunthorpe manager Brian Laws and headed down the tunnel to the dressing room. Minutes later, by public demand, he appeared – minus his famous flat cap – in the Grandstand to swig champagne and acknowledge the applause of the supporters:

As I looked out on all those thousands of supporters, I didn't want to get emotional so I kept thinking about positive things. I tried to be cheery because if I'd stopped to think about it, I would have got a lump in my throat. I didn't allow myself to get emotional. I felt for the supporters at that moment because I knew how they were feeling.

With all the money in the game at the moment, some people have the wrong perception – they think that a manager isn't one of them anymore. But we are all fans, we all get that sense of pride when our team's playing well. I'm ten times worse than them! My whole life is now Cardiff City rather than West Ham. Speak to my missus Wendy – she'll tell you what I'm like after a bad result. I go home and I don't speak for a day or two and then I get over it. I'm worse than the most fanatical supporter because I spend more time working for the club than with Wendy!

After the Scunthorpe result, I tried to make the moment last. I tried to stop the press asking questions about how much money would be available for new players and the future. I just wanted to enjoy the moment. I took my family out on Saturday night and I managed to extend it to Sunday lunchtime.

I'm surprised that promotion arrived within a year of my return because I'd hoped we would be in the top ten, maybe the play-offs, and that I would get some shape and some discipline into the team. Then we would have a right go and win promotion the next season. I tried to pre-empt all the criticism that was going to come my way by saying to everybody that I would be off in two years time if I hadn't been successful.

It was a challenge but it's what I do – I run football clubs, I coach players – and I wanted to see if I could put bums on seats and produce a winning team.

Frank Burrows took a risk, albeit a calculated one, when he forsook his coaching job at West Ham to rejoin Cardiff City in February 1998. By exchanging a comfortable job for life in the Premiership for one of the least attractive manager's posts in the Nationwide Football League, he was putting his reputation on the line. Football is riddled with examples of failed attempts to weave managerial magic for a second time – Howard Kendall at Everton and John Toshack at Swansea immediately spring to mind but, like Watford's Graham Taylor, Frank Burrows has proved that you *can* go back and be successful:

> When I came here in 1986, I had done well at Swindon at Portsmouth but I didn't have a real reputation then. As soon as I returned here in 1998, the expectation level went up because of my track record with Cardiff, Swansea and West Ham – people expected things to happen. I tried to pre-empt a lot of criticism by saying it would take me a couple of years because I genuinely believed that but I never lost sight of the big picture – promotion to the Second Division. If we don't build a platform to Division One, the big boys are going to get bigger and bigger – we've got to get onto their coat-tails.

Len Ashurst had decided to have second go at managing Cardiff City in 1990 when the club was in dire straits and a frustrated Frank Burrows had left for Portsmouth. In his first spell at Ninian Park, the former Newport County manager had arrived in March 1982 as City were heading towards the old Third Division. Ashurst recalls the day they finally went down:

> We managed to get to the last game at home against Luton Town. We had to win to stay up but they beat us 3-2 to confirm their promotion as champions in front of a 10,000 crowd.
>
> After the match, I remember their manager David Pleat walking straight past me to their celebrating supporters in the Grange End which I thought was appalling. When he came into my office, I threw him out although he later wrote me a letter of apology. After he'd left, Bob Grogan came in and we had a drink together.
>
> "Look," he said, "I'm sure you can get us up next season – have a rise!"
>
> It was an incentive bonus to win promotion which we duly did. I

didn't buy a player in the summer but we brought in David Tong, Roger Gibbins and Jeff Hemmerman on free transfers. We then added Jimmy Mullen and Paul Bodin but the backbone of the side was the free transfer lads. I switched Dave Bennett from centre-forward to right wing and, midway through the season, brought in Bob Hatton who was the final piece of the jigsaw. Two games stand out: a 5-1 win away at Brentford when we were powerful and strong and a late season game Chesterfield when we were without five of our special players. I moved Roger Gibbins from midfield to centre-half, we won 1-0 – a result which just about clinched promotion.

Our last match at Bristol Rovers was significant for two things – Jeff Hemmerman's injury which effectively ended his career and a riot which summed up that era of soccer violence. My brother had come down for the game and he was involved in a fight and got his car smashed up. He was an innocent by-stander and I remember wondering what the game was coming to.

Two years after arriving at Ninian Park, Ashurst moved to Sunderland, where he had spent fourteen years as a player. For domestic reasons he'd rejected the Roker Park post while at Newport County but this time the lure was too strong. "I left Cardiff because you have to take opportunities when they arrive in life. I had done well and we were mid-table on a shoestring budget when the opportunity arose to return to Sunderland. Cardiff were never, ever going to press on to anything great."

After a brief, unhappy spell in the North-East, Ashurst coached in the Middle East, first in Kuwait and then Qatar before being tempted back to Ninian Park. Working under Jimmy Mullen, he had helped Blackpool avoid relegation and seemed destined to stay at Bloomfield Road for the new 1989-90 season. But in the absence of a contract, the phone call from Cardiff chairman Tony Clemo meant that, this time, domestic considerations worked the other way:

I decided to come home because I live near Monmouth. It was an ideal opportunity for me but unfortunately the whole package turned sour within weeks when I realised that the picture wasn't as rosy as I'd been told. Coming back to Cardiff for a second time under Tony Clemo was probably the biggest mistake of my life. The difference for Frank this time is that he had a new chairman who was prepared to help a little bit, whereas Tony was going the other way.

After a terrific fight, we were relegated on the last day of the season at Bury. I decided then than if it wasn't going to be any different the following season, I'd quit, which is what I did. By the same token, Cardiff wouldn't have kept me on anyway because Rick Wright came in. He was hovering behind the scenes and was obviously going to put money in but I didn't think he wanted me as a figurehead because I would have been too strong for him. I would have been fighting him all the time so he cleared me out and I was happy to go.

After leaving Ninian Park, Len Ashurst returned to the Middle East for three years and then had a spell as consultant with Weston-super-Mare. He now looks after nine Premierhsip club academies in London, Southampton and the Midlands. He rates his second spell with Cardiff as the hardest time of his career:

The players were excellent, I had good staff around me in Bobby Smith, Jimmy Goodfellow and Gavin Tait who were all very support- ive. They were all on buttons for wages but they did a great professional job and to me it's testimony to their quality that they're still in the game.
I'm now with the Premier League. I couldn't be better off. As well as the academies, I'm also going to be regulating a new Premiership reserve league starting this season. I don't miss club management but I always believe in never closing the door on anything, so who knows what the future holds?

Len Ashurst's replacement was the former Wrexham and Swansea defender Eddie May who he had appointed as his assistant in October 1990 to succeed Bobby Smith. Officially Cardiff's coach rather than manager, May assumed full control of first team affairs at the start of the 1991-92 season and, like Ashurst, would later return to take charge of Cardiff for a second time.

Having led the club to a Third Division Championship and Welsh Cup double, May was unceremoniously dumped by the consortium who tried but failed to buy out Rick Wright. Terry Yorath took charge of team affairs as James Cadman and Michael Boyce struggled to come up with an acceptable pack- age and May moved to League of Wales side Barry Town. But in early 1995, he received the call from Wright to return to Ninian Park until the end of the season:

I agreed to go back as long as Rick paid me everything I had lost since the consortium's temporary takeover. I made it clear that I would be the one to decide when I was leaving and that gave me back a bit of credibility because the consortium had pushed me on my way.

I wasn't worried about the danger of returning to a club where I'd been successful. I'd been very happy at Cardiff and had a very good relationship with the supporters. Although I'd said I would leave at the end of the season, I always liked to think that if we got a few good results then perhaps the new owners would keep me on. I would probably have sat down and talked to them and had we beaten Wrexham in the Welsh Cup Final and then gone into Europe, perhaps Samesh Kumar would have had a different view – who knows?

Eddie May had the misfortune to be caught up in one of the most unsettled and unsettling periods of Cardiff City's history. After leaving for the second time, he'd returned to Barry and has since managed Brentford, Torquay, Haverfordwest and Merthyr. During another financial crisis, he was installed as manager at Penydarren Park on three occasions – all of them for very brief spells – and he now runs a guest house in Cardiff.

"I haven't applied for a job in English football for a couple of years now," says Eddie, "and I wouldn't go back into management here – I'd always go abroad where I've managed nine clubs in the past and never had any problems because there's no politics. They just let you get on with the job, you're judged on results and that's how football should be."

The other manager to return to return to the Ninian Park hot seat is the club's director of football development. Kenny Hibbitt played for Bradford Park Avenue, Wolves and Coventry, and coached at Bristol Rovers before spending four years as manager of Walsall.

"Personally, I think the 'never go back' theory is a myth," says Hibbitt. "There's nothing wrong with returning to any club either as a player or manager. If you've had success with them, there's no reason why you can't go back. You know the club, the supporters and the potential – and that's why a lot of people do go back. I think it's a stupid thing to say because things change – as they have here at Cardiff since the time Frank was here last."

Although he is listed in *Rothmans Football Yearbook* as having managed Cardiff City in two separate spells, Kenny Hibbitt, in fact, never left the club during the period involved. Having replaced Eddie May for the 1995-96 season, he moved upstairs to become director of football when Phil Neal arrived in January 1996. Neal's abrupt decision to jump ship and join Manchester City in the following October led to a brief recall for Hibbitt before he stepped aside again when Russell Osman was appointed manager. Osman was then demoted to assistant and together the pair led City to the 1997 Third Division play-offs. Osman was sacked in January 1998 and Hibbitt resumed control again:

I knew Cardiff had potential but I was flabbergasted by the problems I found when I came here in 1994.I didn't find it difficult being manager again because the players respected me and vice versa. They knew I wasn't going to be long-term on the second and third occasions.

I think reaching the play-offs in 1997 flattered us a little bit. It wasn't the quality we had on the pitch which got us there but the hard graft that we all out in. We lost 3-2 at Northampton and 1-0 here in the semi-finals but it was probably closer than the scoreline suggests. I didn't think we were good enough to have gone up but if we had done I told Sam that we would have had to have changed things. Some of the criticism we received was unjust but some of it was fair.

We didn't have a big board at that time but new investors have since come in who have helped Frank. There's no comparison between his budget and mine but I knew there wasn't much money when I came.

My job as director of football development involves me bringing kids into the club and brainwashing them about Cardiff City. We have tremendous youngsters here – from 11 upwards to 16 – and I think the foundations for the future of the club have been laid. Long-term, it looks very bright.

I do miss the day-to-day banter with the players. I loved coaching and being with the players – it was just three o'clock until a quarter to five on a Saturday afternoon that I found a nightmare!

Frank Burrows will never tire of that Saturday afternoon feeling – win, lose or draw. He freely admits that football is an all-consuming passion and profession to which he is totally devoted. His enthusiasm for the game and its glorious uncertainty is not so much infectious as endemic. Watch him during any match and you cannot fail to be swept along by his passion. Leaning on the dug-out roof with arms crossed one minute, he springs forward to the edge of the pitch, those same arms flailing the next, imploring his players to perform better. When a chance is wasted or a move breaks down, frantic Frank becomes frustrated.

The impact of his return to Ninian Park has been felt by everyone working at the club. From the first-team regulars to the young hopefuls dreaming of a career in football; from the groundsman Wayne Nash as he installs a new sprinkler system to the chairman Steve Borley as he attempts to find the money needed to take the club forward, everyone has been touched and inspired to improve.

Youth development officer and director of the club's centre of excellence, Gavin Tait, was appointed to the coaching staff by Frank Burrows during the manager's first spell at Ninian Park. He has observed the transformation of Cardiff City over the last eighteen months:

> Frank has brought an organisation and sense of purpose to the club. He has restructured it from top to bottom. Colin Pascoe has arrived as youth team coach and I've moved more into the recruitment and development of youngsters at a younger age level. Frank's put me in charge of scouts and there's more money to employ them.
>
> We know now that all the players – from eight-year-olds to those in the first team – are going to get good quality work and facilities and be well looked after. We've upgraded everything and we've employed more people to do the job properly. Already, youngsters are wanting to come to Ninian Park because their parents can see they get a good package.

Physiotherapist Mike Davenport is the most recent recruit to arrive at Ninian Park. He spent three years working with Frank Burrows at Swansea before joining him at Cardiff towards the end of March 1998. "Frank might well be a bit more relaxed, less frantic and a bit more mellow now," he says, "but he's still a very determined man. He'll tell you what he wants and if you don't do it, then you'll know about it."

Mike Davenport will provide round-the-clock cover for all the club's players in conjunction with Jimmy Goodfellow, the longest-serving member of the City staff. The Sunderland-born physiotherapist came to South Wales in 1972 to work with Len Ashurst at Newport County, and followed him to Ninian Park in 1982. After a brief and unsuccessful spell as Cardiff's manager, he left to work at Roker Park before linking up with Frank Burrows with City in 1986.

"I don't think he's changed at all," says Jimmy. "He's still as intense as ever and the mellow bit has come with losing his hair! I remember him as a rough, tough centre-half at Scunthorpe. I was playing for Workington and I chipped the ball over his head but he won't admit it! He had fiery locks then – hair sticking out all over the place – but his attitude towards winning has never diminished from that day to now. The intensity of wanting to win means that until you're two or three goals up in the 89th minute and the opposition can't beat you, you can't relax – and he doesn't."

Frank Burrows has often paid tribute to his assistant Billy Ayre who almost helped Jan Molby take Swansea City into the Second Division via the 1997 play-offs. The former Blackpool manager's knowledge of the lower leagues is second to none and he has just signed a two-year contract with the club:

> The good thing is that you know where you stand with Frank. As a coach he puts you on the spot, he expects high standards and you must respond or he won't tolerate you. It's the attitude he has with us all and it gets the best out of everybody he employs.
>
> Frank's turned Cardiff around so quickly because he's managed the club in every sense of the word – from the political side through dealing with directors to the medical side where he's reformed the structure by bringing in another physiotherapist, a nutritionist and a sprint coach.
>
> He's worked the Bosman Ruling to good effect and used his contacts with players like John Williams, Jason Bowen and Andy Legg who he's brought here to improve the standard of the squad. Frank makes the final decision but he discusses ideas with me. I'm not a 'yes' man and I think Frank likes that – at least he says he does! – and he knows he'll get a true opinion from me. We don't always agree but we thrash it out behind the four walls and then he makes the decision which he feels is best for the team.

Cardiff City's chairman, Steve Borley, is particularly impressed by the team his manager has assembled at Ninian Park. He claims that the extra cost is a price worth paying to keep the club moving forward:

> The wages bill has gone up, but it's all part of the modern game – it's

a case of making sure that the players get the right attention. They're earning about 27 per cent more every year and they're like any piece of equipment – you have to keep it in tip-top condition if you're going to get the best out of it. We must make sure those players stay fit and available to the football club.

Director Philip Jardine says a strong degree of trust exists between manager and board. When Frank Burrows asks for another member of staff, his request is met – on the strength of his track record:

> Frank is transparent – what you see is what you get and the club is safe in his hands. Bill Shankly was the right man for Liverpool in 1959 when he turned a mediocre Second Division side into a team which would later dominate English football over the next three decades, Don Revie did a similar job with Leeds and Frank Burrows is the man for Cardiff City as we enter our second hundred years.

While the support of a board of directors and his backroom staff is essential for any football club manager to be successful, his most important relationship is inevitably with the players – the people who perform out on the pitch from August to May. The well-being of the entire club depends on the rapport struck up between the manager and his charges. He must gain their respect and in return be able to motivate them to play to the very best of their ability.

Mike Ford is the only member of the Cardiff City first team squad who has played under Frank Burrows in his two spells at Ninian Park. His return from injury for the run-in last season did much to calm jangling nerves as promotion was finally secured. The club captain says his manager is more cheerful these days:

> In his first spell here, he'd be very unhappy when we lost. On one away trip, a couple of lads at the back of the coach were making a bit of noise and he told them to shut up because we'd just lost. 'I don't want to hear anybody for the rest of the trip!' barked Frank. It was a five hour journey! Fortunately, we've just had a good season so that didn't happen much in 1998-99.
>
> Without being physical with us, he lets you know what he wants in no uncertain terms. He doesn't pick on individuals and by doing it on front of the lads, I think everyone else takes on board what he expects.
>
> We have tremendous respect for him and Billy. They work well as a pair but everyone knows that the Gaffer is the Gaffer. There's no

question at all about that. Basically, what he says goes – whether you agree with it or not.

We've got players in the squad who can play or have played at a higher level and Frank doesn't want us just to boot the ball upfield. He wants us to play the game a certain way – along the floor. He wants to bring the best out of the players so we work very hard on shadow play, team patterns and set pieces. We're very well organised.

We used a different system with three central defenders and the two wing-backs in the 1998-99 season and it worked quite well – especially with our midfield three.

Jason Fowler's form in the Cardiff City midfield is a source of continuing delight to his manager and supporters alike. His deft chip in the team's outstanding 4-1 win over Brentford at the end of January 1999 provided the Ninian Park regulars with one of the goals of the season. It was no surprise when he was named in the Professional Footballers Association's Third Division team by his peers. He recalls the dressing-room reaction when Frank Burrows returned:

There were a lot of rumours that he'd be very stern but he's been absolutely brilliant with me. He's encouraged me to play football. He's very professional, not nasty, sometimes a little mad but he's gets behind the players one hundred per cent which is what you want in a manager. He's someone who you want to play for, not one of those managers who looks after himself and stays out of the way. He's there for you when you want him.

I had a problem with my weight and Frank put me on a special programme. I had to build myself up and he worked very, very hard with me on it – standing on top of me as I was doing the weights, shouting at me and making sure I did every single one! You don't get that from most managers.

John Williams has more reason than most to thank Frank Burrows. After launching the striker's league career by signing him from Cradley Town in the West Midlands while manager at Swansea, he sold him to Coventry City. In the summer of 1998, Burrows then rescued Williams from obscurity in Exeter via Wycombe:

I owe everything to Frank. He brought me out of non-league football and then turned me into a Premiership player within a year. Now he's resurrected my career at Cardiff. We have a huge amount of respect for Frank because he's achieved a lot with quite a few clubs. He got us up last season because of his professionalism and the way he is as a person. The Gaffer is a winner and he gets that through to the players who respond to him and to Billy as well. They're a good pairing – a bit like chalk and cheese – one's aggressive and one's really angry. I'll leave it to you to find out which one's which!

According to John Williams, Cardiff's second top scorer last season behind Kevin Nugent, Frank Burrows has calmed down a little since his time at Swansea. In particular, John remembers a midweek evening game against Darlington when the manager showed his powers of motivation:

I was absolutely petrified of the man when I was at the Vetch Field. It was my first season in league football and I was so laid back that some people thought I didn't care. I remember sitting in the dressing room at half-time against Darlington. It was nil-nil, I was staring at the floor when I looked up and saw Frank holding a big tub of petroleum jelly which suddenly started coming straight towards my head! I managed to avoid the tub which smashed up against the wall.

Frank was ranting and raving and I've never been so scared of a manager in my whole life. But we won 4-2, I got two goals and afterwards he came up to me:

"See what I made you do?" he said. "That's what I can get out of you – you just need a kick up the backside!"

Frank Burrows was criticised for bringing John Williams to Ninian Park. The former postman's main claim to fame was that he was once football's fastest man following a sprint race at Wembley in the early Nineties. Some doubted if he could reproduce his early-career form – even in the Third Division – but Burrows backed his judgment and Williams delivered:

Everyone forgets that I played eighty games in the Premiership when they say I've done well in the Third Division. The Gaffer likes building up competition for places and when Dai Thomas hit a drought last season, I was brought back. I made sure I did what strikers should do – score goals – and I ended up with something like 10 in 11 games! I know I'm a frustrating player – you either love me or hate me. I'll either score or I'll miss, having done all the hard work!

Frank's a great believer in team spirit and building relationships with the players and everyone goes out there and does their best for him. His tactics are second to none.

The scenes after the Scunthorpe game were amazing. The only

thing I've ever won in my career was the sprint challenge at Wembley when I picked up £10,000, but winning promotion put that in the shade. I'm so happy that we went up in my first season at Ninian Park.

After that result on Saturday May 1st, messages of congratulation poured into Ninian Park from many of the manager's contacts in football. The faxes, letters and cards came from everywhere and everyone – including Premiership managers and the chairman of West Ham. It was left to Frank's personal assistant Jackie Rockey to suggest that they could be displayed in his office:

Frank doesn't live in the past. We got promotion on the Saturday and by the Monday, it was all gone, it was history. He doesn't dwell on things. I know he was touche by all the messages but he didn't want to put them up on the wall. Eventually he pinned a few up for all of five seconds and then took them down!

I get on well with him because he's of the old school. We have an old-fashioned boss-secretary relationship, I go in and take dictation with shorthand and everything has to be exactly so-so.

"As much as I love you Jackie," he says, "if you cock something up, then I'll sack you".

The other managers, Phil Neal, Kenny Hibbitt and Russell Osman weren't as organised and particular as Frank – and Billy Ayre's the same as Frank. Everything has to be spot-on. For example, when Kenny or Russell were busy, they would give me a few notes and ask me to finish off their thoughts for the programme but I always write down precisely what Frank says. The first thing he does when the programmes are printed is turn to his column to make sure it's alright – I've go to be on my toes all the time.

I can sum Frank up in one word – unique. He's a hard taskmaster but he generates a good atmosphere in the club – quite often, he'll arrive in the morning with a big box of chocolate eclairs for all the girls in the office. I can't fault him – I love him to bits.

"Staff at a football club are important," says Frank, "from the football side all the way through to the administration and secretary Ceri Whitehead. Jackie Rockey is my eyes and ears – if she didn't keep my paperwork in order then I would be a lost ship."

As he prepares for the 1999-2000 season, Frank Burrows has set everyone at Ninian Park a series of challenges – including himself. He's determined to make sure that history doesn't repeat itself. Cardiff City must build on their most recent

promotion rather than frittering it away. He wants to exorcise
the ghosts of 1976, 1983, 1988 and 1993 when the club failed
to capitalise on a winning position.

> The first challenge falls on my chairman and his board of directors.
> They've got the most difficult job to keep this club financially stable
> but they've also got to raise enough money so that the team can be
> strengthened and the ground can be developed. I can attract better
> players here if we've got a bigger budget. My directors are back in the
> same position they were at the start of last season. They've got to find
> more investors and more money.
>
> We lose a fortune through not having proper hospitality. Cardiff is
> a growing, vibrant city and there are loads of companies coming in
> here. If we could give them four-star corporate hospitality then this
> club would benefit. The ground has to grow with the team – you can't
> spend all the money on players because you've got to give the fans
> better facilities – seats, toilets and washrooms, burger bars. It too pat
> to say that if you've got a good team, the fans will come and stand in
> anything. There are a lot of go-ahead young executives and they want
> to get involved in success with good facilities and good football which
> represent value for their money. At the moment, we're not in a posi-
> tion to offer that.

The resignation of former chairman Samesh Kumar in May
1999 left Frank Burrows a little confused. Like the club's
supporters, he hadn't expected the announcement, especially so
soon after promotion had been won. "It made me wonder
where the club was going. Luckily, it was close season, so we
weren't winning or losing games. I don't know why he resigned
– that's directors' business – but it did have an effect. The
timing was right as far as I was concerned because we've had
the summer to stabilise the club."

The £500,000 received from Aston Villa for full-back Mark
Delaney went a long way to doing that. Despite criticism by
some supporters, Frank Burrows believes the decision to sell
Delaney was right. "In an ideal world, I would liked to have
kept Mark because we were in a good position but I'm the
manager who also wears a business hat. Bank managers have
friendly smiles but they don't support football clubs – they're
not charitable people."

As Cardiff's promotion drive started to falter in the last
month of last season, the club were also criticised for not solv-

ing their goalscoring problem by buying Eifion Williams from Barry Town. The Wales B striker hit a hat-trick on his debut for Torquay after his £70,000 transfer from the League of Wales champions. Burrows had certainly done his homework:

> I had watched Eifion because no one can fail to be impressed with his goalscoring record. I found out when his contract at Barry was up and how old he was to see whether he would be available under the Bosman Ruling. I was told that Barry wanted £100,000 and I didn't have that kind of money so there was no point in chasing lost causes. The Mark Delaney money went to stabilise the club. I knew and accepted that so there were no complaints from me. The only complaint would have been had we sold Scott Young, Richard Carpenter, Jason Fowler or Danny Hill. I would have questioned what I was doing here if that had happened. I don't mind helping – it's part of my job to help the directors run the club.

The manager's second challenge has been thrown out to his players. After the Scunthorpe game, more than one armchair critic aired the view that Cardiff needed at least three new players to survive in Division Two. If Frank Burrows didn't spend some money, the argument went, then City would be in real danger of justifying their reputation as a yo-yo club. At the end of June, the first close season signing arrived. Having played over sixty games for Coventry City, midfielder Willie Boland signed on a three-year contract. No fee was involved, but in July Cardiff paid £100,000 to bring Matt Brazier back to Ninian Park from Fulham. The wing back played thirteen times during a loan-spell in the 1998-99 season. A further £20,000 was was to Connah's Quay Nomad's for Jamie Hughes, the former Tranmere Rovers striker. Frank Burrows knew he would have to strengthen his squad:

> The challenge for me now is this: can I coach my players into a system and make them rise to the challenge of keeping us in Division Two? I thanked them all for last season, I gave them all the credit for winning promotion, but that's over now. I've got to be clever and use my skills to pick up players and improve the ones I've got. Because I thought it would take two years to sort out this club, I signed a two-year contract and so did twenty-three of my professionals.
>
> I thought that by the end of the 1999-2000 season, they'd all be out of contract and I'd know who'd be good enough to stay in Division

Two and who I'd let go. Success has come a year early so I'm in a difficult position with all my players under contract for another year.

Some of the players will get a fair chance because they're under contract but, somewhere along the line, I'll have to make painful decisions. It's not hard for me because I'm doing it in the best interests of the club, not for petty or mean reasons. The hardest bit of my job is getting money to raise standards all round.

How quickly the players adapt to the Second Division will determine the number of fresh faces I need. Proven goalscorers cost megamoney which we haven't got, so Kevin Nugent will have to do better this season – so will Jason Bowen. He started to show flashes of form but he should have had ten goals last season instead of two. The onus is on him but I know he can play comfortably in the Second Division.

John Williams, David Thomas, Robert Earnshaw and Christian Roberts they will have to rise to the challenge if they get the chance.

This club is tightly-run and we're as ambitious as our money allows us to be. My message is simple: I will not do this on my own. Everyone's got a major part to play. I've got to ignite it but the business community have got to come on board if we give them good facilities and a winning team. I would like these companies to join in – we're only in Division Two but take a gamble and back us! Back the board, invest your money into the club and be part of it.

Despite the general air of optimism around Ninian Park, Len Ashurst doubts whether the businesses of South Wales will come out in support of Cardiff City. Sixteen years ago, he heard the same arguments when he won promotion. Nothing happened then and he fears nothing will happen now. But with Frank Burrows at the helm, the former manager says the club is in good hands:

When I was at Newport and then Cardiff for the first time, I used to go around scouting and whenever I went to matches, Frank was always there working. That showed me he was a grafter and he was interested and so I had no hesitation in picking him to join me at Sunderland. I was proved right because he's gone on and done very well. He was an exceptionally good assistant for me at Roker Park – he took a lot of the weight off me as I dealt with the pressures of the press up there and he's justifiably got a career for himself since then.

John Gregory also employed Frank Burrows as his number two – in the Scotsman's second spell at Portsmouth in 1989-90. The Aston Villa manager's relationship with his former assistant proved crucial when Mark Delaney moved from the League of Wales to the Premiership in less than a year in early March 1999. Gregory believes that the three years Frank Burrows spent at West Ham were a very important part of his career:

> That spell gave him the chance to get back to coaching and not have the responsibility of running the club. It whetted his appetite. I wasn't surprised that he came back to Cardiff or that he's been successful.
>
> At Portsmouth, I knew that if I wasn't there for training, I could leave Frank to run everything. He wouldn't change things because I wasn't there. When you ask him to do something, you know he'll do it to the best of his ability. He expects the best from all his players, he doesn't take any rubbish from anybody and he's the kind of man that Cardiff City are lucky to have – I hope they can hang onto him.
>
> I think he's proved that he can spend money wisely. Being a typical Scotsman, he treats it like his own and doesn't like to part with it very often. I think he's a man the board can trust with a cheque book.
>
> Frank's a good judge of a player – as you can see from what he's done with John Williams. I had John at Wycombe and I couldn't get the best out of him so I let him go but Frank brought him here and he helped take Cardiff up.

Second time around, Frank Burrows is obviously as committed as ever, he appears more able to bring out the best in the people he works with: players, directors, press and media and supporters. His dry sense of humour and honest approach to everything ensures total respect and endears him to everyone: people implicity trust his judgment.

> I'm not the most patient of men and I'm not the best with the press but I try to give them my time and be fair with them. I need to earn their respect by what we do out on the field. We did it in the middle part of last season and the press responded because our crowds went up from 3-4,000 to 12,000. The message came across. It's important to have enthusiastic reporters because the pen is mightier than the sword. The message goes out and then the supporters come in. They start to get animated about this football club. Then it's important that I keep proving to them and the press that we're going forward.
>
> I would like the club to stay in the Second Division and build a platform to get to Division One. I don't want to be in Division Two for the next four or five years – I don't think the fans would tolerate me and I certainly wouldn't tolerate it.
>
> I think we'll stay in Division Two and when I leave this club, I'd like them to have a good enough squad to be in Division One. A good

manager can be judged not on the state the club is in when he joins but when he leaves.

If the finances fall into place, I would say we could be in the First Division within two years. If they don't, it could be longer. But I'll be trying to do it Route One! Don't worry – we won't be playing that type of football but I wouldn't mind promotion in one year again.

Frank Burrows is a proud and professional man. After spending forty years in football, he has made his mark on the game which has been his life – on clubs and players alike. As the 1998-99 season drew to a close he was surprised to read about a team picked by the current England manager Kevin Keegan. Frank's former team-mate at Scunthorpe United was asked by *Match of the Day* magazine to pick the greatest eleven players from all the sides he had turned out for at club level. Alongside some of the biggest names in the game – Alan Ball, John Toshack, Tommy Smith and Emlyn Hughes – were two former Scunthorpe players: Terry Heath and a certain Frank Burrows. His inclusion led to a lot of good-natured ribbing from his players and no doubt, deep down, Cardiff City's manager was chuffed to bits to receive such recognition.

Frustrated, frugal, frantic and now friendly – there are no flies on Frank Burrows, the Scotsman in the cap who made history. Under his guidance, and with the backing of a largely local board, Cardiff City played rather than kicked their way out of the Third Division. They may have missed out on the championship but there could hardly have been a better way to celebrate their centenary. Here's to the next hundred years. Cheers Frank.

# Epilogue
# Last Thoughts on Bart Wilson

When I began writing this centenary celebration, I knew very little about the founder of Cardiff City. From what I'd read, I was aware that Bart Wilson was a disabled lithographic artist from Bristol who had started it all in the summer of 1899.

There was a very grainy photograph of him sitting in full kit in the middle of the Riverside Club's cricketers and he could later be spotted – usually standing on the end of the back row wearing a flat cap or a hat – in Cardiff City's team line-ups. There were a few pictures of him working in the club office in the early Fifties just before his death, but that was about all.

That Bart Wilson was the driving force behind the formation of Riverside F.C. is beyond dispute. The books and pamphlets about the club all pay tribute to his pioneering work at the turn of the century. A slim paperback published by the *Western Mail and Echo* after the 1947 Third Division South championship success is typical. *A Short History of Cardiff City A.F.C.* was compiled by 'Citizen' of the *Football Echo* and produced by public demand:

> No one dreamt in those days that Riverside was really the seed which would give birth to a club whose meteoric rise to fame was to astound the football world. Mr. Bartley Wilson was undoubtedly the soul of this amateur organisation.

In fact, Bart Wilson was the one person who allowed himself to dream. He was the soul – and the heart – of the club which became Cardiff City. As I started to work on the centenary book, a couple of questions nagged away at me. Who was Bart Wilson and why did he want to set up a football team in the Welsh capital at the turn of the last century?

The more I thought about them, the more inquisitive I

became and the more determined to find out more about Bart and the origins of Cardiff City. I decided to begin at the end – with Bart's death. Having discovered a tribute in a club match-day programme, I knew he had died some time between two home games on the 13th and 27th November 1954.

Cardiff Central Library was my first port of call and the *South Wales Echo* my starting point. Sure enough, on page 3 of Friday 19th November edition, I found what I was looking for – 'Bart Wilson, "G.O.M." Cardiff City, dies' read the headline. There followed a short article about the Grand Old Man's life and times, details of the funeral arrangements and a clue or two to Bart's immediate family. The service at St John's Church in Canton had been followed by burial at Western Cemetery. It was a start – something to work on.

Western Cemetery lies on the outskirts of Cardiff – not far from the Culverhouse Cross roundabout and the Ely Link Road. The next day, as I drove along Cowbridge Road, I decided to try to find Bart Wilson's grave.

The assistant on duty that early December day, Keith Chadwick, couldn't have been more helpful. Within a couple of minutes, we were striding through the middle of the cemetery towards Section I where Bart was buried. As we approached the area, I wondered what we were going to find? Keith looked at his piece of paper on which the section was divided into plots – number by number – and then he looked at me.

"This is where it should be," he said, pointing to the two numbers of the headstones either side of Plot 246. We bent down to confirm their position in relation to Bartís grave. It was nothing more than a mound.

"Are you sure?" I said, half-anticipating the answer to my question.

"Yes, I'm sure," Keith replied, "I'm afraid this is Plot 246."

My heart sank. How desperately sad! The man who was responsible for forming Cardiff City lay in an unmarked grave. How could this have happened? But in half a minute, the journalist in me took over. What a story! In the year of the club's centenary, their founder was lying in one of the city's cemeteries but nobody knew he was there.

My immediate concern was to contact any surviving relatives

and, through them, to discover more about Bart Wilson. Several people had told me that Bart's son Jim had died in the early Nineties in a Cardiff nursing home but I wondered if there were any living grandchildren?

The newspaper report of Bart's death mentioned a daughter, a Mrs. S. Head, and her two children, John and Alma. There were quite a few Heads scattered around the city and the first one I rang initially didn't sound too hopeful. Eventually, she told me that John Head lived in Wenvoe, a village about a mile from Western Cemetery.

I returned to the phone book. She was right. I dialled the number, mentioned the name Bart Wilson and struck gold. I was talking to the grandson of the founder of Cardiff City.

After explaining the reason for my call, I broached the question of the unmarked grave. From the moment I told John, and later his sister Alma Vosper, about my discovery, I received nothing but their co-operation and support. Initial shock soon gave way to appreciation and when I suggested that a new headstone should be commissioned as part of Cardiff City's centenary celebrations, they were immediately enthusiastic – as were the club's officials.

From her home in Croydon, Alma proved a tremendous source of encouragement. After providing valuable information about Bart's early life, she then unearthed details of his marriage to Sarah Ellen and the Wilson family tree. She told me she that remembered visiting her grandmother's grave with her mother but when they returned to lay flowers after Bart's death, they couldn't find either the grave or the headstone.

I then enlisted the help of Simon Morgan, managing director of Mossfords, the monumental masons, who had provided the original headstone and Cardiff City's chaplain, Father Joe Jordan. A plan gradually evolved to ask representatives of the club and close members of the family to attend a short re-dedication ceremony in early June which would be filmed as part of my BBC Wales television documentary to accompany the book.

A month before the service, cameraman Tony Yates and I visited the cemetery to plan our schedule. It was pouring with rain – as it had been on the day in 1954 when Bart should have been buried. We searched in vain for the grave, looking for plots

245 or 247. After about ten minutes, Tony drew my attention to a plinth with some writing on it which lay at the base of a nearby tree.

My heart started to pound as I went to investigate. The base provided conclusive evidence – 'Mossfords', 'I', and '246' were the crucial pieces of information it contained. We had found one part of the memorial but where was the headstone? As we started to look around, Tony noticed a slab of marble, largely covered by grass, lying a few yards from the plinth. My pulse was racing.

It was too heavy to lift so Tony borrowed a crowbar from a nearby skip and carefully eased up a corner. I grabbed another one and, as we pushed the headstone up to rest it against the tree, all was revealed. Sarah Ellen Wilson's details were displayed on the stone above an empty space left for those of her husband.

It took only a few moments to take in what we had stumbled across. After nearly forty-five years, the mystery of the missing headstone had been solved. There would be no need for a new one now that the original had been found. With the family's full backing, the headstone was refurbished with Bart's details being carved by hand above a simple tribute: 'The founder of Cardiff City A.F.C.' On June 7th 1999, the re-dedication service took place at Western Cemetery and Bart Wilson finally received his long overdue recognition.

The other mystery I was keen to unravel was the origin of Cardiff City's nickname, 'The Bluebirds'. From my research, I knew that it had started being used, along with 'The Cardiffians', 'The City' and 'The Citizens', after the club changed their colours from chocolate and amber to blue, sometime around 1910.

The *South Wales Echo* again came up with the answer – or at least the most likely one. An appeal through their sports pages led to two readers suggesting there might be a connection with a classic children's play, *The Blue Bird* written by the Belgian playwright Maurice Maeterlinck in 1909. The bird, a symbol of happiness, is pursued by children who want to imprison it in a cage and the play's theme urges us not to try to hoard happiness for ourselves.

My consultant, Richard Shepherd, suggested I should look through the *Echo* archives to discover whether the play had been performed in Cardiff after 1910. So, back to Cardiff Central Library I went and, after a day's searching through the paper's back pages, I discovered that the play had indeed come to the New Theatre in late October 1911. It received good reviews during its six-night run and a week after the production had left town, Maeterlinck was awarded the Nobel Prize for Literature for his symbolist plays including *The Blue Bird* and *Pelleas and Mesilande*.

No positive proof exists but it would seem probable that the publicity surrounding the play's arrival in the Welsh capital and then Maeterlinck's honour led to an unknown Cardiff City supporter deciding to call the team, resplendent in their blue strip, 'The Blue Birds'. Gradually, it emerged as the favourite nickname before being adopted officially by the club.

The nickname would surface again nearly ninety years later as Cardiff City became caught up in the current craze for mascots. They had the bluebird outfit and the person to wear it but they didn't know what to call their creation. So a competition involving members of the Junior Bluebirds was held and their entries were taken into the dressing room for the players to choose.

It was the suggestion by Jacques Aviles, an eight-year-old supporter from Cardiff Bay, which took the first-team's fancy and the mascot was christened Bartley. Bartley the Bluebird. It does have a nice alliterative ring to it – as all mascots should. Jacques had come up with the name because he'd read somewhere that a man called Bartley Wilson had founded Cardiff City back in 1899.

As Bart Wilson always manintained that the club belonged to the people of the city, it seems fitting that Cardiff City are now being run by a group of local buisnessmen rather than a wealthy individual. For the builder, dairyman, electrical engineer, printer and clerk of the original 1910 board read the builder, soliticor, property developer, I.T. expert and engineer who are part of the 1999 line-up. We have come full circle, the enthusiasts, Bart's successors are back in control and no doubt he would have approved.

As the Bluebirds celebrate their centenary, it is also appropriate that Bart's crucial role has now been officially recognised. He was the man with the mission, someone who dared to dream – and it's tempting to do that just now. With the new Millennium approaching, some supporters are hoping that the club might, as one of football's élite, one day play in the stadium being built to mark the turn of the century.

Cardiff City in the Premiership?

Dream on!

But isn't that just what Bart Wilson did a hundred years ago?

# Select Bibliography

'Citizen': *History of Cardiff City A.F.C*, Western Mail, Cardiff 1947 (Revised edition published in 1952)

Corrigan, Peter: *Hundred Years of Welsh Soccer*, Welsh Brewers Ltd, Cardiff 1976

Crooks, John: *Cardiff City Chronology 1920-86*, Cardiff 1986

Crooks, John: *The Bluebirds – A Who's Who of Cardiff City Football League Players*, Cardiff 1987

Crooks, John: *The Official History of the Bluebirds*, Yore Publications, Harefield, Middlesex 1992

Jackson, Peter: *The Cardiff City Story*, Brains Ltd, Cardiff, 1974

Jenkins, Derrick & Stennett, Ceri: *Wembley 1927*, Cardiff 1987

Shepherd, Richard: *The Archive Photograph Series – Cardiff City Football Club 1899-1947*, The Chalford Publishing Company, Stroud 1996

Shepherd, Richard: *The Archive Photograph Series – Cardiff City Football Club 1947-71*, Tempus Publishing, Brimscombe Port, Glos 1997

Toshack, John: *Tosh, An Autobiography*, Arthur Barker, London, 1982

# Index

of Players, Officials and those closely associated with the club

Abley, Tom 42, 45
Allchurch, Ivor 155, 156, 157, 160, 164, 180
Allen, Bryn 136
Alston, Adrian 179, 198, 199
Anderson, Willie 186, 190, 195 197
Andrews, Jimmy 179, 192, 193, 194, 195, 196-97, 199, 200, 201, 202-03
Ashurst, Len 179, 204, 205, 206, 208, 234, 237, 255, 256, 261-62, 253, 266, 274
Ayre, Billy 247, 259, 267, 271

Baillie, James 83
Baker, Billy 133, 135, 137, 140, 149
Baker, Colin 152
Barrett, Stanley 17
Bater, Phil 257
Beadles, Harry, 76, 79, 80
Beare, George 50, 59, 60
Beecher, Ron 170
Bell, Gary 174, 179, 180, 189
Bennett, Dave 186, 205, 208, 224, 262
Bennett, Gary 205, 207, 208
Bird, Ronnie 167, 168, 172, 174, 176, 179, 180
Blackburn, George 83
Blair, Davy 147
Blair, Jimmy 55, 69, 78, 79, 80, 118, 122
Blake, Nathan 154
Blenkinsop, Ernie 125
Bodin, Paul 205, 262
Boland, Willie 273
Bonner, Mark 259
Bonson, Joe 151
Borley, Steve, 241, 242-43, 244, 245, 247, 249, 250, 251, 266, 267-68
Bowen, Jason 267
Boyce, Michael 239, 263
Brain, Joseph 39
Brazier, Matt 273
Brignull, Phil 208
Brittan, Charlie 49, 55, 59, 60, 74

Brown, Bobby 163, 180, 185, 214
Brown, Tommy 65
Brownlee, Alex 98, 139
Buchanon, John 179, 186, 194, 195, 203
Burfitt, Frank 17, 36
Burns, Micky 202
Burrows, Frank 11, 180, 234-35, 237, 241, 242, 244, 245, 247, 248, 254, 255-59, 260-61, 265-66, 267, 268, 269-70, 271-75
Burton, Jack 45

Cadman, James 239, 263
Campbell, Alex 198
Canning, Danny 135, 140
Canter, Billy 17
Carlin, Willie 192
Carpenter, Richard 259, 273
Cashmore, Arthur 61
Cassidy, Pat 46, 52, 56, 59, 64
Castle, Fred 83
Charles, Clive 179, 192, 195
Charles, John 146, 150-51, 156, 157, 160, 161, 164, 165-66, 171, 180
Charles, Mel 154-55, 160, 164
Chisholm, Ken 145, 146
Clemo, Tony 196, 201, 208, 223, 231-33, 234-35, 236, 237, 247, 249, 250-51, 253-54, 256, 257, 262
Clark, Brian 9-10, 159, 161-63, 164, 167, 168, 170, 171, 172, 173, 174, 175, 176, 177, 178-79, 180, 182, 183-84, 188, 197, 214
Clarke, Joe 47
Clarke, Roy, 134, 136, 137Clayton, Lew 190
Collins, Jimmy 125
Crichton-Stuart, Ninian 33, 41, 42, 54
Curtis, Alan 256
Curtis, Ernie 83, 84, 88, 92, 93, 95, 99, 108, 119, 155

Dalton, Tom 58

Davenport, Mike 259, 266
Davidson, Billy 47
Davies, Fred 164, 166, 167
Davies, Len 58, 67, 69, 73, 75, 77, 78, 84, 86, 94, 100, 110, 113
Davies, Stan 109
Davies, William 70, 78, 79, 84, 108
Dean, Norman 165-66, 167, 173
Delaney, Mark 154, 227, 244, 245, 247, 258, 272-73
Derrett, Steve 177
Dewey, Fred 169, 170, 171, 181, 188, 190
Dewey, Vivian 170
Dibble, Andrew 205, 207
Doncaster, Tommy 46
Donnelly, Peter 153
Drake, F. 17
Duffy, Jock 42
Durban, Alan 156, 207, 208, 209-10, 211, 227, 234, 256
Durham, Ron 198
Dwyer, Phil 10, 55, 185-88, 189, 191, 192, 194, 195, 196, 197, 198, 199, 201, 203, 204, 205, 206, 207-08, 209-11

Eadie, Jim 176
Earnshaw, Robert 274
Edwards, George 144-45, 146-47, 149, 157, 170
Elliott, Dave 203
England, Mike 197, 198-99, 217
Evans, Herbie 64, 74
Evans, Jack 'Bala' 40, 41, 42, 45, 59, 61, 67, 69, 75, 77, 82
Evans, Tony 179, 197

Farquharson, Tom 55, 67, 69, 81, 87, 104, 107, 114, 121, 123, 238, 204, 206
Farrell, Greg 161
Farrington, John 192, 194
Featherstone, Harry 45
'Fels Naptha' 48, 49-50, 52, 53, 54, 56-57, 58-59, 60, 61, 62, 63, 64., 66, 28, 74, 76, 77, 78, 79-80, 85, 98, 109, 110, 112-13
Ferguson, Bobby 166
Ferguson, Hughie 82, 84, 85, 86, 88, 89, 91, 94, 98, 99, 100-01, 109, 159

Finnieston, Steve 194, 195
Finney, Jim 238, 250
Flynn, Brian
Foggon, Alan 189, 190
Ford, Mike 207, 248, 257, 258, 268
Ford, Trevor 1, 149, 150
Forse, Tommy 119, 124, 125
Fowler, Jason 269, 273
Francis, Gerry 207
Friday, Robin 186, 199-201

Galbraith, John 112, 114
Gibbins, Roger 205, 211, 221, 222, 237, 238, 262
Gibson, Colin 134, 136, 137
Gibson, Ian 177, 178, 182, 188
Giles, David 221
Giles, Paul 203
Gill, Jimmy 64, 67, 75, 78, 80
Gilligan, Jimmy 257
Goddard, Arthur 50, 52
Goldstone, David 181, 190, 191, 192, 194, 196, 197, 231, 248
Goodfellow, Jimmy 206, 207, 234, 256, 263, 266, 267
Goodfriend, Sue 212-17, 219-20, 221-22, 223, 224, 225-26, 227-28, 229
Grant, Dave 209
Grant, Wilf 145, 146, 155
Grapes, Steve 200
Griffith, Cohen 225
Grimshaw, Billy 58
Grogan, Bob 196, 201, 218, 223, 233, 234, 252, 261
Guy, Paul 241, 243

Hagan, Alfie 71
Hamilton, Leslie 227
Hampson, Tom 83
Hansforth, Percy 36
Hardy, Billy 45, 49, 52, 56, 58, 72, 94, 108, 110, 115-16, 126
Harris, Brian 161, 163, 166, 167, 177, 180, 203, 234
Harris, Frank 108
Harrington, Alan 151, 153, 156
Harrison, J. Bell 33
Harvey, Henry 'Kidder' 46, 56, 59, 64
Hatton, Bob 205-06, 262
Healy, Ron 179, 192, 198

Hemmerman, Jeff 205, 206, 207, 208, 221, 262
Henderson, Jim 47
Hibbitt, Kenny 241, 255, 264-64, 271
Hill, Freddie 120
Hill, Joan 226, 227, 240, 241, 245-46, 247
Hill, W. 17
Hillier, Joe 108, 117
Hitchens, Gerry 149, 150
Hobby, Jimmy 186
Holder, E.W. 17
Holder, J. 17
Hole, Barrie 156, 164
Hollyman, Ken 133-34, 135, 136, 137, 140, 142, 147, 150
Howells, James 120
Hughes, Jamie 273
Hughes, Wayne 203
Husbands, Ted 41, 45

Impey, John 186
Irving, Sammy 86, 108

James, Billy 133
Jardine, Philip 241, 242, 243, 245, 247, 249, 250, 253, 268
Jenkins, Eddie 111
Jenkins, Eddie J. 111-12, 114, 116, 118, 121-22, 123
Jenkins, W. 17
Jennings, Bill 125, 128
Jennings, John 'Jack' 117
John, Dilwyn 160
Jones, Barrie 105, 182, 214
Jones, Bill 145, 151, 153, 155
Jones, Bob 125
Jones, Herbert Frew 22
Jones, Ron 207, 208, 217-18, 222-23, 226, 252, 257
Jones, Vaughan 207

Keating, Albert 130
Keating, Reg 130
Keenor, Fred 10, 49, 52, 55-58, 60, 66, 67, 69, 82, 84, 86, 90, 92-93, 94, 95, 96, 97, 98, 99, 108, 109, 110, 111, 112, 113-14, 116, 138, 139, 204
Kellock, Billy 186

Kelly, Mark 259
Kneeshaw, Jack 46, 52, 59
King, Jake 207
King, Peter 156, 160, 163, 172, 185
Kumar, Samesh 226, 239, 240, 241, 242, 244, 245-46, 247, 249, 264, 265, 272
Kyd, Charles 24, 25, 36, 39

Lamour, Albert 179, 188
Latham, George 46, 58-59, 66, 67, 85, 90, 98, 115, 116, 122, 124
Lawrie, Bob 42, 45, 46
Lawson, Dennis 73
Layton, Arthur 50, 52, 60
Lea, Les 164, 166, 180
Leah, Bob 45
Leckie, Jock 123
Legg, Andrew 267
Lever, Arthur 'Buller' 134, 135, 136, 137, 147
Leonard, Jack 196, 208, 234, 256
Lewis, John 205, 221
Livermore, Doug 197, 203

MacAulay, Bob 124
Malloch, Jimmy 42
Mann, T. 17
Matson, Tom 83
May, Eddie 237, 238-39, 255, 263-64, 265
McCandless, Billy 135, 140, 144, 151
McCulloch, Andy 186, 190, 194
McDermott, Brian 257
McDonald, James 42
McDougall, Davy 41, 45
McGill, Job 36
McInch, Jimmy 186
McKenzie, James 42, 54
McLachan, George 84, 86, 89, 94, 110
McLaughlin, Bobby 145
McLoughlin, Paul 207
McNeill, John 140
Mellor, Jack 124
Merrett, Sir Herbert 126-28, 134, 135, 139, 140, 142-43, 144, 145, 147, 149, 150, 230, 253
Milne, Alec 151
Mitchell, Graham 258
Montgomery, Stan 136, 145, 155

# Index

Moore, Beriah 133
Moore, Graham 151, 154
Morgan, David 120
Morgan, Richie 165, 202, 203, 204, 216, 234
Morris, Trevor 138-39, 140, 141, 142, 147, 148, 149-50, 151
Mort, Enoch 122
Moseley, Graham 256
Moss, Frank 110
Mullen, Jimmy 205, 206, 209, 234, 262
Munro, Jim 110
Murray, Don 156, 160, 161, 165, 166, 167, 176, 177, 179, 181, 182, 183, 185, 189, 192-93, 194, 197, 214

Nash, Lew 36
Nash, Wayne 216
Neal, Phil 241, 265
Nelson, Jimmy 74, 77, 82, 94, 109
Nicholls, Jack 76
Nicholls, Sid 39, 40, 47, 48, 67-68, 73, 76, 98, 253
Nicholson, Joe, 78, 70
Nicholson, William 127
Nugent, Kevin 259, 270, 274

O'Farrell, Frank 191-93, 204
Osman, Russell 241, 265, 271
Owen, Gordon 207

Page, Chris 139
Page, Willie 65
Parker, Ivor 32, 36
Parker, Walter 36, 48, 84, 98, 109, 118, 119, 120, 121, 122, 126, 127-28, 253
Parsons, Harry 97, 136, 173-74, 186, 199, 200, 227
Pascoe, Colin 266
Peake, Bob 42
Pearce, George 17
Pearce, J.F. 17
Peck, Trevor 160
Phillips, Bob 242, 243
Phillips, Leighton 177, 194
Pirie, Tom 87
Poland, George 135
Pontin, Keith 205
Postin, Eli 130

Powell, Dave 178
Price, Mike 242, 243
Pritchard, Jackie 133
Pritchard, John 39

Ramsay, Jack 42
Rankmore, Frank 156
Redfearn, Jimmy 17
Reece, Gil 178, 189, 195
Rees, Mel 257
Rees, Nigel 159, 174, 175-76, 186, 187
Richards, Stan 134, 135, 136, 161
Riden, Walter 39, 98, 139, 149
Ridgeway, John 108
Robb, William 71
Roberts, Bill 108
Roberts, Christian 274
Roberts, Dave 202
Robertson, Norman 33, 35, 38
Robinson, Matthew 108
Rockey, Jackie 271
Rodrigues, Peter 156, 160
Rogers, Alan 256
Rogers, Liz 224-25, 227
Russell, George 123
Rutter, Charlie 145-46

Sayer, Peter 196, 197, 201, 216
Scouler, Jimmy 97, 157, 160, 161, 163, 166, 167, 168, 169, 170, 171, 172, 173-74, 175, 176, 178, 179, 180-82, 183, 186, 187, 188, 189, 190, 191, 193, 194, 204, 232
Sheen, Andrew 17
Shepherd, Sol 141
Sherwood, Alf 134, 135, 136, 137, 144, 147
Sloan, Tom 84, 87, 109
Smith, Bobby 263
Smith, Ernest 'Bert' 58, 60, 69
Smith, George 190, 195, 196
Spiers, Cyril 128-19, 131, 134-35, 136, 138, 140-41, 144, 145, 146, 147, 148, 149, 180, 255
Stansfield, Fred 134, 135, 136
Steer, Tudor 134, 139
Stephenson, John 52, 57
Stevenson, Ernie 145
Stevenson, Nigel 257
Stewart, Alex 58

Stewart, Fred 45, 46, 47, 50, 51, 52, 53, 56, 58, 60, 63, 64-65, 68, 70, 71, 74-75, 76, 82, 83, 88, 93, 108, 109, 110, 111, 112, 114-15, 116-17, 122, 147, 180
Stitfall, Ron 151, 155
Stone, A.J. 17
Stone, B. 17
Sullivan, David 230
Sullivan, Derek 151
Sutton, Mel 170, 180
Swan, Maurice 156
Swindin, George, 155, 156, 157, 160

Tait, Gavin 263, 266
Tapscott, Derek 151, 153-54, 160, 161, 164
Taylor, John 36
Temme, David 242, 243
Terlezki, Stefan 196
Thomas, D.A. (Lord Rhondda) 33
Thomas, Dai 270, 274
Thompson, Eddie 45
Tiddy, Mike 145
Tobin, Bobby 133
Tong, David 205, 262
Toshack, John 10, 154, 163, 164, 167, 168, 169, 170, 171-72, 173, 180, 184, 201-02, 203, 214, 215, 244, 261, 276
Tracey, Harry 45
Travis, George 18
Turner, Bert 125

Vearncombe, Graham 161
Villars, Tony 193
Vincent, Johnny 190, 195
Vivian, H.C. 33
Viard, Ted 30, 31

Wake, Harry 71, 77, 81, 82, 89, 91, 92
Walker, Kim 242, 243
Wall, Charles 33, 37, 39
Walsh, Brian 151
Walton, George 125
'Wanderer, The' 81, 85, 91
Warboys, Alan 170-71, 172-73, 178, 188
Watkins, Johnny 151
Watt-Jones, Ben 120, 121, 122, 124

Waters, Arthur 45
Watson, Tom 109
Watts, Billy 42
Went, Paul 201
Wheeler, Paul 225
Whitcombe, P. 17
Whitehead, Ceri 250, 271
Williams, Billy 58
Williams, Gareth 156, 160
Williams, Graham 204, 234
Williams, John 259, 267, 269-70, 274, 275
Williams, Robert 170
Wilson, Walter Bartly 9, 12-13, 14-15, 16-17, 18, 19, 20, 21-26, 27-28, 29-30, 31, 32, 34, 35-36, 37, 38, 39, 40, 42, 45, 47, 50, 54, 56, 58, 63, 64-65, 66, 68, 72, 98, 104, 109, 114-15, 117, 118, 119, 120-21, 122, 126, 138, 139, 140, 141, 142,-43,147, 148, 213, 277-82
Wilson, Bob 166, 167
Withy, Graham 207
Witts, Tom 47, 54
Wood, George 259
Woodruff, Bobby 174, 189, 243
Wooller, Wilf 126
Wright, Rick 225, 236, 237-38, 247, 249, 253, 263

Yorath, Terry 239, 263
Young, Scott 273